Praise for *China in Another Time*

"How do we gain some perspective on China after four decades of the fastest economic growth in world history? One way is to enjoy this engaging account of one intrepid woman's half century of life there in the early 20th century. From childhood through becoming a nurse in a society where political turmoil and social insecurity created challenge and misfortune for so many, the author's memories allow the reader to touch the texture of people's daily lives. This is a moving introduction to the world the Chinese were fortunate enough to leave far behind."

> – R. Bin Wong, Distinguished Professor of History, UCLA,
> and author of *China Transformed: Historical Change and the
> Limits of European Experience*

"Lintilhac's fascinating, masterfully edited collection of vignettes, sidebars and archival photos is as intimate as a diary and as endearing as a scrapbook, allowing us to experience China through the lens of a privileged Western girl-becomes-nurse-midwife who was born in rural China as it convulsed in revolution to cast off foreign empire-builders. A wonderful, detailed addition to the genre of memoirs chronicling the birth of modern China."

> – Helen Zia, author of *Last Boat out of Shanghai: The Epic Story
> of the Chinese who Fled Mao's Revolution*

"This deeply human and moving book immerses us in a time that seems much more than just a generation away; in a culture and way of life that has disappeared forever; and in the dangerous and courageous lives of service that people not so very different from us were brave enough to pursue. How fortunate that Claire's observations and photographs have survived to remind us of that recent yet irretrievable past."

> – Andrew J. Nathan, Class of 1919 Professor of Political Science,
> Columbia University; co-author of *China's New Rulers: The
> Secret Files* and *China's Search for Security*, and author of *China's
> Transition, China's Crisis* and *Chinese Democracy*

"This memoir of a Western woman who was born in China in the time of the Boxers and lived there throughout most of the next half century, part of it as a traveling nurse, offers a fascinating window on a country undergoing a series of dramatic transformations. China in Another Time is enlivened by firsthand details, enriched by sidebar materials that help orient readers unfamiliar with the setting and the history, and filled with evocative visual materials."

> – Jeffrey Wasserstrom, Chancellor's Professor of History, University of California, Irvine, and co-author of *China in the 21st Century: What Everyone Needs to Know*

"Born in 1899 to a Canadian medical missionary and his wife in a rural Chinese village, the author lived through the Boxer Rebellion, the first national government takeover and collapse, a decade-long period of warlord rule, a successful national government takeover in 1928, and finally, the Communist takeover in 1949. Throughout her narrative, she focuses on how such instability affected the Chinese people, as well as her own daily life as a 24-hour duty nurse."

> – *Kirkus Reviews*

CHINA
in Another Time

A Personal Story

Claire Malcolm Lintilhac

CHINA
in Another Time

A Personal Story
Claire Malcolm Lintilhac

Edited, with additional articles, by Doug Wilhelm

Introduction by Nicholas R. Clifford, Ph.D.
Late Professor of History, Middlebury College

Rootstock Publishing

Hardcover ISBN 9781578690190
Softcover ISBN 9781578690183

Published by Rootstock Publishing
www.rootstockpublishing.com
An imprint of Multicultural Media, Inc.
info@rootstockpublishing.com

Front cover design by Laughing Bear Associates
Book design by Stride Creative Group
Front cover photo by Donald Mennie, "Eve the Mist Had Altogether Yielded to
the Sun," National Galleries of Scotland. From *Glimpses of China*, published by
A.S. Watson & Co. Ltd., Shanghai, 1920.

Printed in the USA

The ultimate principle
of life is love.

From one of Claire's journals, 1960

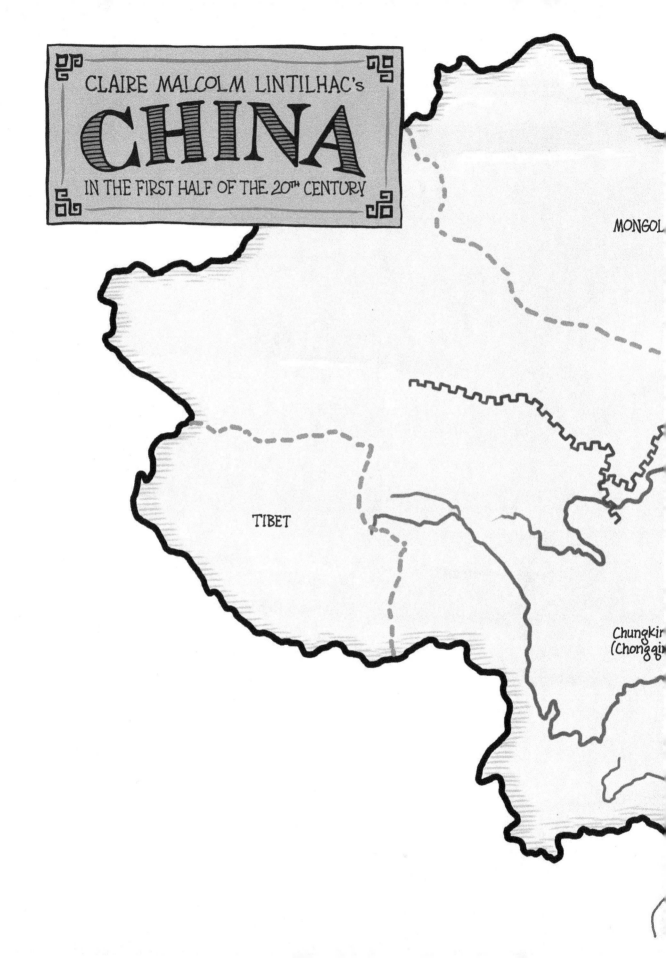

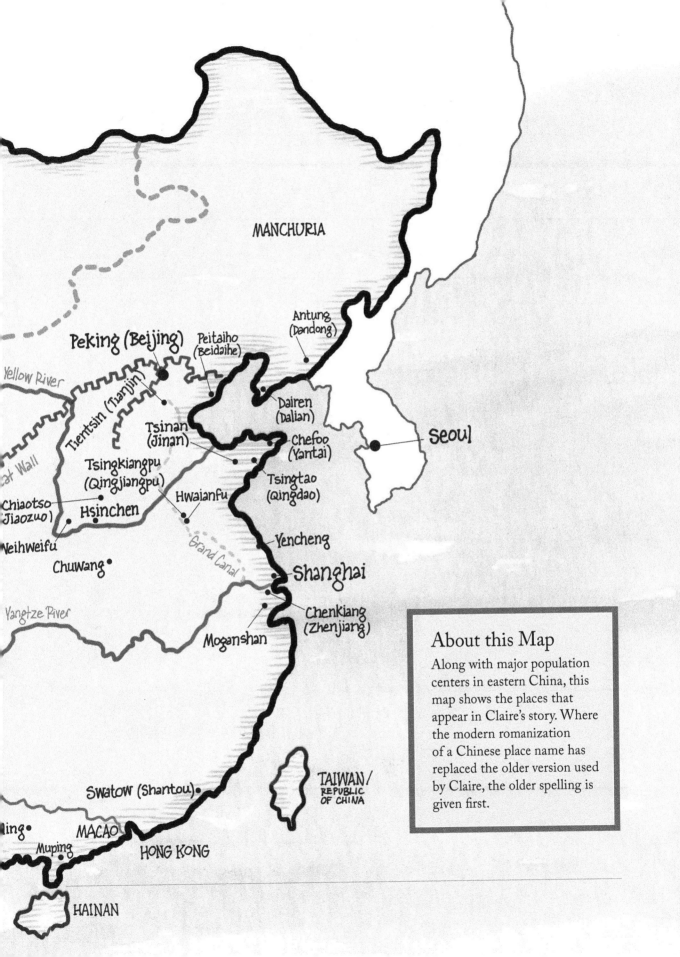

MANCHURIA

Antung
(Dandong)

Peking (Beijing)   Peitaiho
(Beidaihe)

Yellow River

Dairen
(Dalian)

Tientsin (Tianjin)

Seoul

Tsinan
(Jinan)   Chefoo
(Yantai)

Tsingkiangpu
(Qingjiangpu)   Hwaianfu   Tsingtao
(Qingdao)

Chiaotso
(Jiaozuo)   Hsinchen

Neihweifu

Yencheng

Chuwang   Grand Canal

Yangtze River   Shanghai

Chenkiang
(Zhenjiang)

Moganshan

About this Map

Along with major population centers in eastern China, this map shows the places that appear in Claire's story. Where the modern romanization of a Chinese place name has replaced the older version used by Claire, the older spelling is given first.

Swatow (Shantou)   TAIWAN/
REPUBLIC
OF CHINA

ling   MACAO
Muping   HONG KONG

HAINAN

China in Another Time
A Personal Story

by Claire Malcolm Lintilhac

Contents

Claire Malcolm Lintilhac
in Stowe, Vermont

Preface

by Philip M. Lintilhac

The book you hold in your hands has its own history. The original unpublished version was written during the time of the Vietnam War. Claire Lintilhac was deeply affected by the profound lack of cultural understanding underlying the promulgation of the war. She began to see her own life story as something that could be used to break through the institutional arrogance that was being used to justify the war. What began as a simple memoir for the benefit of family and friends became a remarkable window into a turbulent time, and a unique commentary on the roots of social conflict.

My mother Claire was born in 1899, in a remote village in North China during the last days of the Qing Dynasty. In those days life in North China, at the farthest eastern end of the ancient Silk Road, was a complex juxtaposition of cultures that had percolated across Asia for millennia. Government, complacent in the past glory of empire, was incestuous, corrupt and confounded by the relentless pressures of modernity that had been brought by strangers from across the ocean. The immediacy of China's constant upheavals made life uncertain at best, and communication with the outside world was minimal.

Claire lived for much of the next 50 years in small communities, working either as a freelance traveling nurse or in local hospitals. Her favorite work was maternity care, and although most of her contract jobs were in the isolated communities of Westerners spread across the North China coast, she made herself available to local Chinese wherever she lived. A knock on the door in the middle of the night would take her down through the alleyways to make the best of some desperate situation.

Claire was not a professional writer. She never went to college beyond the basic nurse's training she received in Shanghai, but she was organized and resourceful. She collected family documents, her diaries and her extensive correspondence, and she began to create a personal chronicle of the family from the materials at hand. First she sat down with a reel-to-reel tape recorder and began to recount a chronological oral history. These recordings amount to some 15 hours of lively storytelling. Then she began to assemble her stories into the first written draft of this book, supplementing the narrative with her own drawings.

Claire was a good storyteller, but there is not a word of fiction in this book. Her chronicle provides a remarkable and completely authentic view of early 20th century China — a period in the country she loved that has, for the most part, been lost to or edited out of history. Her chronicle grew out of her ability to see her former life through the filter of her new American consciousness.

After we moved to Vermont in 1958 following the death of my father, Claire found a community of people that welcomed her into their lives and trusted her for who she was. She took the time to educate herself more deeply, not only about her new home but also about the country where she had lived most of her life; yet under the surface she was always aware of a deep existential gulf that set her apart from even her closest friends. Many times she confided in me: "People think that because I look like them, and speak like them, that I must *think* like them; but how can I?" The world she grew up in was not measured by a Christian yardstick. It was measured by cultural necessity.

To compile this book, Doug Wilhelm has woven together Claire's recorded and written materials, and has added carefully researched historical notes. My mother's drawings, and many photos from her and my father's family collections, are supplemented with additional photographic material from a variety of sources. We have also made available selected audio clips from her recorded storytelling at the book's website, **www.chinainanothertime.com**.

China in Another Time is the personal recollection of a woman who came to understand the value of her own experience, and who took the time to document and interpret it. To hear these stories in Claire's own clear and expressive voice is a gift. Some are tragic, some are astonishing, and to a Western consciousness some are appalling. All are interesting and thoughtful, and all of them are true.

Philip M. Lintilhac, Ph.D., is associate professor of plant biology at the University of Vermont.

Introduction

by Nicholas R. Clifford

Though memoirs are not history, they can become the building blocks of history. True, they must sometimes be used with caution, as when, for instance, two (or three?) different generals each claim credit for a great battlefield victory. But memoirs can also be valuable in enlivening history — shedding light on its shadows, reminding us of those too-often ignored aspects of the past, helping us understand how events looked and felt to those living through the times that we now try to understand.

Such are the virtues of Claire M. Lintilhac's memoir of China. She claimed no great battlefield victories, nor did she mingle often with the rich, the famous or the powerful. The daughter of Canadian missionaries, she was no missionary herself in the conventional sense, but devoted most of her working life to nursing. She was an itinerant nurse, traveling through large parts of eastern and northern China to follow her calling, and doing so during a particularly troubling and dangerous time in modern China's history.

These were the last decades of foreign privilege in China, the years that saw the growth of a new nationalism, the years of almost continual civil strife by rival warlords. They were the years too of foreign invasion, which ultimately helped lead to the Communist victory in 1949. Claire noted carefully what she saw among her fellow Westerners, and among her Chinese friends at different levels of society. Do we come away wishing she had written about yet more aspects of her life, her adventures, her travels? Of course; but what she did write captivates her readers, introducing them to a life and a time that is past.

When Claire Malcolm was born in a small North China town in 1899, the country was still in a drastic slide from its former position as the world's greatest empire, little over a century earlier, to what some commentators of the day called "The Sick Man of Asia." Until roughly 1775, China had had the world's largest economy, and its standard of living, at least in its more prosperous regions, compared favorably with that emerging in the West. Since 1644 it had been under foreign rule, but its Manchu conquerors from the north had become well-adapted to Chinese culture and politics and for the most part ruled China as it had been before. The Manchu, or Qing, empire also brought under Beijing's control, in theory at least, such large, non-ethnically Chinese regions as Mongolia, Tibet and Xinjiang, and of course Manchuria itself.

But by the end of the 19th century, much of this structure of power and authority was in decay. Historians give many reasons for this collapse. Population growth was beginning to outstrip the ability of Chinese agriculture and technology to support it: the 18th and 19th centuries brought a rapid increase, from a formerly stable 140 million to 450 million people. After the brilliant reign of the Kangxi emperor (1661-1722), the quality of imperial leadership declined. Internal rebellions broke out, some of them in part religiously inspired, from White Lotus Rebellion of the late 18th century to the massively destructive Taiping, Nien and Muslim rebellions of the mid-19th century and later.

Then there was the coming of the West. Though traders and missionaries had arrived in China by the 16th century, they had by and large at first been included within China's foreign and trading relations. Then the early 19th century brought a Western attempt, largely British-led, to absorb China into the West's own patterns of imperial and trading relations. China's capitulation to the British in the Treaty of Nanjing of 1842 set the pattern, and was copied by others — Americans, French, and eventually the Japanese.

These foreign assaults on China's sovereignty took many forms. Most obvious were the openings of the treaty ports: five at first, from Guangzhou (Canton) to Shanghai in 1842, but the number had grown to more than 80 by the time of Claire's birth in 1899. In these ports, merchants from the treaty powers — the nations that had signed the appropriate documents with China — could live and do business free from earlier restrictions. In some of the larger ports (Shanghai, Hangzhou and Tianjin, for example), foreign concessions and settlements were established, administered and governed by foreigners under foreign law. (A concession is a place, in these cases often a portion of a city or a town, within a nation that is administered by another nation.)

Thanks to the practice of extraterritoriality, foreigners were subject to their own laws rather than those of China. In 1854, the Chinese Maritime Customs Service was established to collect revenues on foreign trade; and while this was technically a Chinese agency, it was run and staffed in its senior positions by foreigners. In the meantime, China was allowed to impose no more than a 5 percent tariff on foreign imports. In the later 19th century, when China became a recipient of large foreign loans, the foreign-run Maritime Customs insured that bondholders in London, Paris, Berlin and elsewhere outside China had first claim to the Customs revenue.

China moreover found itself victimized by foreign wars, which it inevitably lost, first against the British and French and later against the Japanese, to whom they had to cede the entire province of Taiwan in 1895. Another aspect of this foreign presence was the emergence of the so-called spheres of influence. Though these had no official or diplomatic existence, those who came under the influence of a strong foreign presence in such regions would show special partiality to those foreigners. Many spoke of a British sphere radiating out from Shanghai and Hangzhou through the Yangtze River Valley, or through Guangdong from the colony of Hong Kong. The French had a sphere down near the borders of French Indochina, and the Germans in Shantung province, while the Russians and the Japanese contested for a sphere in North China.

Finally, foreign missionaries had new rights under the treaties. Their activities, earlier outlawed, were now permitted, first in the treaty ports and soon in all of China. It's unlikely, of course, that Claire's father, a Canadian Presbyterian medical missionary, thought of himself as a domineering foreigner; but seen through a certain Chinese vision, that's what he was, every bit as much as a powerful Catholic or Anglican bishop.

Modern Chinese often call this period *Bainian guo chi*, the Century of Humiliation. It stretched from the 1840s to the 1940s, from the British victory in the first Opium War until the Western nations finally surrendered rights they had appropriated under what the Chinese quite accurately call the Unequal Treaties. This dating puts all the blame for China's humiliation on the foreigners, overlooking domestic reasons for the weakening of its own polity. But there's no doubt that foreign derogations of Chinese sovereignty — economic, legal, social and otherwise — were the most visible and tangible evidences of China's fall.

Inevitably there was a reaction to all this. Why was China now so weak when it had been strong, when it had been *Zhongguo*, the Middle Kingdom, and middle not just in some geographic sense but in a cultural and moral sense as well? Civilization had been defined by China, and those who lay outside it — British, Italian, Peruvian, Arabian and so forth — had all been to some extent uncivilized or barbarian.

How had China become subordinate? Was it simply because of the strength of Western weapons technology, or did the fault lie in China itself, now ruled by Manchu foreigners? Perhaps it was even more basic than that, going back to the antiquated ways of Confucius and his disciples?

Understandably enough, a strong nationalist agenda developed. After the suppression of the Boxer Rebellion at the turn of the 20th century, this nationalist movement, especially among young intellectuals, took on determinedly modernist stand. The fall of the Manchus in 1911 gave rise not to the formation of a new dynasty, but to the brief emergence of a new republic along western lines. The slogan "Science and Democracy" was its watchword, even as the political disintegration of the republic continued under the warlords.

This was the China that Claire saw and knew as a young woman. She remained there, first as a traveling nurse, then as the wife of a British business executive in Shanghai during the time when the two great political rivals, Nationalist and Communist, emerged to fight out their last battles. And she was there, finally, for the victory of Mao Zedong and his Red armies in 1949.

Nicholas R. Clifford, Ph.D. (1930-2019), was a longtime professor of history and chair of the History Department at Middlebury College. He was the author of The House of Memory: A Novel of Shanghai *and* Spoilt Children of Empire: Westerners in Shanghai and the Chinese Revolution of the 1920s.

Editor's Note

In her account of living and working in China during the first half of the 20th century, Claire uses some terms that were common in that place and time, but which may upset or even offend readers today. Although we very much don't wish to cause offense, we decided to keep those terms as Claire wrote them, to maintain the historical accuracy of her story. This note offers our reasoning, and some explanation.

Claire uses "coolie" to describe both a manual laborer and certain types of household servant. (For example, the water coolie took care of bringing in the day's water supplies, of purifying water for drinking — a painstaking, time-consuming process, as Claire describes — and of keeping the home's water containers filled and maintained.) And she occasionally uses "boy" in reference to a male domestic servant.

The trouble with using "boy" to describe a Chinese man is obvious. "Coolie" is nearly as troubling, as this today can be received as racist if applied to someone of Asian descent. In putting together Claire's account from the writing and oral storytelling she left behind, I tried out neutral substitutions for "coolie," like "laborer" and "servant," but these were not true to the culture or the history she relates — and to make an account of history carefully inoffensive can often make it misleading, and less useful. These were the words that, for better or worse, foreigners who lived in China were using at that time.

"Coolie" appears to have originated in India, and during the colonial era of the 19th and early 20th centuries it spread from Asia to Africa, the Caribbean and the U.S. It generally described a laborer or an indentured servant, usually Indian or Chinese. It's plain enough why the term became resented; the Chinese rendition of "coolie" translates to "bitter labor." In the China of Claire's time, "boy" referred, ironically enough, to a senior employee of a foreign family. "Number one boy" was the chief of the household staff.

Claire was in many ways an independent soul, honest and clear-eyed about the world she knew — but she was also a person of her time, and her book portrays a very different era in China. In these pages, she is never shy about describing events, customs and people, both Western and Chinese, exactly as she experienced them. It's in that spirit of honest portrayal that we chose to keep these terms, outmoded though they are, in *China in Another Time*.

One final note: The system that was commonly used, in Claire's era, to write Chinese place and personal names in the Roman alphabet was different from today's "pinyin" system of romanization. Claire called the Chinese capital Peking, while today we use Beijing; she called the leader of the Chinese Communist Party Mao Tse-tung, while today we write Mao Zedong. We decided to keep these and other names as Claire knew them, with the modern, pinyin version following in brackets on first reference.

Doug Wilhelm

The Audio Project
Hear Claire Tell Her Stories

Appearing in the margin of a number of pages in this book is a small image, or icon, of a pair of headphones. Each of these is numbered — and each icon lets you know that you can find on the book's website, **www.chinainanothertime.com**, a recording of Claire talking about the story, situation or character that's described on that page.

At her home in Stowe, Vermont in the late 1970s, Claire recorded some 15 hours of oral history and storytelling from her years in China. Using a reel-to-reel tape recorder, she spoke about growing up, about her nursing career and adventures as a traveling nurse, and about her experiences during the civil conflicts and warlord years of the 1920s, during the Japanese attacks on Shanghai in the 1930s, and during and after the Communist takeover of the country in 1949. In her lively and down-to-earth way, she also described many of the memorable people, Chinese and Western, who appear in these pages.

Twenty-two exceptional segments from Claire's recordings were selected, edited and mastered using today's technology to produce the audio clips on the website. Each selection is numbered to correspond with its icon in the book. Each is accompanied on the website by one or more photos.

We hope you'll enjoy these audio presentations — and we hope they will greatly enhance your appreciation for Claire and her unique story.

 When it appears on a page margin, this icon refers the reader to a numbered audio clip at **www.chinainanothertime.com**.

PART 1

A Doctor's Daughter
and a Dynasty's End

1899 – 1918

China was catapulted into the 20th century virtually unchanged for 3,000 years. Today, to make her urgent need for change possible, she has made a complete break with her age-old traditions — traditions that had shackled her for so long to her rich but archaic past. Hers was an ancestor-worshipping past that frowned on change; a past that included nearly a thousand years of foot binding among women; a past in which young people were taught that what was good enough for a father was good enough for the son. Today that past is not only not good enough for the son, it is no longer even good enough for the father.

The West tends to be sentimental about the ancient civilizations, but the romance of Asia — her rich art, culture and philosophies, especially in China — is inextricably linked with the nightmare of misery, cruelty and degradation. To change the habits and thinking of 800 million people is a task unprecedented in history. In coming to grips with her problems, China is gathering a momentum that, when she reaches the standards long enjoyed by the West, will not let her stop there.

Since making my home in Vermont in 1958, I have had the opportunity to reflect on a lifetime spent in China. Not until I began to see my childhood there unfold against the pattern of life here did I begin to suspect that there was anything very different about it. While I was there, China was for me the norm. I was born there, and from the ages of nine to 28 I never left China. I had all my schooling and my nurse's training there. After that, when I did leave, it was just for short home-leave visits by boat to England, and when my son Philip and I were evacuated while my husband was interned during World War II.

Left: Claire Malcolm was born in this room, on this bed, in 1899 in Hsinchen, China.

Until we finally left Shanghai in 1950, China was home to my husband Lin and me. Both our families were born there, and we thought we would live there permanently. When I first arrived in Vermont, friends would say, "It must have been quite an experience to have lived for 50 years in China!" But for me the *experience* was what I was having in Stowe. I still can't take for granted the pure, cold water that comes out of the tap. On the other hand, what I did take for granted at first, as everyone spoke English, was that we automatically understood each other. But slowly I began to realize that this was not necessarily so.

While people understood what I was saying, it did not follow that they always understood what I was talking about. I grew up in a Christian home in a small foreign (Western) community, it's true, but otherwise I was a product of a way of life totally different from that in the West.

My son Phil asked one day how it was that we had all been born in China in the first place. I explained that it was a long story — that in fact it was two separate stories, his father's and mine. His dad's family had been silk merchants from England in China for two generations. My father was a medical missionary from Canada, stationed in China since 1892.

I was born on December 20, 1899 in Hsinchen, a small mission station in the interior of Henan province in North China. During the following nine years the family twice traveled back and forth across the Pacific, finally returning to China in 1909 to stay. I was then nine years old. The next time I left China, I was 28 — and that trip was for only a few months in England, then back home.

Claire (right) and Dorothy as young girls in China.

Except for three years in a small Canadian missionary boarding school in Henan, I had all my schooling in the Shanghai American School. I finished in June 1918. After a summer at home in Chefoo (known as Yantai in English today), my sister Dorothy and I entered Shanghai's Municipal Hospital to commence our nurses' training. Three years later, in September 1921, Dor left to be married. I stayed on, finishing that December.

I nursed a total of 17 years before I was married in July 1936 to Francis Eugene (Lin) Lintilhac. During all this time I was the only foreign private-duty nurse between Shanghai in central China and Peking [Beijing] in the north. I called myself a "tramp nurse" — I went anywhere that patients or their families called me. There was never another nurse, foreign or Chinese, who did this kind of freelance nursing, either before or during my time. So all my nursing was 24-hour duty.

My nursing was among isolated foreign communities in small ports in Manchuria and along the China coast. These communities were composed of Westerners representing the many foreign interests in China: shipping firms and banks, big oil and tobacco companies such as Standard Oil, Shell and British American Tobacco, and business firms engaged in both import and export trade with China, including DuPont and its German and British equivalents, I.G. Farben and Imperial Chemical Industries (my husband was with I.C.I.). The chemical companies imported mainly fertilizers, drugs and dye stuffs. The Chinese Customs, Postal and Salt Revenue services and cable companies were administered by Westerners. Last but not least were the different consulates, there to protect the interests of their own nationals.

To reach these foreign communities I had to travel on small Chinese cargo boats, sharing the only cabin with Chinese men, and the toilet with all comers. If I was lucky and the cabin had six bunks, I always chose an upper bunk. Pushing my hat forward and leaving my shoes on, I would to go to sleep, for I was always tired.

If I was *un*lucky and the cabin had only two bunks and the other one was occupied, I would spend the night out in the public saloon, sleeping on the settee. Only once was there ever another woman on board, in that case a Russian. Chinese women never traveled on these boats in those days.

Claire at work as a nurse in China, about 1932.

One hears all kinds of stories about China. Some are about her rich and sophisticated culture. There are other stories of poverty and misery, so we often wonder what to believe. The truth is they are all true, and they often existed side by side.

China is so large, and her history is so long, that she's had time to rise to all kinds of heights, and to fall to levels of oppression and poverty and misery that are hard to believe. When the West first made contact with her, China had really reached an all-time low in her social order, so we still suffer from those initial impressions that our first traders and missionaries had. It's hard to get rid of those.

China has always loved America — not just her great generosity, which is proverbial, but her concern for the dignity of the individual. That's what the missionaries went to China to teach. Where did this get lost? Well, we were pretty rigid and inflexible, and the West was inflexible with some of its attitudes. We took our Christianity for granted, and we identified it with business — big business, and politics for that matter, and … Oh, it's such a long story. To tell my story properly I should relate how I happened to be in China. To do this I must go back even farther, and describe briefly how Mother and Father first went there.

A Mission in Medicine

My mother, Eliza Pringle (1869-1942), was born in Chambly, Quebec, of Scottish parents. My father, William Malcolm (1861-1946), was also of Scottish descent; his father was a farmer who settled in Bruce County, Ontario, where he and his four sons cleared the land and built their own home. It still stands today. With his three brothers, my father grew up on the farm.

Father's mother died when he was only 15. He always felt that if she had had proper medical care, she need not have died. From that moment he vowed to become a doctor — but he was reckoning without his Scotch Presbyterian father, who was determined that one of his sons should be a minister.

Claire's parents, Eliza and William Malcolm, in 1901.

Despite many arguments, Father was sent to study theology at Knox College, Toronto University. After two years, his heart still set on medicine, he came home to talk it over with his father, who finally relented. So in 1887, my father enrolled in the University Medical College in New York City.

After two years of study, old Grandfather Malcolm could no longer afford the tuition, so my father took a year's leave of absence from his studies to work as a nurse. He finally graduated in 1890, after which he did a year as house physician and surgeon at St. Barnabas Hospital in Newark, New Jersey. His heart's desire was fulfilled at last: he was a doctor of medicine.

After marrying Christina Ann McArthur in 1892, Dr. Malcolm offered his services to the Canadian Presbyterian Mission as a medical missionary. That year he and his bride left for China, to be stationed in Chuwang, in Henan [Honan] province in North China.

Many years later, after World War II in the summer of 1948, we were about to be transferred from Tientsin [Tianjin] back to Shanghai. A few days before leaving, Lin and I and our son Philip, then eight years old, were invited to a farewell luncheon given for us by some old friends.

My host's very old mother was seated beside me at the table. She spoke of planning to go that afternoon to visit her husband's grave in the little British cemetery there. Then she surprised me by saying, "You know, your mother's grave is just beside my husband's."

I didn't know what to say, for my mother had died in New York shortly after Pearl Harbor. I explained gently that there must be some mistake.

"Oh, no," she replied, "I knew her quite well. And besides it is clearly written on the gravestone, 'DIED OCT. 1, 1894. CHRISTINA ANN, DEARLY BELOVED WIFE OF WILLIAM MALCOLM.' That's your father, isn't it?"

It all came back to me then. Yes, of course, that was my father — but Christina was not my mother.

Father and his first wife had been in their station a little over a year when she came down with the dreaded smallpox. Father nursed her through. When she was well enough to travel, he took her down the Hai River to Tientsin so she could convalesce among other foreign women. While they were in Tientsin, an epidemic of cholera broke out nearby.

In those days there were no western-trained Chinese doctors, so all available foreign doctors were sent to the affected area to try and contain the epidemic. Father was away about three weeks. When he got back to Tientsin, he found that his young wife had suddenly contracted cholera and died. That was indeed in October 1894.

The same year, 1892, that Father was married to his first wife, Mother was married to her first husband, the Rev. Herbert McKitrick, an American. Their honeymoon was spent on a trip to Tarsus in Asia Minor, where they were stationed for a while. Rev. McKitrick was later transferred to the American University of Beirut, in Lebanon, as professor of languages there. The following year he was suddenly taken ill and died of what was diagnosed as malignant malaria. A month later my mother's first baby was born, but lived only nine days.

Two months after this, Armenian massacres broke out and all foreigners were evacuated to London. Eventually Mother found herself back with her family in Ontario. My mother and father had known each other as young people, and they exchanged letters of sympathy. Thus began a correspondence.

In 1896, alone, my mother traveled all the way out to China. Father met her in Shanghai, where they were married in the lovely Episcopal cathedral there. (In 1936, Lin and I were married in this same church, and in 1940, Philip was baptized there.)

Six months later, in Chuwang, my father came down with a third undiagnosed attack of what turned out to be appendicitis. Mother took him all the way back to Canada to be operated on. After a long convalescence, back they went to China.

Above: William Malcolm (top left) and his first wife, Christina (bottom left), with fellow missionaries in Weihweifu, 1892. Below: Bill, Claire, Dr. Malcolm, Dorothy, Eliza Malcolm and Mary, in Chiaotzo, 1915.

Who Were the Missionaries?

The first Christians to gain entry into China were Jesuit Catholics. Between 1582 and 1800, about 900 Jesuits taught Western science, astronomy and visual art at the Imperial Court. But the era when thousands of missionaries could work across the country did not begin until 1860, when a treaty legalized Christianity and gave missionaries the right to settle inland.

In the years following that 1860 treaty, missionaries built compounds, mostly in rural China, that often included schools and hospitals, or medical dispensaries, along with Western-style homes. By 1900, China had about 2,000 Protestant missionaries — almost half of them American — along with about 1,000 Catholic priests and nuns.

The missionaries of the late 1800s often arrived knowing little or nothing about China. Their strident efforts to win converts met with little success and created a lot of resentment, which largely sparked the bloody Boxer Rebellion of 1900 (see pages 10-12).

Canadian missionaries in Henan, China, 1898: Dr. William Malcolm, Claire's father, is seated second from left. When the Boxer Rebellion broke out in North China in 1900, Jonathan Goforth (standing, second from left) and Dr. Percie Leslie (seated second from right) were attempting to lead 30 carts full of missionary families away from the violence when attacking villagers slashed Goforth's pith helmet to pieces, and gave Dr. Leslie 15 wounds. After escaping by night, they and their caravan made a month-long journey to safe haven.

After 1900, the missionaries focused largely on building schools, colleges and hospitals, battling the opium epidemic, and promoting what they saw as positive changes in Chinese life. They continued to be controversial, but in many ways they helped educate and motivate a young Chinese generation that wanted a government which cared for its people, and a way for China to join — not just serve — the modern world.

Missionary doctors like Claire's father built health care facilities, practiced Western medicine to generally high standards, and introduced China to Western medical innovations. China had a sophisticated medical tradition, but it had no surgery, and little awareness of the link (only recently accepted by Western medicine, thanks to the germ-theory work of Louis Pasteur and others) between the lack of cleanliness and disease. So missionary doctors commonly saw the most advanced cases of disease and infection in their Chinese patients. Often they were able to help; for example, they restored sight to many through cataract surgery.

Missionaries like Dr. Malcolm usually came from rural backgrounds, and were supported by donations from congregations and organizations back home. Claire's parents were far from wealthy, but Chinese servants were part of their family life, as they were in almost every missionary household.

In China in the early 20th Century, household work was very time-demanding; it could take much of a person's day just to do the wash or purify the water. Servants were inexpensive to employ, and they were pretty much essential to running the household of a family like Claire's.

Listening to a preacher at an American missionary station. To the right of the U.S. flag is the Manchu imperial banner, a black dragon and red sun on a yellow ground.

The Family's First Station

Missionaries were encouraged to take their families away from the isolated interior stations for the hot months. The favorite North China summer resort was Peitaiho [today's Beidaihe, a district of the city Qinhuangdao] by the sea. Here my older sister, Dorothy, was born in September 1898.

As soon as my mother was able to travel, they returned to their new station, Hsinchen, sixty miles farther inland beyond Chuwang, a six-week journey by houseboat from Tientsin up the Grand Canal and Wei River. Here, in 1899 in Hsinchen, I was born.

With the men away all day, Mother often got lonely for someone to talk with. I recall her saying "at least the chickens clucked in English." She spent long hours studying the language, and struggled to introduce foreign cooking to the cook. He became particularly deft at decorating cakes. One day, Mother went into the kitchen to watch how he did this. She found him busily creating elaborate designs on the icing, with the aid of a hair comb! When she diffidently questioned this, the cook assured her that he didn't in the least mind using his comb, as the sugar could be washed off quite easily.

Chinese people and missionaries *Image courtesy of Peter Lockhart Smith and Historical Photographs of China, University of Bristol.*

Many times during the long days there would be loud bangings on the compound gate by crowds outside. The gateman explained that all they wanted was to see a foreign woman, and that it might be wiser to let them in than try to keep them out. So my mother would stand patiently on the terrace to be stared at.

This usually ended in the bolder ones coming up close and examining her clothes — even lifting her long skirts just enough to catch a glimpse of her feet and confirm for themselves the unbelievable rumor that they were big like a man's. In this part of China, even the beggar women had bound feet. They wondered too at Mother's "colorless" eyes, for they were very blue.

Above: Dr. William and Eliza Malcolm with Dorothy, their first child, in Chuwang, China, 1898.
Below: William (top center) and Eliza (left) with fellow medical missionaries Dr. and Mrs. Mendes in Hsinchen, 1899. Eliza Malcolm was pregnant with Claire when this photo was taken.

"North China Became a Tinderbox"

Meanwhile, trouble was brewing in rural China — especially in Shandong, an ancient province along the north coast and the lower Yellow River that for centuries had played a key role in the country's economy, culture and history.

"The rather dense population had become so poor that few gentry lived in the villages, and banditry had become a seasonal occupation that inspired intervillage feuds. The Qing government and gentry were losing control," wrote the late Harvard historian John King Fairbank in *China: A New History* (Merle Goldman, co-author, Second Enlarged Edition, Belknap Press, 2006).

During the 1890s, German missionaries used very assertive tactics to recruit converts, then claimed Shandong as a German sphere of influence. Their arrogance, Fairbank writes, fueled an anti-Christian, anti-Western sentiment that had been building in the country as missionaries set themselves up in the interior, and as China was again and again forced to sign humbling treaties with Western powers and Japan (see p. 11).

Riots against the missionaries began to erupt. Chinese courts sought to protect the foreigners, further inflaming the rural poor. Villagers in Shandong began forming secret groups for self-protection.

Then in 1898, a ruinous flood was followed by a long drought — and Shandong was ready to erupt. "North China," Fairbank writes, "became a tinderbox."

The Boxer Rebellion

All this time, the anti-foreign feeling and anti-Christian feeling was increasing in China and the old Manchu Empress Dowager, a rascal, was whipping it up. The feeling was very anti-Manchu government, because she was so unscrupulous with taxes and all. But she cleverly deflected this into an anti-foreign feeling that was never very far under the surface anyway, and what followed was the Boxer Rising.

In Hsinchen there were no newspapers or any other way of getting the news, so they had no idea the rebellion was underway. There was a lot of hostility, but there always had been. But my mother was nervous — and the three other men at the station prevailed on my father to take his little family for a trip to Tientsin on the coast. This meant a three months' journey; it was a six-week trip along the canal by houseboat, just the one way.

They got on the houseboat and set off. My father would ride his bicycle along the towpath. But when they came near Tientsin, people started stoning him on the bicycle, so he had to take it onto the boat and stay inside. My parents didn't know why the stoning was going on, but they were used to adversity. They arrived in Tientsin to find the whole foreign community armed and the Boxer Rebellion in full swing.

Above: Rural Chinese men took up arms in the 1900 uprising.
Image courtesy of Jim Williams and Historical Photographs of China, University of Bristol.
Below: Foreign soldiers, including the Russians shown here, were sent by eight nations to crush the rebellion.
Image courtesy of the UK National Archives.

As the Boxers approached, all foreigners were evacuated to Peitaiho, where a British gunboat, the *HMS Terrible*, lay at anchor, ready to take off all British nationals if necessary. Every house had a flag showing its nationality. Our house was on the beach opposite where the boat was anchored, and they sent in a couple of sailors to set up a signal station. The sailors were billeted in our house; their job was to keep track of the movements of the Boxers and to signal their arrival.

Somebody became very ill onboard the gunboat. My father went out, and while he was aboard, the arrival of the Boxers was signaled. There were no radios in those days, so the Boxers must have been pretty near before the sailors knew they were coming. Foreign civilians were evacuated immediately.

The Violent Start to Claire's China Years

In the hot summer of 1900, the first year of Claire Malcolm's life in China, resentment and anger in the country caught fire.

The Boxer Rebellion erupted among struggling farmers in North China and spread fast across the nation. The rage was aimed largely against the foreigners, especially missionaries and their families. Also fueling it was frustration with the greedy, corrupt Manchu government, China's last dynasty, which did virtually nothing to ease the struggles of peasant communities with drought, floods and economic depression.

Before they were beaten back by foreign soldiers that summer, the rebels, who rose out of rural secret societies and called themselves Harmony Fists, or Boxers, had killed about 300 Westerners, 243 of them missionaries and their families. Many other families, including the Malcolms, made often-harrowing escapes. In the aftermath, an untold number of Chinese were killed in reprisals by the foreign soldiers — British, American, European, Russian, Indian and Japanese — that were sent to quash the rebellion. Numbering some 55,000 in all, the foreign soldiers captured the capital, Beijing (Peking), and freed some 1,000 besieged Westerners.

After 1900, China was never the same. Just over ten years after the Boxer Rebellion, the Manchu Qing Dynasty finally collapsed, ending 21 centuries of autocratic rule by a succession of monarchies. Decades of struggle followed over what kind of modern nation China would become, and Claire's story gives a window into those turbulent years. But to understand her world, it's important to mention an earlier conflict — one that opened the gate for thousands of Westerners to enter China, beginning its time of turbulent change.

In 1839, the Manchu Qing government went to war against Great Britain to stop English traders from importing opium into China from India. The drug had addicted a great number of Chinese people. But China lost that war, and the treaty it was forced to sign in 1842 set a pattern for many more treaties in the years ahead.

Each of those agreements gave a foreign power the right to make its own settlements in Chinese ports. Foreigners — at first British, then Europeans, Americans and Japanese as well — would do business in these ports, and Chinese laws would not apply. This was called *extraterritoriality*, and it became a huge issue.

At first there were just five "treaty ports" on the Chinese coast. Each was a new community built on the edge of a Chinese city, and protected by the navy of its home nation. This caused great resentment among many Chinese; it also led to the growth of big, prosperous Western settlements in Shanghai and other cities. (Hong Kong had become a British colony after the opium war.)

By the early 20th Century, there were more than 80 treaty ports up and down the coast, and foreigners owned property in nearly every major Chinese community. The foreigners who lived in China did business with the Chinese — but except for the missionaries, they generally lived apart, confined inside the international settlements that grew up in the treaty ports.

Captured Boxer Rebellion fighters.

My mother, with two babies to care for, took off her petticoat, stitched it up along the bottom and filled it full of baby napkins. She wasn't allowed, much to her distress, to take her *amah*, or household servant. Mother and others got into lifeboats and went out onto the HMS *Terrible*. Before the ship got underway, our house on the beach was in flames.

Our next stop was Chefoo [Yantai], also on the coast, where all the foreigners were refugeeing until they had boats to get them out. The mission compound was crowded with refugees. With ten others, we, now a family of four, shared one large room in a mission boarding house. By this time my sister Dorothy, just two, was seriously ill with dysentery.

I don't know how long we were in Chefoo, but eventually the Boxers arrived there too. This time we traveled steerage, the lowest-fare accomodations, on some boat to Japan. Mother had to sit up at night to keep the rats off her babies. In Japan, kind friends took us in until we were able to get passage to Vancouver, where my mother's family now lived.

Ruins after the foreign soldiers' siege of Peking.
Image courtesy of Billie Love Historical Collection and Historical Photographs of China, University of Bristol.

Washington, D.C.

In February 1907 we moved to Washington D.C. My father developed a successful cardiac practice on I Street. He had all kinds of affluent patients, including President William H. Taft. At last my mother was able to get the music she so loved and had missed for so many years. Life here was just nicely settled when my father unexpectedly suffered what at first seemed a minor injury.

While fooling about in the office one day, a patient accidentally stuck the blade of his penknife into the palm of my father's right hand. Father became desperately ill with blood poisoning; two or three operations followed. Poor Mother — my brother Bill and I were very sick with measles at the same time.

In time my father got better, but his hand was rigid and largely crippled. This left him at times discouraged and depressed. While in Washington, my parents had joined the Southern American Presbyterian Church. It so happened that this church was looking for a doctor to go to China to establish a hospital in Hwaianfu, one of their mission stations on the Grand Canal.

Whereas the Canadian Mission field was located in Henan province, the Southern American Presbyterian Mission field was in Kiangsu [Jiangsu] province, just south of Henan. Both my parents spoke Chinese, at this point, and the Henan dialect that they were familiar with was not unlike that of Kiangsu.

Back to China

I suspect that the sense of loss following his accident, combined with the thought of establishing a much-needed hospital among the desperately poor and sick in China, appealed once again to Father's pioneer spirit. Mother loved Washington, and she knew only too well the hazards of living in remote places in China. She had had enough of that.

But in November 1909, my father sold his practice and our home in Washington and, with my mother and their three children, set out once again on the long trek back to China. Little did I dream then that it was to be 19 years before I stepped foot outside of China again, and then for only a few months in unfamiliar England.

My mother was one of a family of ten, seven sisters and three brothers. The third brother, James, had become a Mountie in what was then known as the Royal Northwest Mounted Police. Before leaving Washington to commence our long journey across Canada, my mother sent word to Uncle James, stationed in Regina, Saskatchewan, that our train would be passing through at a given time and would he try to be there to see us.

The train arrived on time. We all poured onto the platform, hoping to see Uncle James. I still recall how eagerly we looked and waited, for he had said he would be there. Time was running out. The whistle blew. With a heavy heart, Mother bundled us all on board again.

The train slowly started up and as it pulled out of the station, in the distance my mother spotted a figure approaching, a horseman in (believe it or not) a cloud of dust. He got to the station and dismounted, but the train was gathering speed too fast for us to distinguish who the rider was. Months later, in China (for there were no telephones in Vancouver in those days), she learned that it had indeed been Uncle James. The next year, while he was out on a routine assignment with his Indian guide, the two men were caught in a blizzard and were frozen to death.

Shanghai: Confusion in the Rain

Early in November 1909, we set sail from Vancouver on the SS *Korea*. My most vivid memory of that trip was being awakened in the middle of the night to see Halley's Comet — that and the confusion on the dock when we arrived in Shanghai.

It was pouring rain, and the minute we put foot ashore we were surrounded by what seemed like hundreds of rickshaw drivers. As my father tried to round up all our bags and boxes, men grabbed at each piece as it appeared, hoping to secure the job of carrying it to our destination. They were competing with so many others. Father was trying to count his bags and baggage; he put Bill and me into a rickshaw, and the driver put a tarpaulin over our feet and legs to protect us from the downpour.

That was my first impression of Shanghai.

Bill and I sat there patiently, just our eyes peering over the top of this tarpaulin. In all the confusion, Father seemed to be at his wit's end about something. Finally I called out to him, "What's the matter?" He turned and said, "Oh — there you are! I thought I'd lost you." All he could see was these two pairs of eyes, peering over the tarpaulin.

Claire and her brother, William, almost hidden in the rickshaw. This and all other drawings in this book are by Claire.

From the dock we were whisked in a caravan of rickshaws to the Missionary Home in Hongkou district. Here we stayed for about a week. My recollections are a blur of morning prayers, long dark corridors, Ningbo varnish, wide verandas, and my brother Bill getting his head stuck between the bars of the veranda railings. Panic! He had been watching the changing scene below, then found he couldn't get his head back. As always, Dr. Malcolm came to the rescue.

We got in a sort of houseboat caravan, with a launch that towed the houseboats to Chenkiang [Zhenjiang], where the great

Rickshaws and pedestrians in Shanghai, early 1900s.

Image courtesy of Alison Brooke and Historical Photographs of China, University of Bristol.

Yangtze joins the Grand Canal, a man-made waterway of about 600 miles that runs from the mouths of the Yangtze River up to pretty near Peking. The Grand Canal was dug not for the convenience of the masses, but for transporting tribute rice from the provinces up to the Imperial Court and all its retinue. Rice does not grow in North China.

Before it entered the Grand Canal, our houseboat ran afoul of a rock or something and the whole bottom of the boat was ripped out. They had to throw the babies from one boat to the next. They jumped for it, but nearly everything they possessed went to the bottom in the muddy water.

They did recover one box. In it my mother had a bolt of red cloth that she was planning to use; but unfortunately, in those days red was not colorfast. She said everything she owned after that was red. She could not afford to throw it away, so she just used it the way it was.

Two-Sided Bargains

At Chenkiang some kind missionary friends put us up for a few days. On another occasion we stayed with the Sydenstrickers, Pearl Buck's family. Pearl herself had left for college in the United States. [An American missionary's daughter, Pearl S. Buck won the Nobel Prize for Literature for her novels, especially *The Good Earth*, portraying peasant life in China.] Later I got to know her younger sister Grace, in the Shanghai American School.

In Chenkiang the days were full of the excitement of engaging a new houseboat, complete with boatman and family, to take us up the Grand Canal to our destination, Hwaianfu. Here too is my earliest memory of the elaborate business of bargaining. Bargaining for the hire of the boat. Bargaining over the amount of "wine money." (Perhaps the best definition of wine money is *cumsha*, or tip.) There was no such thing as a fixed price for anything. Every price had to be gradually arrived at, after much gesticulating and polemics.

The cook, newly engaged for the trip, became a self-appointed middleman. First he would support my father by remonstrating with the boatman, exhorting him to be more reasonable in his demands. We were good customers and had no desire to beat anybody down. The next minute he would appeal to my father's generosity on behalf of the poor hard-working boatman, who had such a big family with so many mouths to feed and times were hard.

At long last all was settled and we started on our two-week journey up the Grand Canal to Hwaianfu.

At a ferry crossing on the Grand Canal.

"Cash" Coins and "Mexican Dollars"

Chinese money in those days was all in metal coins, beginning with the small brass "cash" with the square hole in the center. The next denomination was the copper cent, about an inch in diameter. Then came the silver 10-cent piece, 20-cent piece, 50-cent piece and finally the silver dollar, called the Mexican dollar.

The origin of the Mexican dollar goes back to the New England trading-ship days, when those ships sailed to the Orient via Cape Horn with a cargo of rum, ginseng and pots and pans. When they reached Mexico they traded their pots and pans for the Mexican silver dollar. Their next stop was the British Columbia coast, where they traded their rum to Indians for fur pelts. Their final destination was China, where they traded their ginseng and silver dollars for silks and tea and porcelains.

People in China rarely used silver money in those days, as the brass cash and the copper cent were ample for one's daily needs. Mother's household accounts were always kept in cash, though they did run into the thousands.

For some reason the exchange rate fluctuated every day. There were 13 cash to the cent, from ten to 13 cents to a silver ten-cent piece, and from ten to 13 ten-cent pieces to the dollar, all depending on whether one was dealing in "big money" or "small money."

Brass "cash" coins, from Claire's collection of mementos.

The Boatman's Family

A houseboat, while a bit slow, can be a cozy and comfortable way to travel. We had a large living-room cabin in the main part of the boat, with a wide deck forward. Behind the main cabin were two small sleeping rooms — and that is all they were. The floors, on which our quilts were unrolled, were knee-high and about the area of a large double bed. Shoes remained outside on the floor of the corridor.

In the stern were the quarters of the boatman and his wife and three children. The little ones were usually tied by ropes around their waists to some fixed object on the deck. The older ones had inflated pigs' bladders attached to their backs. There were in addition two grown men, also members of the family, to help with the boat.

If the wind was favorable, the sail was hoisted. If it was not and the water was shallow, the men would get out their long bamboo poles and punt or pole us along. Two men started at either side of the bow, plunging their poles to the bottom and thrusting the weight of a shoulder to the top end of the pole. They would then pace slowly in step down the narrow decks on either side of the boat till they reached the stern together. Here the poles were sharply withdrawn from the muddy bottom and trailed leisurely through the water back to the bow, there to begin all over again.

If the water was too deep to pole and there was no wind, we would have to be towed or pulled. To do this the boat was maneuvered to the bank of the canal, where the men would jump ashore or cross on a narrow plank, carrying with them a large coil of rope, one end of which had already been secured to the top of the mast.

Uncoiling the rope as they walked forward, one boatman would thrust his chest against the wooden bar or yoke at the end. Each of the other boatmen would then take up a branch rope, which stemmed at intervals from the main rope, and lean against his yoke. Throwing their combined weight against these bars, they began to track in unison.

As the boat began to move, the trackers would trudge slowly forward. To guide the boat back into midstream, the wife would man the rudder.

We children used to get out and help the boatmen. We would hitch ourselves onto the rope and plod along, step by step, for we traveled at a slow walking pace. Sometimes this towing went on for days.

Rowing a river houseboat.
Photograph by G. Warren Swire. Image courtesy of John Swire & Sons Ltd and Historical Photographs of China, University of Bristol.

The sail was hoisted at the merest suggestion of a breeze. Without interrupting the towing, the head boatman would take his place at the foot of the mast and with a high-pitched, tremulous note, gently "call" to the wind, "*Loo-loo-loo-loo-loo-loo!*" We didn't need much encouragement to sit beside the boatman and help him whistle up the wind. Children are children the world over, and the Chinese are so patient and indulgent with them.

Towing a river houseboat.

A Baby on the Grand Canal

One day while we were walking along the bank — the boatmen were well ahead, pulling — Mother said, "I can hear a baby crying." They looked around and couldn't find it. We finally came to a little square hole that was cut into the ground and covered with straw, right in the middle of the path.

Mother and Father pulled the straw up, and there in this hole was a baby. It was covered from head to foot with black grease. To my father's surprise it was a boy, about two weeks old. While girl babies were often abandoned, rarely did this happen to a boy.

What do you do? You don't just leave it. Mother and Father decided to take the baby on board. The boatmen didn't like this at all, but my parents insisted on carrying it into our cabin.

The baby was completely covered with black lard and soot. Mother cleaned this stuff off, and Father was puzzled to find a deep, charred wound in one of the baby's thighs. The wound seemed to have been made by a red-hot needle. Then, as though in answer to their mounting suspicions, the baby was seized with a violent convulsion.

The needling had been done to let the devil out

So this was the answer — the baby was "possessed by a devil." The needling had been done to let the devil out. They had blackened it so the devils would recognize their own and claim it.

We had brought the baby on board, and this was very bad luck — the boatmen were upset about it. They went around with torches, with some tar on the end, flaming all through their quarters to drive away the evil spirits that were probably looking for this baby.

In spite of all my mother's care, a few days later the baby died. Then we had another fuss because we had to bury it, somewhere along the bank of the canal. This was followed by more elaborate flaming by the boat people.

Hwaianfu and the Ancestor's Weasel

We arrived at Hwaianfu, a typical walled city. Its high, crenellated city wall and impressive battlements were encircled on the outside by a moat and supported on the inside by a wide sloping embankment, rising to within five feet of the top of the wall.

From the top of this embankment we could see the countryside for miles around. Narrow footpaths divided the cultivated fields, where all too large a portion of the precious arable land was taken up by the big earth-mounds of family graves. Some of these graves were of ancestors, dating back many generations. Thus the dead were still monopolizing land that was scarcely enough to support the living.

This same embankment also overlooked the teeming city within. The narrow cobblestone streets were endlessly sandwiched between ten-foot-high walls, built of gray brick. The streets were dirty and drab — but these walls sheltered the compounds, with their luxurious homes and picturesque courtyards, of many wealthy officials.

Hwaianfu was the seat of government of the local prefecture. It was near the confluence of the Grand Canal and the Yellow River, connecting China's two great waterways, the Yangtze River in central China and the Yellow River in the north. Hwaianfu was one of the main distributing centers for tribute rice, to be transported to the Imperial Courts. There was a great deal of wealth in the city.

When we first arrived we stayed with the only other missionary family there, the Rev. Dr. Henry Woods and his wife and son and daughter, Josephine, who had just recently returned from college in the United States to join her parents in mission work. She wore Chinese clothes, which somehow looked out of place with her "large" feet.

Dr. Woods was a Chinese scholar, tall, distinguished-looking and autocratic. He wore a long, plum-colored silk brocade gown with a short black brocade *'k'an-chan-enh* (waistcoat) over the gown. His long white queue, or braid, was crowned by the traditional black brimless hat, with a little red button on the top. Mrs. Woods was small and completely overshadowed by her patriarchal husband.

A site had already been purchased to build a house for the new doctor and his family. Like all Chinese homes, this property was surrounded by high walls. The place had been up for sale because it was believed to be haunted by the spirit of an ancestor in the shape of a weasel.

While the old one-storied buildings were being pulled down to make way for the foreign house that was to go up, we lived in three rooms that were left standing temporarily. My mother and father were constantly on guard — not against the spirit of the ancestor but against scorpions, centipedes and rats and the like, continually being disturbed by the demolishing of the old

The "queue," or long braided ponytail, was a widespread custom during the time of the last Chinese emperor. Originally from Manchuria in the north and known as the Qing dynasty, the Manchus ruled from 1636 until the Nationalist Revolution of 1911.

buildings. Never a day passed without one of the workmen coming to Dr. Malcolm in agony from the sting of a scorpion, to be relieved by an injection of novocaine.

I remember one evening picking up a stack of books, and when I looked where my hand had been, there was a great big scorpion. Evidently I hadn't disturbed it, so it hadn't stung me.

Our vigilance never relaxed until we crawled under our mosquito nets at night, always trailing our bedroom slippers and dressing gowns in after us to make sure they would be safe to put on again in the morning. We didn't dare leave the slippers outside, because otherwise, in the morning if you put your foot in, like as not there would be a centipede curled up there, and centipedes were deadly.

As all these creatures were being disturbed in their natural haunts, they were coming out into the rest of the house. They would drop from the rafters, even onto unsuspecting heads below. My father took to wearing his large pith helmet when he sat reading at night. For Mother, he fixed an umbrella attached to the back of her desk chair.

None of us was ever stung or bitten — but every evening we were visited by the ancestor's "spirit." After supper when all was quiet, a long red weasel would come slinking out along one of the beams under the ceiling and lie there, motionless, watching us. It never bothered us, except once.

Our father had bought each of us children three little baby chicks. We kept them in a little coop he had made for them, and we showered on them all our surplus energy and affection. Then one morning we awoke to find nine lifeless little bodies lying in the bottom of the cage. Our childish indignation was high, for we knew at once who was responsible.

Looking out from the walls of Hwaianfu.

The Work of Cleaning Water

The complicated routine of preparing water to make it safe to drink was a full-time job that Father trusted to no one but Mother.

The canal was our only source of water. To say it was polluted doesn't begin to describe it, for it was not only the major waterway but the place where everyone along the canal washed their rice, vegetables and laundry. All refuse was thrown into it indiscriminately. The "night-soil" pots of human waste were not emptied into it, because that precious commodity was carefully collected and saved for fertilizer, but the pots

were washed in the canal. This was done in the early hours of the morning before people were about.

Water was carried in wooden buckets from the canal to the house. Here the water carrier emptied it into the first of a series of three *gongs*, large crocks three feet in diameter and about as deep. Into each was stirred a measure of alum, an astringent that drew the mud to the bottom. When it had settled, the first gong was literally half mud. The water from the top was then syphoned off into a second gong and more alum was added. After it had settled for a second time, it was syphoned once more into the third gong. Although the water now looked clear, it was just as polluted as ever.

Now began the tedious business of purifying it. First, bottles had to be found and scoured, then boiled. We didn't have the beautiful wide-necked bottles of today but instead dark green, narrow-necked things. After the water had boiled for a good 20 minutes, it was filtered through cotton into a jug which too had been boiled beforehand. When the water had cooled a little it was poured into the bottles.

Still hot, the bottles were hung by their necks in the breeze, with wet cloths wrapped around them to encourage cooling by evaporation. I was forever drinking lukewarm water, especially in the hot weather when the supply of cool water could never keep pace with the demand.

When we got properly settled in our new house, my father called in the local tinsmith and together they designed and made a copper still. It was very big and stood permanently on the back of the brick stove in the kitchen, for distilled water was needed for preparing medicines. Before it was even put into the still, the water was first boiled to be on the safe side. We also drank this water; it had an unpalatable, flat taste because of the lack of minerals in it. As a special treat, occasionally our mother would add a dash of precious lime juice to give it a little taste.

Tien-Sui.
(Sweet water)

In Peking, where the water was so brackish, *tien-sui* (sweet water) from special wells was trundled along the cobblestone *hutungs* in large wooden barrels on wheels, to be sold by the bucketful at the gates of homes.

Summer in the Mountains

Summer was stifling hot, and Mother was expecting a baby. In July, Father took the family to Moganshan, a mountain resort not far from Shanghai. We traveled, as always, by houseboat. We spent one night at the foot of the mountain in a Chinese inn, where my recollection was of Dorothy being bitten by bedbugs that left a trail of vivid red spots across her little white back.

The next day we set out for the settlement at the top of the mountain, traveling in a caravan of sedan chairs — parents, children, servants, bags and baggage. The bearers crossed the short, flat plain almost at a run, gradually slowing down as they commenced to climb. The narrow winding mountain paths often followed turns so sharp that a chair was momentarily suspended over a sheer drop of what seemed like thousands of feet, as the bearers carefully maneuvered around these acute angles. To look down then literally took one's breath away.

The chair for carrying people up the mountain was very different from the more substantial, closed-in sedan chair used for regular travel. The mountain chair was made of the slenderest bamboo framework. With every step it bent and swayed and creaked as though it were about to break in two. But bamboo is incredibly strong, as well as being light in weight and endlessly versatile.

What I recall most vividly about the bearers was two things: the large lumps on their shoulders, a result of a lifetime of heavy pressure there, and the enormous, bulging veins in the huge muscular calves of their legs.

All sorts of missionaries had built houses at the resort at the top of the mountain. I suppose it was emotionally important for them to get together occasionally, to exchange news and experiences. It was cool and clean there and the streams provided the rare luxury of pure, cold water to drink. Here in a little rented bungalow, my youngest sister, Mary, was born on September 1, 1910.

In the courtyard of a Chinese inn, early 20th Century.

This little house was almost completely engulfed by towering bamboo trees that swarmed with cicadas whose shrill, deafening note pierced the air. At times this noise became so unbearable that I would bury my head in a quilt. The amah sometimes caught the cicadas and ate them, after first roasting them in hot ash. We children tried them, too. They tasted like a bit of crisp, without any particular flavor.

Chinese and Western Medicine

There were no signs of a hospital. My father did his work in a couple of small, mud-floored buildings that served as dispensary and outpatient clinic. Although Mother had no technical training, Father taught her to do most of his dispensing and to look after the women patients, for women were always reluctant to have a man examine them.

The outpatients' waiting rooms, one for men and one for women, were always overflowing with all kinds of diseases — leprosy, smallpox, advanced cases of venereal disease, deformities and skin diseases, streaming sore eyes, and those sick with fevers and the dying. In those days the Chinese didn't come to the foreign doctor unless they had given up all hope, having tried every kind of cure practiced by their own medicine men.

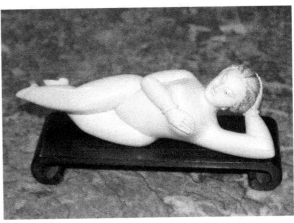

Because he could not examine female patients directly, Dr. Malcolm carried this figurine. Patients pointed to where their pain or discomfort was.

The Chinese medicine men had knowledge of the use of herbs, drugs and acupuncture, and of the principle of counter-irritants handed down from one generation to the next by the apprentice system. But it has never ceased to puzzle me that so highly civilized a people, after so many thousands of years, had made so little progress in understanding anatomy, physiology, hygiene and the true functions of the body. They knew, for instance, that to drink cold water would make them sick, so they drank boiling water. But they thought it was because the water was cold that it was dangerous. They didn't connect purifying to the act of boiling.

Ancestor worship automatically precluded any study of anatomy, because it denied the grim necessity of the dissecting room. Man was believed to have two spirits. One inhabited his stomach; the other was represented by his breath of *ch'i*. At death the ch'i stayed on earth, hovering over the grave of the deceased. This spirit had to be placated at given intervals by the offering of food and wine and the burning of incense, accompanied by mourning at the graveside. If this ritual was neglected, it was believed the ch'i would turn into a malign thing, haunting the lives of the bereaved.

The other spirit left the body at death, going directly to join its ancestors in the spirit world. This spirit was believed to represent exactly the shape and form of the body it had just left behind on earth. This is why beheading, and all other forms of deliberate mutilation of the body, was such an ignominious way to die — one was then condemned to arrive before one's ancestors without a head or whatever parts had been removed. This belief made the study of anatomy, by autopsy, unthinkable.

The Doctor and His Patients

In our new home in Hwaianfu, Father had one room set aside as an office and consulting room for special patients. One day I couldn't find Mother and went to the office in search of her. From behind the closed door she called to me that she was busy. Listening for a bit, I thought I heard some funny noises that I couldn't quite make out so I put my eye to the keyhole. I saw a man lying on a table and my mother holding a foot while my father sawed away at what must have been a leg amputation.

Another time, Mother sent me to call Father from the dispensary for something. I went into the enormous waiting room, full of people with illnesses of all kinds. The man in there said Father was busy, so I sat down between two waiting patients. Eventually Father came out, and he grabbed me and he pulled me out. I'd been sitting between a man falling to pieces with leprosy and I don't know what the other patient had, and Father just was so upset about this.

I was once allowed to watch him do a cataract operation and, among other things, often watched him pull teeth. I recall one day being in the clinic when an old man came in and elaborately explained about an aching tooth. Father asked him to open his mouth and point to exactly which tooth it was that was aching. Then, with his forceps held out of sight behind his back, my father resorted to his commonest form of anesthetic, the element of surprise! In a flash he had the offending tooth out.

When the old fellow recovered from his surprise, he gasped, "Oh, but it wasn't *my* tooth I was talking about, it was my wife's!"

The Hwaianfu beggar whose nose tumor Dr. Malcolm removed.

Our mother "taught" us for a couple of hours each day, for there was no school. We also had some lessons in reading and writing from a Chinese teacher that year. But we missed a whole year of formal schooling.

I have one vivid memory of a professional beggar who sat day after day outside our front gate. Suspended from the end of his nose was a large tumor, only a little smaller than his head. He had the thing neatly tied up in a faded blue cloth bag, with a purse-string around the top where it joined onto the nose. We children occasionally dropped a cash into his eternally proffered bowl, and sometimes prevailed on the gateman to give him something to eat — then stood watching, fascinated, while he maneuvered this thing to one side as he lifted the bowl to his mouth to eat.

One day my father spoke to him, asking if he might examine his "nose." He then asked if the man would be willing to let him remove the tumor. At first the man demurred, saying that without it he would be deprived of his livelihood. But in the end, he agreed.

I wish I still had the pictures that Father took of the man before and after the operation. He had looked like an old man, his brow permanently furrowed from the strain of this heavy weight that had hung there for many years. After the operation, he looked the young man he really was, no more than 30 or so. His happiness was unbounded and his countenance radiant. He must have stayed around the compound for some time, for I remember him so clearly.

Street Calls and Compound Life

As in all walled Chinese cities, the streets in Hwaianfu ran north and south, east and west, or as the Chinese say, east-west, south-north. As there was never any heating in the homes, it was important, in North China especially, for all living quarters to face south to embrace as much of the low winter sun as possible. To further conserve warmth, there were no windows on the north walls of rooms. All main rooms faced south, giving onto an enclosed courtyard which not only embraced the sun but also was a protection against the never-ending winter winds. The courtyard's side rooms were used for kitchens and other utilities, and for the "lesser" members of a family.

A street scene, 1920. INTERFOTO / Alamy Stock Photo

A street barber gave the family's gatekeeper his weekly shave.

In the city, life within a family compound was a unique and private world all its own. Women and girls rarely left the seclusion of their high compound walls. All their needs, whether food or services, were met by peddlers who routinely passed by the front gate during the course of the day and even at night.

These peddlers, or hawkers as they were called, had regular beats, so we got to know when we could expect them. Their approach was always heralded by their distinctive street-calls, whether by gong, horn, rattle, cymbal or voice. They had mastered the art of pitching and throwing their voices over the high walls that everywhere surrounded the homes. Of all these cries, the night calls, when all was still, were the most haunting and uncanny.

A whole book could be written describing the variety of the hawkers' cries. I learned to recognize the different calls and would rush out to look, or buy, or to ask the gateman to get a bowl mended or a shoe-sole stitched. Better still, I would help the amah choose a length of cloth, or enviously watch her shoo the flies away from the sticky *tze-ma-t'ang* (malt and sesame-seed candy) as she bargained for these sweet morsels, strictly forbidden to us children. Usually, after a fair amount of coaxing, she would succumb to our entreaties and give us each a piece, first blowing on it to make sure no dust or fly clung to its sticky surface.

Then there was the traveling Punch-and-Judy show, all confined within a four-foot-square cloth stage. I could never understand what they were saying in their high-pitched falsetto voices, but there was no mistaking their gestures, which often finished up being plainly lewd.

But what fascinated me most of all was to watch the street barber give our gateman his weekly shave and comb his long, handsome queue, of which he was justly proud. This done, the barber would apply a steaming hot towel to the gateman's face. The towel was wrung out of boiling water in a brass basin that stood on a brazier of glowing coal-balls. The towel was gray from long and constant use, but the service was nonetheless refreshing. Last but not least came the ear-cleaning, deftly done with the aid of a little ball of lamb's wool (non-disposable) on the end of a sliver of bamboo.

When it was all over, the gateman would stand and flick the barber's towel around his neck and shoulders to remove any hair or dust that might be there, gradually working his way down his long garment to his shoes. These too got a quick flick just for good measure.

Then with a smile and a friendly nod, the barber would take back his all-purpose towel, shoulder his pole and move on, twanging his brass tongs as he went, announcing his coming to his next customer, on whom the same faithful towel was used.

Girls were confined within their compound walls, it's true — but there was never a dull moment, for they helped with the chores and were taught the tasks necessary to become a wife and mother. Then there was the fun of watching the world go by from the front gate; until, that is, she came "of age." After that it was considered unseemly for her to be seen hanging around the gate for all to eye.

Another feature of city life was the night watchman. He did his rounds at regular intervals with the tick-tick-tack of his bamboo clock, announcing the watches of the night. It was not unusual for a watchman to make special arrangements with the Robbers' Guild by paying them regular "protection money."

Rice in the South, Noodles in the North

The days were filled with the routine of daily living. Breakfast, in South China, usually consisted of a bowl of *hsi-fan* (rice congee, a gruel or porridge), with perhaps a few small chunks of salt radish to add a little flavor, with green tea to drink. I'm speaking of the peasant. The very poor ate plain rice and drank *pai-ch'a* (white tea), which was simply plain boiling water. The affluent would likely have egg with their congee, or chicken broth and a little fish — or anything they desired, as do the affluent anywhere.

In North China, the peasant didn't eat rice for the simple reason that rice doesn't grow in the dry, cold north. The peasant eats what he grows. In the north he eats mil-

A midday meal of noodles in north China.

let and wheat flour, made into various kinds of breads, and noodles boiled in plain water. I recall when nurses were admitted to the hospital to commence their training, we had to give them five meals a day of noodles or *mant'o* (steamed bread). Only three meals of such plain diet just didn't sustain them for the kind of work and study expected of them. And their digestion couldn't at first tolerate a richer protein diet, for they had never been accustomed to it.

Millet, the even commoner diet in the north, was cooked in different ways, from a soft gruel to a solid cake. Rickshaw pullers ate this cake during the day when they were

on the job. They stored it in the space under the passenger seat of the rickshaw. Between fares they would take it out, break off a chunk and eat it with no trimmings. Sometimes this cake had become so dry and hard that I have seen them try in vain to break it with their teeth. They would have to hammer it into small pieces with a stone. But fresh millet, especially the glutinous variety, was sweet and so delicious. As children in school, this was easily our favorite hot cereal.

Chores in the Women's Courts

On sunny days — and it was usually sunny in North China, where it rained all too seldom — the *pei-wos* (quilts) were hung out to air. (Sheets, as we know them, were not used.) One of the major preoccupations for women in the spring was the taking apart of all their winter quilted bedding and quilted garments. The covers were washed, then smoothed out on straw mats to dry. The cotton padding had to be fluffed out before the quilts could be made up again.

The fluffing process of this old, matted, by now gray cotton was something to see. It was done by a man using a long bow made of bamboo that crossed his back, from over one shoulder to under the other arm, with its taut cord passing across and down in front of him. With his two hands he would twang this cord while applying it to the matted cotton. The cotton fell apart and fluffed up — and so did the operator, for in time all that was to be seen of him was an animated apparition completely covered with fluff.

Boys in the home were usually apprenticed to their fathers, or, in the wealthier homes, were taught the elements of reading and writing and the use of the abacus. Girls learned to cook and to sew. An important part of their sewing was the making of shoes. Each girl had to make her own; only she knew the shape and size needed for her own little bound feet.

To make soles for shoes, a piece of cardboard about two feet long and a foot wide leaned permanently against an outside wall, facing the sun. Whenever there was a scrap of torn or discarded cloth, no matter how small, it would be saturated in a mix of flour and water, then pasted smoothly onto this cardboard. Gradually this became thick and firm, always drying in the sun. Layers of this were then cut out in the shape and size of the required shoe sole, stitched firmly together, then finally covered with strong new cloth. To be strong enough for this work, thread made from fresh new cotton wool had to be hand-spun with the aid of a spindle.

Foot Binding: The Crippling Custom

The custom of foot binding among the women of China existed for over 900 years. What was its origin? Many romantic theories have been postulated, but for a custom of this dimension to have persisted for so long, there can be no question of romance. It was clearly a repressive measure imposed by men over women.

I have often heard Chinese men wish for the good old days of the onetime-close family life. But never does one hear a woman yearn for those days.

At the time of the Nationalist Revolution in 1911, foot binding was legally abolished, and among the student class it was soon abandoned. But it took much longer for the masses to give up a custom that had prevailed for so many centuries. A girl was permitted to run free until she was about five years old, then the painful and crippling business of binding began. It had to be done very carefully, if serious complications such as gangrene were to be avoided.

Slowly but firmly the four small toes were folded under, gradually embedding them into the ball of the foot, leaving the big toe free. As the foot grew longer, the instep was bent under and back, giving the foot its abnormal arched appearance. Bathing, powdering and rebinding had to be done at careful intervals — but as long as the foot was still growing, the intense pain was always there.

A woman's bound feet.

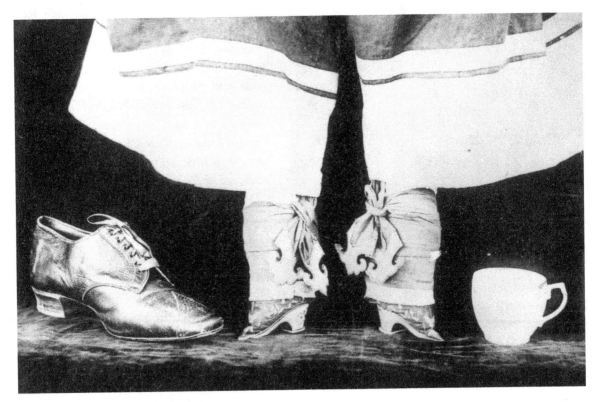

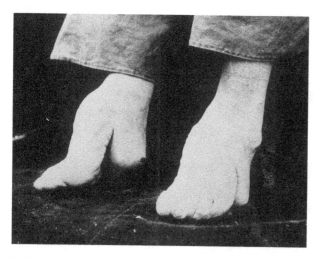

As the foot grew, the instep was bound under and back, giving the foot its abnormal arched appearance.

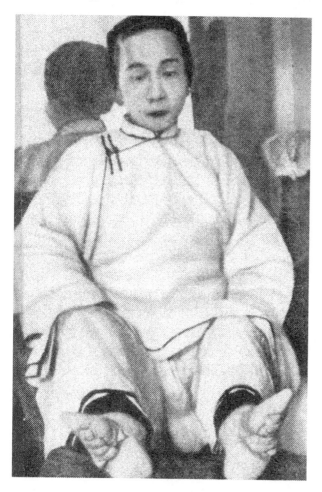

A Chinese woman's bound foot was such a private and personal thing that rarely did anyone, except a husband, ever see it without its bindings. As a hospital nurse I have had occasion to see women's feet with the bindings off. In the women's wards it was still dark in the early pre-dawn when they began the care of their feet, always bathing, powdering and re-binding. Even the woman in the next bed couldn't see her neighbor's feet. By daylight the women would all be cheerfully combing their hair.

I recall as late as 1925, a country woman patient whispering to me, asking what nationality were the Chinese girl nurses who were taking care of her. I asked what nationality she thought they were. She replied that while they looked Chinese and spoke Chinese, they couldn't be — "Look at their big feet!"

Manchu women never bound their feet. It was not a Manchu custom. Nor did the hill women of the south, who had to climb all the time. The boat women worked side by side with their men, and went barefoot most of the time just like their men. But all other women, rich and poor alike throughout the length and breadth of China, had bound feet. I've seen little homeless girls on the street, binding their own feet with tears running down their faces. They thought they would never get a husband if they had great, big, male-sized feet.

But ironically, it was the women of the leisure class who suffered most. With serving maids to wait on them hand and foot, they had less need to walk, so could afford to have their feet bound very early and thus kept very small. It became a status symbol. Physical exertion of any kind was looked upon as menial. Another status symbol was the pale whiteness of a lady's skin, indicating that, unlike the peasant woman, she didn't have to toil in the fields all day under the burning sun.

So a lady of leisure hobbled, with the aid of maids, from her bed to the mahjong table. [A tile-based game, mahjong is still popular throughout much of Asia.] With almost total illiteracy added to their bound feet and long, long fingernails, their activities were very limited. It was no wonder so many spent their nights in gambling and intrigue.

When you bind the feet of a nation's women for so many centuries, you bind more than their feet. And when you release those feet, you release more than just feet.

The Beggars' Guild

As in all Chinese cities at that time, professional beggars abounded in Hwaianfu. They were part of a highly organized guild. They had their regular beats, roaming the streets begging from passersby, following them with whining pleas that only thinly veiled their threatening manner. As children we were never allowed on the streets without both the amah and a gateman. More than once I have seen a "crippled" beggar, leaning heavily on his crutch, suddenly straighten up, pick up his crutch, and use it to menace a timid pedestrian.

Crippled and deformed people were stationed at strategic spots to beg, while their takings were closely observed from a discreet distance. Favorite baits for this ploy were helpless old people, who sat by the hour where they were left, and crippled women with nearly naked babies on their laps, crying feebly in the bitter weather.

We never dared give to these beggars. If one did, one would immediately be surrounded by more that seemed to materialize from nowhere, all demanding money. More than once in Chefoo, years later while riding through the city to get to the hospital on the far side, I was followed by a husky beggar, running alongside my rickshaw with his restraining hand on the mudguard, whining for money. Trembling inside, I would feign unconcern. Rarely did the rickshaw man dare to brush him off, lest he be ganged-up on at some later date. As this became my regular route to the hospital, I dared not risk ever giving them anything.

A street beggar.
Photograph by Hedda Morrison. Image courtesy of the President and Fellows of Harvard College.

Flying Kites in Spring

In the early spring, our greatest treat was to be taken out onto the city-wall embankment to fly our kites, and to watch groups of young men fly their many kinds of large kites. Of these the most fascinating was the many-sectioned dragon kite. These varied in size and length, consisting of as many as 12 or more sections. The first section, the head of the dragon, was about four feet square, with each succeeding section tapering off in size, finishing up with a long tail made of string.

To fly this thing took careful organization. Each section was held separately by one man, while the anchor men — sometimes two or three or even more, depending on the size of the kite — held the strong ground-cord. At the first sign of a favorable wind, the whole team ran together into the wind. At the second signal, each section was released almost simultaneously, with the head section slightly in advance of the next and the next. The whole performance had to be sensitively timed, for a miscalculation meant the ruin of hours of preparation.

After the kite was up, it took strength combined with a sixth sense to hold it and keep it flying. Sometimes it went so high that it was scarcely visible. That kind of kite-flying was no child's play.

Flying little kites from within compound walls sometimes turned out to be a cutthroat sport. Once a kite was up, there was no way of preventing its string from extending above and across neighboring compounds. If the kite was a handsome model, it was often watched with envy from below.

Suddenly from behind some wall, up would soar a menacing slingshot, consisting of a length of string with a stone attached to each end. Skillfully aimed, this would straddle the kite string — and in a twinkling the kite would

A steet vendor, making and selling kites.
Photograph by Hedda Morrison.
Image courtesy of the President and Fellows of Harvard College.

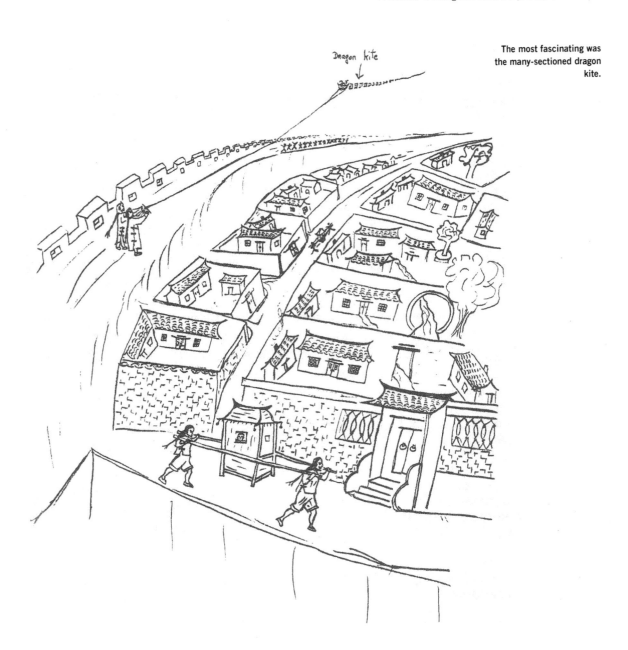

Dragon kite

The most fascinating was the many-sectioned dragon kite.

be down and out of sight, the string cut and released, leaving nothing but a loose end dangling in the owner's hand, with no clue as to the culprit. There was no question of hopping onto the wall to get a quick look round, for to discourage intruders these walls were crowned with broken glass embedded in cement.

Another lovely sign of spring was the sight and sound of flocks of pigeons. With whistles tied to their legs, these birds wheeled and circled back and forth across the sky, their whistles singing a cheerful note as they flew.

The Gu Family

In time we moved into our new, foreign-style house and it was lovely, with wide verandas, a living room and dining room and kitchens at the back. On the right side of the house, Father had a sort of waiting room; behind that was his consulting room, because the hospital hadn't been built yet.

One day in autumn 1910, a wealthy local government official named Mr. Gu came to call on my father, saying that his wife was very ill. He said he had called in Chinese medicine men, but they could do nothing more for her.

To prescribe for a person after medicine men had been treating them was always risky — for if the patient died, the last one to touch the patient was considered responsible for the death. This was one of the hazards that foreign doctors faced. But my father went with Mr. Gu to his home. As always, when he was to attend a woman patient, he took my mother with him to do the intimate examining.

I don't recall what it was that ailed Mrs. Gu, but it was something that Western medicine understood, for Mrs Gu got well — and from then on, Mr. and Mrs. Gu were devoted to my parents. A friendship developed between the two families which became very close on both sides, and soon included the children.

I recall my first visit to the Gu family home. Dorothy and I were asked to take off our shoes, while one of the maids traced the shape of each foot on a piece of paper. On our next visit we were each presented with a pair of dainty, black satin slippers with delicate flowers embroidered on the toe of each shoe. "*Hao-kan, hao-kan*" (pretty, pretty), we exclaimed.

Dorothy and Claire.

Dorothy and I came to know the ladies of the Gu family very well, and spent many happy days with them in the secluded women's courts of their lovely Chinese home, where we were often invited to spend the night with the girls. At the time, we took all this for granted. But looking back on it now, I realize that in 1910 and 1911 it was a rare exception for foreigners in China to be admitted into the intimate circle of a family of this social standing.

Whenever Mother invited the Gu family to our home, they would arrive escorted by a couple of gatemen and accompanied by a maid-servant each. The girls were always filled with curiosity and amusement at our very different way of life — and there were shrieks of laughter when Erhsiaochieh, the middle daughter, dressed up in some of my mother's clothes. Later she asked Mother to order for her a foreign dress, complete with a hat to match. I don't know where Mother got it from — Montgomery Ward, I imagine.

The Love and Loss of Daughters

There is a belief in the West that the Chinese do not love their daughters as much as they do their sons. The importance of having sons in the family becomes clear when one realizes that the only form of old-age security was to have sons who would stay in the home and carry on the family affairs.

Daughters were equally well-loved, but no sooner did a girl begin to be useful in the home than she was given in marriage at the early age of perhaps 15 or 16. She then left to live in her husband's home. Also, the obligation of a dowry and the cost of a wedding were heavy expenses to the bride's family. So especially in the poorer homes, a daughter had to be regarded as an extra expense.

When I went back to Shanghai in 1946 after the war, our old gardener, Yin, was still there. One day he asked me to come to his home nearby to see his wife, who was sick. I remembered that they had five children, two boys and three girls, but I also recalled that when I was evacuated in 1941, the mother had been expecting another baby. Hesitatingly I asked Yin where the sixth child was.

There was a short silence. Slowly the old man explained that, during the Japanese occupation, times had become very hard especially after *Lao-pan* (Mr. Lintilhac) was interned but before the Japanese took over our compound as a military residential headquarters. With no money coming in, there was less and less for the family to eat. The new baby was a strong, healthy girl. As long as she was on mother's milk, it had been all right, but soon she became another mouth to feed.

With his head bowed, he assured me that she was in a good home. They had sold her to buy food for the family. I sat down beside the mother and put my arm around her, then changed the subject.

Women in the courtyard of a home in Peking.
Photograph by James Ricalton. Image courtesy of Billie Love Historical Collection and Historical Photographs of China, University of Bristol.

Mornings with the Gu Girls

Mr. Gu was a man of about 45. His wife was exactly the same age. They had three daughters but no sons. The oldest daughter, Tahsiaochieh, was 25. Erhsiaochieh, the second daughter, was 19, and Sanhsiaochieh was a year younger than me.

In many ways the Gu family was very unusual, especially for a Chinese family; for although Mr. Gu had no sons, he had never taken another wife or concubine. Even more unusual, he was in no hurry for his daughters to marry and leave the home. And — this was almost unheard-of, in China in those days — Mr. Gu had never permitted his daughters to have their feet bound.

The two older daughters shared a three-room suite, with a bedroom each and a common living room in between. Like all living quarters, this suite faced south, giving onto a courtyard that seemed always flooded with warm sunshine.

In wealthy homes such as this, each daughter had her own *ya-t'ou*, or slave girl, bought by the mother for the daughter as her personal maid as well as companion and personal property. Usually this maid was the same age as her mistress, for they were bought when the girls were very young so that they grew up together. While on the one hand they were playmates, at the same time it was the duty of the ya-t'ou to care for the intimate needs of her mistress. In the Gu home these slave girls were treated with the greatest kindness, almost as though they were members of the family.

Whenever we spent the night there, Dorothy would share the room with Tahsiaochieh while I roomed with Erhsiaochieh. Each morning on arising, the ya-t'ou would come in with a kettle of boiling water. Pouring it into an enamel basin that stood on a wooden stand, she would then wring out steaming hot towels for our faces. While I dressed, I recall watching the ya-t'ou binding her mistress's breasts with a firm flat breast-binder, for it was considered immodest for a girl to show her figure.

Each daughter had her own ya-t'ou, *or slave girl*

Among the toilet articles in the girls' rooms were a box of chalk-white face powder and a little pot of rouge, used to tint not only their cheeks but also the palms of their hands. The dainty soft hands of Chinese ladies-of-leisure were so delicate and shapely. Their hands are traditionally compared to the petals of the lotus blossom, and rightly so. (One of the first things I noticed when I came to live in the West was the splendid strong hands of American women, accustomed to doing everything for themselves.)

One of the many other things that puzzled me was a skein of wood shavings that hung from a nail on the windowsill. One day I watched the ya-t'ou take a couple of these shavings from the bunch, place them in a bowl and pour boiling water over them. After letting this stand for awhile, the water, though remaining quite clear, became thick and glutinous. This was hair-set lotion. The shavings were from the wood of the slippery elm.

After a breakfast of soft rice congee, and perhaps a poached egg or a little fish or salt vegetable, the business of hair-combing began. My hair was fairly long by Western standards, but it was a reddish color, of all things. What with that and my glasses, the sight I made with my hair pulled straight back caused a bit of polite merriment. Dorothy's hair, on the other hand, was brown but irrepressibly curly, and no amount of brushing and braiding could straighten it out.

Most Chinese have an abundance of long raven-black hair on the head, but a very minimum of hair on the body. In fact, hairlessness, certainly among women, is considered a measure of refinement. It is no wonder that the Westerner with his hairy chest and legs, not to mention his bushy beard, was commonly referred to by Chinese as a "hairy barbarian." An uncouth, even revolting sight to a Chinese.

The serious combing of a girl's hair was done by her maid. With the aid of a toothbrush she first applied a little of the slippery elm hair-set lotion. The raven black tresses were then combed and combed with a fine bamboo comb until every hair was in place. Now, gripping the hair firmly at the nape of the neck, a red silken cord was wound round and round till it was the shape and size of a large spool of red thread. Once this was securely fastened, the braiding began. Each fold of hair was as smooth as satin. Toward the end of the braid, another length of red cord was braided in, then fastened in the same way.

In those days the unmarried girl always wore her hair in this long braid, or queue, hanging down her back, while in front she wore a straight fringe or bangs, covering most

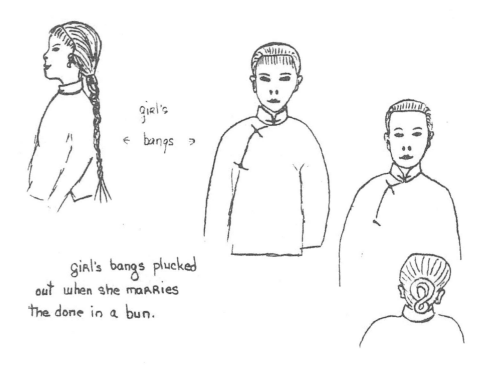

girl's

← bangs →

girl's bangs plucked out when she marries the done in a bun.

of her forehead. After she was married her hair was done in a neat bun at the nape of her neck. But part of the wedding preparations was first to have her fringe or bangs plucked out hair by hair, leaving a severe, square line outlining her face.

Although I have yet to see a Chinese lady with a single hair on her face, nevertheless it was also the custom to go over the bride-to-be's face with a kind of twisted thread to remove any suggestion of fluff that might be there. To do this the maid, or whoever was skilled at it, would take a yard of fine silk thread and twist it until it doubled back on itself, creating a tight double twist. With one end in her right hand, the other end held firmly between her teeth and the loop in the middle spread out with the fingers of her left hand, she ran this contrivance over the face, alternately pulling and releasing the two ends. It worked something like our childhood game of spinning a button on a loop of twisted string. By pulling and releasing this thread, it picked up every suspicion of hair, however fine.

This was a sensitive ordeal for the girl, but a fascinating thing to watch. With tears in her eyes, the bride-to-be would sit patiently till the performance was over. For the rest of the day her face would be blotched with vivid red from the sharp irritation. But it was all in the cause of beauty.

The bride-to-be.

The Braided Queue

The old Western habit of referring to the Chinese man's queue as a "pigtail" was not only a misnomer, but was considered by the Chinese as a form of ridicule. Nothing could have been less like the tail of a pig than a Chinese man's long, handsome queue.

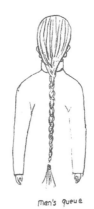

girl's queue   man's queue

The main difference between a man's and a girl's queue was that the man's was not fastened at the nape of the neck, but was braided evenly right down to the end and there fastened with a black silk cord. When the man was in mourning, his queue was fastened with white cord. In the front, the man's hair was shaved back a couple of inches to give him a sharp hairline, leaving a short, inch-long fringe that stood straight up from the head.

On the other hand, the European custom in the pre-Victorian era of a man wearing powdered hair or a wig, with its little curly braid at the back, looked exactly like a pig's tail. This is where the expression originated. It didn't apply to the Chinese man's queue.

The queue was the token of allegiance to the Manchu throne. It was imposed on Chinese men for the duration of the Manchu rule, which was about 300 years. After the government was overthrown in the Nationalist Revolution of 1911, in theory the Chinese abandoned the custom of wearing a queue.

Men at a meal, each with the braided queue and the shaved forehead that were common in the last years of the Manchu dynasty.
Photograph by Lai Fong (Afong Studio). Image courtesy of Special Collections, University of Bristol Library and Historical Photographs of China.

The Jewel Box

Erhsiaochieh, the middle Gu daughter, would indulge me by allowing me to investigate all her pretty things. One favorite pastime was exploring her little carved wood jewel box, composed of tiny drawers filled with the most fascinating jewelry. Everything went in identical pairs, whether rings, bracelets or earrings. Then there were hair ornaments of every kind — intricately designed gold-filigree butterflies, overlaid with the delicate blue feathers from hummingbirds' breasts, and straight stickpin hair ornaments with heads of carved jade.

There were many other things, but to me the strangest were the long, intricately carved, curved fingernail shields made of tortoise shell. Made to protect the nail, these were slipped on over the long fingernail and fitted snugly over the end of the finger down to the first knuckle.

I don't recall Erhsiaochieh's nails as being unduly long, but some of the ladies in the family wore them one or more inches in length. This was the vogue for women of fashion, and a positive hallmark of a lady of leisure — for with these long nails and their little bound feet, they could do very little for themselves and had to be waited on hand and foot.

Although maidservants, with all their work, couldn't possibly cultivate long nails, they nevertheless managed to let the nail of the little finger on each hand grow to a very useful, all-purpose length. It came in handy for many things, such as scratching the head and cleaning the ears.

In recalling these days my memory darts about, conjuring a kaleidoscope of feminine occupations. My sister and I were taught how to cut out dainty paper flowers, symmetrically designed, to be embroidered-over on the toes of ladies' shoes. And from a handful of cotton wool we learned to spin strong thread, for stitching the cloth soles of shoes.

We were also shown how to spin a Chinese bamboo *diabolo* until it hummed its high musical note. I learned, too, how to kick a shuttlecock made of chicken feathers tied to a couple of brass cash, the kind with a square hole in the center. This was a boy's game, not for girls with bound feet, but Sanhsiaochieh had natural feet like mine.

Aside from the gardener and the water-carrier and an occasional visit from Mr. Gu, no men were ever admitted to the women's courts.

A Chinese girl, late 1800s.
Image courtesy of Dr Jocelyn Chatterton and Historical Photographs of China, University of Bristol.

In the Family Room

One delightful memory is of the Gu home's large formal reception room. Against three of its walls were arranged the usual formal sets of little square tables, flanked on either side by straight-backed, carved, black wood chairs. On the fourth side of the room, at the far end, was a raised dais about four inches high. Side by side on this stood two regular barber's chairs, complete with head and foot rests and screwed firmly to the floor. Mr. Gu regarded these chairs as the last word in modern comfort.

Smoking a water pipe was a social pastime and a graceful art. A pinch of tobacco was taken from a compartment at the back of the pipe and rolled between the thumb and finger of one hand. This was lightly placed in the top end of the tobacco tube in front (rather like a cigarette holder) that extended down into the pipe's water compartment. Now the glowing end of a spill of fire-paper was briskly blown into a flame and held to the tobacco. The smoke, drawn down, made a bubbling noise as it passed through the water in the bowl, where it was cooled.

The two older daughters always joined in these evenings with their parents. They watched the younger girls play, and Mrs. Gu would hail one of us when either of the parents' pipes needed re-lighting. We would have lighted paper tapers, and we'd blow one of these into a little flame and hold it to their pipe while they inhaled this smoke.

Children are children, and mothers and fathers are mothers and fathers in every language — and we would run around having great fun while the two older girls sat and made conversation. This was the family circle after supper at night; it was all so natural and gracious.

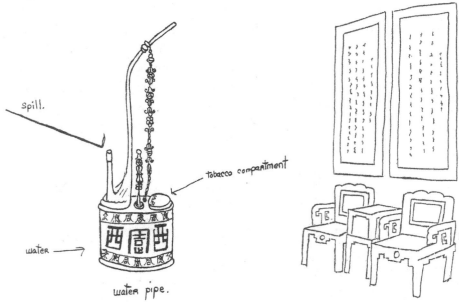

Far left: the Gu family's water pipe. Left: In the family room.

Grandmother Gu's Birthday

One of the important events of that year was the birthday celebration of Mr. Gu's mother. She looked very old and small, dressed in elaborately embroidered and voluminous ancestral robes, sitting in state in a carved ancestral chair on a dais at the end of another large reception room. I remember the fascination of watching the procession of family retainers, filing in to pay homage to the old lady and do their obeisance.

First came the bond-servants, who prostrated themselves full length on the floor before her. Immediately they were up and away as though not deserving of more than a moment of her attention. Next came an endless procession of personal servants and family retainers. One at a time they fell on their knees, knocking their heads three times on the floor; then they too were gone. Next came the poorer relations, and finally the immediate family, beginning with the little children all dressed up in their formal best. Each child stepped forward with hands cupped together and bowed three times without a word, then stepped back but didn't go away.

The very last to pay homage was Mr. Gu himself, the old lady's eldest son. With his hands cupped together, he too bowed three times.

Besides my sister and me, there were other onlookers, adding to the colorful ceremonial scene. The birthday feast was given later in the evening. We children didn't go to that.

Mr. Gu's Concubine

The following year Mr. Gu finally concurred with his wife that there should be a son in the family to observe the rites of ancestor worship. Mrs. Gu herself sought out and found a young, rosy-cheeked country woman, whom she bought from a family that had too many daughters and needed the money. Mrs. Gu presented this young woman to her husband as a concubine.

Mrs. Gu presented this young woman to her husband

In due course a son was born. This child was automatically recognized by Mrs. Gu as her own legal son, while the mother of the baby assumed the role of wet nurse and amah for the child. So at last there was a son and heir in the family.

There was great rejoicing, and the thrill of having a baby in their midst caused a flutter of excitement in the women's courts. The best was just barely good enough for the baby and his mother. She was constantly plied with all the delicacies considered beneficial to a nursing mother.

One of the favorite dishes was a thin gruel made by pouring boiling water over a couple of tablespoons of *ou-fen*, sweetened with brown sugar. Ou-fen is a powder very much like arrowroot, made from the bulbous root of the lotus. Another slightly more substantial dish was the thin congee made from glutinous millet or glutinous rice. Then there was always the *kwa-mien*, fine noodles cooked in delicious chicken broth. (The Chinese never drank milk. Cows were used only as beasts of burden.)

In the meantime the jealous gods had to be hoodwinked into thinking that the sun did not rise and set on this precious child. All sorts of ruses were used, including the custom of never completely finishing the sewing of the baby's little garments. This was to give the impression of not caring whether the child lived or not, lest those jealous gods snatch him away. For the same reason, a boy was often given a girl's name.

There were very strict rules governing the routine of a mother at this time. No visitors were permitted to step across the threshold of her room during the child's first hundred days. In those days, hygiene as such was not understood, but a mother knew that she risked all kinds of bad luck if she ignored these rules.

A mother and child, about 1910.
Image courtesy of Charles Poolton and Historical Photographs of China, University of Bristol.

The Festival of Flower Petals

One day, to join in an early spring festival, Dorothy and I were invited to go with the Gu ladies by houseboat to a nearby town to visit a temple run by priestesses. This temple had a large inner courtyard, completely enclosed on all four sides by two-storied buildings. Overlooking the court, a second-story veranda extended all the way around. Within this enclosure grew three huge magnolia trees, said to represent the spirits of three virtuous nuns. At this time of year these trees were in full bloom; one could reach out from the veranda and touch their fleshy blossoms.

The festival atmosphere was enhanced by the smell of incense and the muffled background sound of deep gongs and high flutes. There were many other women and girls there, and lots of excitement. The main holiday spirit was centered on each girl plucking the blossom of her choice from one of the trees. There followed much rushing about to decide which bloom was the biggest and best.

Finally, each girl carried her chosen flower inside to a temporarily set-up kitchen where waiting nuns, standing behind a vat of boiling sesame-seed oil, would separate the petals of the flower, and, one by one, dip them into batter then plunge them into the boiling oil. When nicely browned and puffed out, the petals were picked out of the oil with the aid of long metal chopsticks, then smothered in soft brown sugar and placed on the girl's plate.

As I recall, the batter and brown sugar were delicious, but the petal itself had a bitter taste. But it was a beautiful day, and all such fun.

The Tide of Change

We spent the summer of 1911 at Guling, a popular summer mountain resort for missionaries from central China. My sweetest memories are of being allowed to run free, and drinking the pure cold water of the mountain streams. What my mother enjoyed most was the music she so longed for, and could never hope to get in a remote mission station. I recall hearing her sing the lead in Handel's *Messiah* that summer.

In September all this came to an end when Dorothy, Bill and I were taken to Shanghai and put into Miss Jewell's Boarding School. This was on the outskirts of the Shanghai International Settlement, and it was the nearest thing to an American School in China at that time. The Shanghai American School was not established till the following year.

In the meantime the tide of change in China was moving forward. It was on October 10, 1911 that the Manchu government, the Qing Dynasty — last of the dynasties, with the old Empress Dowager — was overthrown. With this Nationalist Revolution, the Chinese people ended 300 years of Manchu rule.

Hwaianfu was evacuated. The next thing I knew, Mother and my baby sister Mary were in Shanghai, staying at the Missionary Home next door to the school. Mother offered her

The Nationalist Revolution

The Nationalist, or Republican, Revolution of October 1911 was touched off by a revolt against the Qing government's bid to nationalize railroads that had been built by Western interests with local investors. The revolution spread very quickly, and in January 1912 a coalition of young revolutionaries created the Chinese Republic, with Dr. Sun Yat-sen, their leader, as its first president.

But Dr. Sun was president for just three months. The office passed in March 1912 to a general of the former Qing army, who later declared himself emperor. That government fell in 1916, and more than a decade of turbulence followed as various local warlords competed for power and territory.

Dr. Sun's Nationalist Party, the Kuomintang, continued to be a force in the nation. In 1928 its second leader, Chiang Kai-shek (Jiang Jieshi in the modern spelling), installed a Nationalist government that held power, often precariously, until its defeat by the Chinese Communist Party in 1949.

Sun Yat-sen, often called the father of modern China, was president of the short-lived Republic for just three months in 1912.

services as a substitute teacher, while Father volunteered for the Red Cross and went with the Nationalist troops to Nanking, where the fighting was going on. There he crawled in among the Ming Dynasty tombs to rescue the wounded and give them first aid.

By now an emergency existed in Shanghai. We children were forbidden even to go near the windows, for there was fighting on the streets — but it was always worth the risk to take a peek from time to time, for rumor had it that soldiers with their swords were chopping off men's queues out on the streets. In China the traditional way to make a capture had always been to grab a man by his queue. By quickly winding the queue around the arm, it was simple enough to hold the prisoner secure.

My peeking paid off one day, when I saw a soldier give chase to a civilian with a long queue. As he caught up with the man he made dive for his queue and held on. To the soldier's astonishment, the man kept right on running, leaving his queue, complete with hat, dangling from the would-be captor's hand.

The queue, again, was a Manchu custom, imposed on all Chinese men as a token of allegiance to the Manchu throne. So this symbol now had to go.

Floodwaters and Famine

The fighting had scarcely stopped when the Red Cross called again on my father to help with famine relief work. Heavy rains had swollen the waters of the great Yellow River, long known as "China's sorrow" because of its tendency to overflow and flood the surrounding countryside. Money intended for maintaining dikes had as usual been pocketed by government officials. The bed of the Yellow River was silted up so that it was higher than the surrounding land and the banks — and when the neglected dykes gave way, the river overflowed this low-lying, very fertile agricultural land.

Tens of thousands of people drowned. Those who had anything that would float got onto that and drifted until they came to dry land. There they were with their lives but nothing else, and nothing to eat.

Within a few days, Hwaianfu was overrun with destitute people. The problem was to feed these people until the floodwaters subsided and the families could get back to their land. My father was put in charge of the relief work in Hwaianfu and Tsingkiangpu [Qingjiangpu], another city just ten miles north on the Grand Canal.

In each city, a temple had been converted into a rice kitchen. Work continued from daylight till dark, as over 3,000 refugees were fed in each city every day. I can remember awful scenes in the temple courtyards; they were crowded with thin, gaunt people with grossly distended bellies, so typical of famine victims, for they had been reduced to eating even the bark of trees.

Dressed in Chinese clothes, Mother worked by Father's side. They both wore long Chinese pants, bound tightly at the ankles to reduce the constant risk of picking up lice and fleas, carriers of the dread typhus fever.

The temper of these starving crowds varied between listlessness and desperation. Walking through the courtyards where they worked, my parents had to be accompanied by two soldiers, for these frantic people would reach out and grab hold of their ankles and refuse to let go. I remember the soldiers almost breaking their batons over the knuckles of these poor, starving people to make them let go. This cruel business distressed Mother even more than the exhaustion of the work itself.

The relief system was to admit the people into the rice kitchens by families, with each member receiving a bowl of rice while the father was handed a string of cash for traveling expenses, hopefully to get them back to their homes. To discourage duplication, as he received this money a daub of green paint was applied to the father's back. But families began turning up again, with the father's back rubbed raw by stones where the paint had been scraped off. So my father conceived the idea of stationing a barber at his elbow. As each man was given his string of cash, one eyebrow was shaved off.

Mother and Father were offered horses belonging to the local soldiery, for they had to spend half of each week in Hwaianfu and half in Tsingkiangpu. But these horses turned out to be so vicious that riding had to be given up in favor of the next-quickest method of transport, by wheelbarrow along the canal towpath.

Claire with Luk Sao-tze, who was widowed by the Yellow River flood and was taken in, along with her daughter, by the Malcolm family.

The sights along the way became so harrowing. On one occasion, a refugee woman and her five children were lying across the path. The mother was dead; the father had abandoned the five children and pressed on. The baby was still nursing at the dead mother's breast while the older children sat listlessly by.

To a Westerner, it seems unthinkable that a man would abandon his family like that and go on — but what was his alternative? His wife was dead. He could stay behind and die with the children, or press on. The instinct for survival is very strong. He pressed on.

On another trip, my parents came upon a woman on the path, sitting apathetically beside her dead husband. Her little daughter, my age, was sitting by her mother's side. Mother said to the woman, "What are you going to do?" She looked up and said, "I don't know."

Well, among all these tens of thousands, this was the woman, Luk Sao-tze, that mother arranged to take into our home with her daughter, Ken-hsiao. When Luk Sao-tze got stronger, she became our wash amah. They were soon part of the family, and we came to love them dearly.

In time the wheelbarrow transport had to be abandoned too, in favor of a small houseboat. The plodding pace of the boat took the better part of a day to reach its destination, but the rest gave Mother a chance to gather strength for the next ordeal.

A Coal-Mining Community

Summer came at last, bringing Mother and Father back to Shanghai, where they picked us up at school. From here we went north by steamer to the lovely seaside resort of Peitaiho for the summer. Our father had to go back to Hwaianfu, returning for us in September in time to enroll the three of us in the newly established Shanghai American School.

In Hwaianfu, Father found it had been decided to transfer him to Yencheng, a newly opened mission station where there were three new missionary families and no doctor. This was a blow, for now there seemed little prospect of the hospital that my father had so hoped for. So that winter he resigned from the mission, and accepted a position as medical officer with the Peking Syndicate Mines at Chiaotso [Jiaozuo] in North Henan.

This was a large British coal mining operation, located where the major railways crossed. They had I don't know how many pits, and a large hospital for the laborers; they were in immediate need of a doctor to take charge. So Father and Mother found themselves back again in familiar North Henan, the heart of the Canadian Presbyterian Mission field.

I recall our house in Chiaotso as large and comfortable. Within the compound were generous vegetable and flower gardens and a tennis court. Trees of many kinds included apricot and date trees and two kinds of persimmons, along with a bamboo grove where fragrant purple violets grew in the springtime.

It was hard to grow a flower garden in dry North China. The only flowers we had were hardy perennial zinnias and cosmos. All this was carefully tended by Father's chair-bearers, who doubled as gardeners; the company provided him with a handsome sedan chair and eight stalwart bearers, on call around the clock because he had to be ready to go at any time. The front gate was tended by two distinguished-looking Sikh watchmen in smart navy blue uniforms and red turbans, one on day duty and the other on nights.

Most important, there was a hospital equipped with everything a doctor's heart could desire. My father had a large staff — not nurses, but Chinese male orderlies. They knew as much as Dr. Malcolm had time to teach them. He was kept busy treating miners suffering from fractures, burns and all sorts of other ailments, many the results of explosions and accidents in the pits.

The only servant we brought north with us from the south was Luk Sao-tse, and of course her daughter Ken-hsiao, who was like another daughter to Mother. During the years that she was with us, Mother taught Ken-hsiao to read and write Chinese, so that she was admitted with honors to the mission school for girls, and eventually was graduated as a qualified teacher.

The British mining community consisted of about 50 Englishmen and their families. These men were attached to the company as pit foremen, accountants and overseers. The mine produced a high-grade anthracite coal, but in one of its richest pits they had had the misfortune to strike underground water. To keep this under control, a tremendous Hawthorn-Davy pump had been installed.

One of the Sikh watchmen at the family's front gate in Chiaotso.

While the water was a drawback to the operation of the mine, it was heaven-sent for the surrounding countryside. The volume pumped out every day was enough, not only for the needs of the community, but also for irrigating the crops over a wide surrounding area. In a region so chronically short of rainfall, such abundant water was like a gift from heaven. It also provided us with a beautiful swimming pool, a thing almost unheard-of in the interior of China in those days.

During their three years at Chiaotso, my mother and father built and established a small church, which was later taken over by the Canadian Mission. Every Sunday morning Father would preach in Chinese while Mother played the hymns on her baby-organ. For many years, Mary would conclude her childhood bedtime prayers by rattling off, "and God bless the Soongs and the Changs and the little church at Chiaotso."

A Mission School

Now that we were living in North Henan, instead of being sent back to Shanghai to school, we went to the Canadian Mission boarding school in Weihweifu, only six hours by train from Chiaotso. Weihweifu was the main station of the Canadian Presbyterian Mission. Like most mission stations, it consisted of a church, a hospital and schools for boys and for girls. The homes of the missionaries were grouped within a large and pleasant compound, bounded on three sides by a high brick wall.

This was a Chinese idea. All Chinese homes were behind high walls, for safety and sanitation reasons but largely for protection and seclusion, especially of the women. But this mission compound had one wall that was wire — not barbed wire, just a wire fence, so the Chinese could see in and know that the foreign devils weren't up to any mischief. That side of the compound overlooked the Wei River, and boats of every shape and size passed by on their way to the market towns.

Outside the mission compound's wire fence, onlookers (at left) gaze at a wedding party. Claire is standing at the extreme right.

In our photo albums, I have a photograph of a wedding that took place at the mission compound. We're all gathered together with the bride and groom; I'm standing on the right hand, Dorothy is at the back, and there's a wire fence and a whole crowd of Chinese on the outside. It looks as though they are refugees behind the fence — but, of course, they are outside it and are just passersby, stopped out of curiousity.

Among the more unusual craft, I recall seeing an enormous raft made entirely of a great accumulation of river weed, piled at least six feet high above the water, gently drifting by on the current. On top was a small improvised cabin housing a boatman and his family, casually occupying themselves with the business of living while poling this huge mound of weeds to its destination for sale as fertilizer. There was an eternal shortage of fertilizer, an eternal demand.

Adjoining the main compound was the school for foreign children. With only 25 pupils, there were just enough children to provide companionship for each age group. It seemed more like a home than a school. Besides our regular classes we were taught Chinese. Our Chinese teacher, Mr. Lee, was a dapper little man who stood for no nonsense from his pupils. Once a week as he entered the classroom, the whole class would stand, and bowing in unison with hands cupped together would chant an appropriate greeting in Chinese.

From Claire's family albums, this photo is labeled "Two Bible women."

Among other things, Mr. Lee taught us to say the Lord's Prayer in Chinese and to read from the Gospel of St. Mark. He drilled us in finding our way around the Chinese Bible, for the whole school regularly attended Sunday morning service in the Chinese church.

The Peddlers of Peitaiho

Peitaiho [Beidaihe] was originally an exclusively foreign summer resort by the beautiful northern China sea [the Bohai Sea today]. It was here in September 1898, before the Boxer Rebellion, that Dorothy was born. Now here again, we children reveled in the luxury of running free, enjoying swimming and picnics and donkey rides and the company of lots of other young people our own age.

One amusing feature of Peitaiho was its many peddlers. There were men selling everything from canaries to curios, and there were conjurors and men offering to cut away the calluses and corns from the feet of the poor suffering grownups who never went barefoot. But the most persistent were the men peddling lace and embroidered linens. With their wares wrapped in cloth bundles tied together and slung across their shoulders, they would edge their way up to our wide verandas. Lingering here they would then try, by all sorts of ruses, to catch an eye — for common courtesy forbade their coming up onto the veranda without first having secured some recognition, however small.

The best way to discourage these persistent fellows was to ignore them completely. This was easier said than done, for what could be more natural than to look up when called unexpectedly by name, as these artful men learned to do? The minute they caught an unwary eye, they engaged in a running conversation. No matter how one-sided the conversation was, they then felt emboldened to come up onto the veranda. As they talked they opened up their bundles, spreading their wares all over the floor, every move putting us more and more heavily under obligation to buy.

A street food vendor, early 1900s.
Image courtesy of Peter Lockhart Smith and Historical Photographs of China, University of Bristol. University of Bristol.

Some of these men were born comedians, and as they displayed their wares their sales patter was interspersed with killingly funny remarks. If they could get us into a good mood, their battle was half won. At this stage, one became aware of some member of the household staff hovering in the background. Before even attempting a sale, these men would have already been into the servants' quarters to settle, with whomever was the senior member there, exactly what percentage of each sale would go to him or her. Peddlers well knew that if they did not conform to this custom, they would never be permitted to come near the house again.

Among these men, I recall one who put on a one-man impersonation of a foreign dinner party. He would mimic exactly English conversation and laughter, complete with background sound-effects of knives and forks being used and bottles of wine being opened. It was so realistic that it was hard to believe that he wasn't in fact actually saying anything at all.

World War and Grave Mounds

On July 28, 1914, the First World War broke out in Europe. I remember the intense anxiety, excitement and worry. We used to go and read the bulletins — I suppose they came in by wireless — every day at the community hall, where church was held. War, war in Europe — what did that mean?

Hastily we returned to our home in Chiaotso, and much to Mother's disquiet, Father talked of volunteering for service at the front. Mother pointed out that he would not qualify because of his age and disabled right hand. But he sent in his application to the British Consulate in Shanghai and was accepted. Mother started making plans to take us children "home" to Canada the following spring.

Dorothy and I stayed on at the missionary school. Once we went to the next mission station at the end of the railway, and from there we took sedan chairs to the lovely mission compound. Halfway there we had to stop and get a meal; but what I remember most is the local village latrine. It was a trench with a plank board laid over it. You walked along that board and then you squatted down across it, hung onto a rail, and contributed to the collection of fertilizer that was accumulated all year long. I'll never forget that.

That winter I spent a good deal of time outdoors, going for long walks by myself. One of my favorite haunts was the dried-up bed of a river that had long since changed its course. This gully, worn into the famous loess [soft, wind-deposited topsoil] of north China, must have been a good 30 feet deep. Its precipitous banks were tunneled with cave dwellings which,

A path at a missionary compound where Claire often took walks.

although no longer occupied, were still intact. The mouth of each cave was blocked by a large boulder that all but filled the opening, a protection from both weather and intrusion. You had to squeeze or sidle your way past.

In the center of the cave that I remember most vividly was a solid, round mud table, and a mud stove against the wall nearest to the entrance so the smoke could get out. On either side of this main room were two sleeping recesses, with the whole space taken up by a solid mud platform about knee-high and the size of a large double bed. I don't recall knowing the history of these caves. I was content with the adventure of exploring them.

There were grave mounds, on all the cultivated lands. Each land had its own graves. Once while I was walking along, out from some grave mound darted a stray dog that had a baby's arm in its mouth. The little hand kept flapping up and down as the dog ran. Some instinct made me give chase, until the dog disappeared among the grave mounds.

The level of misery was high indeed

Many circumstances can explain this. In the winter in north China the ground is cold, dry and very hard, so graves were shallow and small coffins were often exposed. Also, people were poor and the death rate among infants was enormously high, so babies were sometimes just left by the wayside or among the grave mounds. At the same time the countryside was overrun with stray mongrel dogs. No matter how starved and diseased these creatures became, because of their belief in the transmigration of souls, no Chinese would ever kill them.

I recall once seeing a dog that had obviously had its back broken, for with its forelegs it was painfully dragging itself along. Foreigners learned the hard way that if they attempted to put these poor animals out of their misery, in no time the nearest village would claim all kinds of damages, insisting that this dog had been their best watchdog and they were now deprived of their security. But the sad truth is that many of the people themselves were very little better off than the dogs. The level of misery in China was high indeed, in those "good old days."

Shipping Labor to France

Having gradually got used to the idea of breaking up her home again, mother was now looking forward to seeing her family in Vancouver. So it came as a blow when, on his arrival in Shanghai, the British Consulate announced that when

The Chinese government created a work-study program so that a number of students who spoke French could travel with the wartime laborers to France, and could serve as their interpreters. Among those who traveled to France with the program, which continued for a time after the war, were Zhou Enlai and Deng Xiaoping. Both later became leaders of the Chinese Communist Party.

Claire, at left behind the first two girls, and classmates at the Shanghai American School.

they accepted Dr. Malcolm for service they had overlooked the fact of his disabled hand, and regretted to inform him that his services could not be used at the front after all.

The war was in full swing and China, as her reluctant contribution to the war effort, was being asked to send thousands of men as laborers to France. They were to be shipped from the North China seaport of Chefoo. At this time Chefoo had no doctor, for the former port doctor, a German, had been interned in Japan.

So after he'd spent a year as physician and surgeon at the Shantung Road Hospital in Shanghai, my father was asked if he would be willing to go to Chefoo for the duration of the war, to serve as both community doctor and quarantine officer to supervise the shipment of these men (and hundreds of mules) to France.

I was in the Shanghai American School. There was a great deal of anti-British feeling in the school, among the teachers especially and even among the students. I was Canadian but they thought I was British, and they were very critical of England, her gunboat diplomacy and her imperialist rule. I didn't know anything about gunboat diplomacy, I didn't know what they were criticizing England for; I was just embarrassed. Not that it got me down, I was sort of an irrepressible creature and carried on.

I was at school with Pearl Buck's sister Grace and with Henry Luce's two sisters. [Luce, born into an American missionary family in China, became the publisher who created the magazines *Time, Life, Fortune* and *Sports Illustrated*.] George Kennedy was there too — he was the only one who studied Chinese. I remember him reading Chinese newspapers. Later he was in charge of Chinese studies at Yale University.

On its face, the International Settlement in Shanghai looked like a true example of foreign imperialism, but in its way it was also a ghetto. The Settlement was on a mudflat, below sea level. The foreigners, far from home in an alien land, pooled their resources for their mutual health, security and entertainment. In no time the International Settlement developed into the most prosperous business area in China.

Anti-British mural, Shanghai.
Image courtesy of Historical Photographs of China, University of Bristol.

The Chinese were enormously resourceful, enormously industrious. What they lacked at that time was mutual trust in each other, which they dared not indulge in. They had reached a point where no progress was made at all, and they weren't proud of it. They were embarrassed by it.

When the war ended in 1918, no one came to relieve Dr. Malcolm. Chefoo became our home till 1939, when my mother and father retired to Shanghai, where my sister Mary Starr and I then both lived.

The Carefree Summer

I finished school in Shanghai in June 1918, and now at last I was home. I had been in boarding school since I was ten, almost without interruption. I was planning to begin my nurses' training in October, but at the moment the whole lovely summer stretched out before me. It was the most carefree summer of my life. My brother Bill attended the Chefoo Boys' School, and Mary, now eight, went to the Girls' School. At last we were all home together.

My older sister Dorothy had already had a year at home, and among the assets she had acquired was a pony. Dor didn't really like riding, so I fell heir to her pony. His name was Porridge, and he looked it.

All the horses on the China coast were a breed of Mongolian pony, a tough, sure-footed little animal. I learned to ride on Porridge, and this summer I learned to dance, too — ballroom dancing! (The Shanghai American School was a missionary school; the Virginia Reel was the nearest we ever came to dancing.)

But my most fun that summer was with Bill's little kayak. I would spend whole mornings draped over the bow of this boat, pulling myself along in the shallow water among the rocky coves watching the myriad life on the bottom, among them the innocent-looking sea anemones that were lying in wait for some unsuspecting, minute passerby to suddenly devour. At other times I would follow the tiny crabs in among the rocks, trying in vain to catch them before they burrowed into the sand.

When I got home, Mother would ask where I had been and what I had been doing, the traditional mother question. My reply was just as traditional — "Nothing special." But I had never been so free.

This view from about 1920 shows the seaport city of Chefoo [Yantai], in northern China.

In the House Above the Harbor

David G. Pearson was Claire's nephew, the eldest son of her older sister Dorothy. He also wrote a memoir, which he titled China and Beyond, An Autobiography. *Here is David's description of Chefoo [Yantai] at this time, and his grandfather Dr. Malcolm, from that unpublished book.*

Our grandparents lived on what Westerners called Consular Hill, at the western end of the town, and their house overlooked the harbor which lay to the west of the headland. The harbor was always filled with vessels, some fairly large but mostly "coasters." Included was usually a sprinkling of naval vessels from the U.K., U.S., Japan, Italy, France and, sometimes, Germany. The really large vessels would anchor outside the breakwater where the water was deeper.

My grandfather, in addition to running a one-man medical practice out of his home, was also Yantai's port health officer, a welcome source of additional income, as my grandmother always accused him of not charging his poorer Chinese patients. These however would never fail to later bring him a gift of eggs, or a chicken perhaps.

... Gramp was also one of the oldest ham (amateur) radio operators in the world at one time. It was his passion, although not my grandmother's, who disliked having the dining room walls covered with the call cards of his "contacts" around the world and his daily habit of jumping up from the dinner table with the shout "*My sched!*", meaning his scheduled contact with some other ham in Russia, or Australia, or South Africa or the U.S. or wherever. While visiting our grandparents we were never surprised, for example, to see one or two American sailors in their summer whites helping Gramp with his radio mast, or this or that part of his set. Then he'd ask them to stay for tea.

The U.S. Navy played a big part in the life of our town during the 1920s and 30s. The U.S. Asiatic Fleet was based in the Philippine Islands during the winter but every summer would head north to Yantai, where it would stay for several months. The fleet usually consisted of a tanker, the *Pecos*, which because of its deep draft would anchor a long way out in the bay; a destroyer and

Above, the family's home in Chefoo; below, Dr. and Mrs. Malcolm at home.

submarine tender, the *Black Hawk*, which was moored in the harbor, usually with a destroyer or two tied up alongside; two minesweepers, the *Finch* and the *Bittern*; three or four submarines and approximately seven "four stacker" destroyers. These were, to the best of my recollection, the *Paul Jones*, *Peary*, *Edwards*, *Alden*, *Pope*, *Pillsbury* and *Ford*.

In addition, for some part of each summer the fleet would be joined by the *Augusta*, a heavy cruiser, and the *Langley*, a flattop. Unfortunately all but two of these vessels were lost during the desperate opening stages of the war against Japan.

"Your Father Wants to See You"

Chefoo is a seaport on the northern coast about halfway between Tientsin in the north and Shanghai to the south. The climate is not unlike that of New York City: the winters are very cold, with almost three months of bitter weather where the harbor freezes over to a depth of almost three feet. There is very little snow, for it is dry in that part of the world, with a minimum of precipitation in summer or winter. The spring is sudden, cold and windy one day, almost too hot the next. Then comes a short but lovely hot, dry summer, followed by an autumn that is warm and clear right up to December. The sea, like the sky, is a beautiful deep blue almost all the time.

The local products and main export were peanuts and soybeans. Melons and grapes in season were abundant, along with other fruits including the apple banana and Bartlett pear, introduced years before by missionaries. The main industries were lace, embroideries, straw braid and hairnets, in the days when the hairnet first became popular. These were made from either human hair or yak tail, so I was told.

One of the strange new sights in those days was to see Chinese girls being taken to work in the many hairnet factories. With their small bound feet they couldn't walk, so they were transported by wheelbarrow. It was not uncommon to see as many as eight girls on one wheelbarrow, giggling and laughing and filled with curiosity — for although they worked 12 long hours a day, they were also out of their confined women's courts, probably for the first time in their lives.

girls with bound feet being taken
to work in a hair-net factory.

Toward the end of this wonderful summer, my father had the misfortune to be thrown out of his rickshaw. Going down a slight incline, the rickshaw coolie lost his footing and the rickshaw went out of control, finishing up against a stone wall. Fortunately the coolie wasn't hurt, but my father landed in a ditch and broke his elbow. It was then only a matter of weeks before I was to leave for Shanghai to commence my nurse's training.

One night I became aware that my mother was shaking me, calling to me to wake up.

"What's the matter?" I asked.

"Your father wants to see you," she replied.

Hastily reviewing my activities of the day before, trying to recall if I had done anything out of order, I followed her into their bedroom.

"Claire?"

"Yes, Father."

"I'm having a lot of pain, and I want you to give me a hypodermic of morphine."

In tears I begged him to let Mother do it, promising to do it for him the next day.

"You say you want to be a nurse," Father said — "well, there's no time like the present to learn to give an injection properly. You will have the advantage of being a jump ahead of the other nurses when you begin your training. Now listen carefully. Are you ready?"

"Y-e-e-e-es."

"On the table in my dressing room you will find my medicine case. The hypodermic equipment is in the left hand compartment." A pause. "Have you got it?"

"Yes," I said, my voice still shaky.

"All right. Now do exactly as I tell you."

Mother gently pressed my arm and went silently off to her bed. I knew she was trembling between the sheets for me.

To give an injection of almost anything in those days was quite an operation, for nothing was pre-prepared or pre-sterilized. Now, with the directions coming step by step from the bedroom, I found the vial containing quarter-grain tablets of morphine. In a few drops of water, in a teaspoon held over the flame of a little alcohol lamp, I dissolved one of these tablets. I waited till it cooled before drawing it into the syringe.

Next, rolling a pinch of cotton wool onto the end of a match, I dipped this into iodine and went in to see my father. He showed me just where to dab the iodine. I returned for the needle, gripped his arm firmly with my left hand, and with my right hand held the needle poised.

"Now," said Father, "don't hesitate. Jab it straight in."

A moment's pause, then, BANG, in it went.

"All right, Claire, just the needle, not the whole syringe."

Now, retracing my steps and still following directions from the bed, I cleaned the needle and put everything back where it had come from, and then went meekly back to bed — but not to sleep.

So ended my first lesson in nursing.

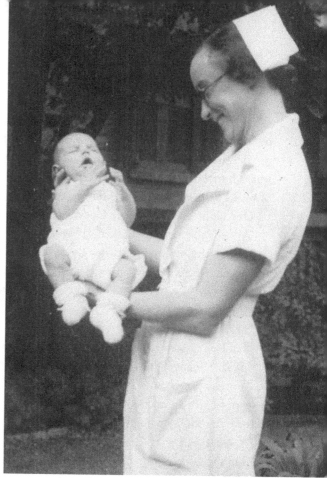

PART 2

Nursing Journeys and Civil Wars

1918 – 1930

Before I left for Shanghai to commence training that October, Mother gave me a "coming out" party, on which occasion I formally put up my long, straight hair. It wouldn't stay up. But I had to get used to it, for hospital regulations required it.

It was 1918, the end of the first World War and the tail end of the Victorian Era in England. As the matron and the nursing-sisters at the Victoria Nursing Home were all English, British tradition prevailed throughout the hospital, dictating everything we did. This included not only having the skirts of our uniforms measure exactly three inches from the floor, but also wearing large, full-length whalebone corsets. These were not optional, and our uniforms were fitted accordingly.

The uniform was of a pretty pale blue-and-white check. Aprons were, of course, white with a bib and full-length skirt that met together at the back. The winter uniform had a long sleeve and a separate, four-inch white cuff that slipped on over the hand and was held together by a stud. To match, there was an equally stiff, two-and-a-half-inch white dog collar fastened by another stud in front. The belt was of the same stiff white material, also two and a half inches wide and fastened at the back by a third stud.

When I first wore this uniform, I felt as if I was in a straightjacket. The only concession to the hot, humid Shanghai summer was a short puff sleeve and flat, detachable Peter Pan collar. The corset was still compulsory.

Shanghai seasons do not conform to England's. Despite this, the date on which we changed from winter into summer uniforms was determined by the English calendar

Facing page, above left: Claire with Yuantasao, her family's amah in Chefoo; above right, Claire as a young nurse. Lower photo: Chinese government soldiers walk past battle-scarred buildings in Hankow, a port city on the Yangtze River that was the scene of several armed conflicts in the early 20th century. Image courtesy of Billie Love Historical Collection and Historical Photographs of China, University of Bristol.

Claire in training as a nurse. Shanghai, 1920.

— come hell or high water, we weren't permitted to change till the end of May. Shanghai's hot weather commences well before that. I suffered through the first year, accepting all this as part of the training.

By the second year, toward the end of April it was awfully hot, and one day I developed a big blister under my chin, caused of course by the hard collar. Utterly miserable, I went to the sister in charge of my ward and showed it to her, asking for permission to take the collar off. She refused. "Regulations!" she said. Before the day was out, the blister broke, and I had blood running down my snow-white collar. Not till then did "Sister" tell me to remove my collar.

By now I was indignant and asked permission to go to the matron to plead for summer collars. The next day we all changed into summer uniforms, but the corsets were still maintained. As mine was permanently damp (wet is a better description), I reluctantly invested (because it was a very expensive thing) in another corset. It was only a matter of 24 hours till both corsets were soaking wet — and they never, ever dried all that summer, for the humidity in Shanghai is always 100 percent. The result was that I broke out in lumps and bumps all over my body and was eventually sick.

Before the third summer, I volunteered to go to the matron to ask, on behalf of all the nurses, that we be allowed to discard altogether these uniforms in favor of an ordinary short white smock with open neck and short sleeve. My request was granted. At last we were free of those inhuman corsets.

Kitty Lyle

I was on duty on the women's floor when a young woman was brought in for emergency surgery. In those days, patients remained in hospital quite a long time after an operation to convalesce. She was a darling patient and such good fun, easily the favorite of all the nurses.

We all came to know who our patient was. Her name was Kitty Lyle. She was also known as "Singapore Kate," one of Shanghai's most sought-after "demi-monde dames." Because she and others of Shanghai's better-class call girls lived in houses on Kiangsi Road, they were popularly known as "Kiangsi Road girls."

One day about a year later, I was invited by some friends to a gala afternoon at Shanghai's elegant Race Club. Fashion in those days called for long dresses and picture hats at these affairs. I had never been to the races before, and knew absolutely no one — but suddenly, among the many guests, I saw a young lady, beautifully dressed, whose face looked very familiar. In a flash I recognized her. It was Kitty Lyle.

I rushed over to speak to her. As I opened my mouth, she drew herself up and fixed me with a cold stare; then she turned and walked away, mingling with the crowd. I was bewildered and hurt. I wondered if I had been mistaken, or if she had perhaps failed to recognize me, for she had never seen me except in uniform.

They were known as "Kiangsi Road girls"

In the meantime another race had begun and excitement was running high. I was standing with my friends at the rail, intent on watching the finish, when suddenly I felt my arm being squeezed. I turned, but already she was walking away, again mingling with the many other guests. Then, from far across the paddock, she turned and waved to me.

Months later I heard that Kitty Lyle was in hospital again. She had attempted suicide. When she was convalescing, I asked for permission to visit her. When I came into her room, she looked at me and, with a wan smile, said, "You young fool! Don't you know any better than to be seen talking to someone like me in public?"

I never saw her again. Years later, rumor had it that she tried again to take her own life. This time she succeeded.

On a Harley to Peking

My brother Bill, now working with a silk firm in Chefoo, decided to spend his Easter holiday in 1919 on a trip to Peking. To my delight, he asked me to go with him. So off we went, complete with his newly acquired Harley-Davidson motorbike.

Peking is a city within a city within a city. Approaching by train from Tientsin in the south, we first saw the city's high outer wall of gray stone, rising 90 feet out of the flat surrounding plain. Its massive ramparts and escarpments, its towering gateways and turreted top had the effect of dwarfing people as they drew near.

Within this wall the crowded Tartar City teemed with life. Here the city's business and commerce was carried on, including the entertainment world of theaters and restaurants. Here, too, was where the historic Legation Quarter was located, and where the residential and diplomatic life of China's capitol was lived.

Within all this lay the Imperial City, surrounded by its wall enclosing the crowded palaces, temples and audience halls of the vast Imperial Household, all dominated by the imposing *T'ien An Men*, The Gate of Heavenly Peace. The roofs of these buildings were of glazed imperial-yellow tile. In the past this enclave was reserved for the Manchu overlords of China.

Finally, completely surrounded by the Imperial City and protected by its own wall of soft ochre-red, crested by the same glazed tiles of imperial yellow, lay The Forbidden City, "The Great Within" (*Ta-Nei*), where lived the Son of Heaven himself. This beautiful wall once guarded the lives, intrigues and strange secrets of an indulgent and introverted court life. Its ambitions, joys and sorrows and relentless conformity were largely at the mercy of corrupt and powerful eunuchs, many of whose stories will never be told, for their secrets died with them.

… their secrets died with them

Peking in my day, on the surface anyway, was still almost untouched by the 20th century. If it hadn't been for the fun of riding on Bill's bike, I doubt if either of us would have taken the time to visit its historical sights. I yearned more for the delight of tea dances at the lovely Wagons-Lits hotel, and at the sophisticated Peking Hotel where we were staying.

Tea dances were strictly foreign pastimes. Almost all Chinese women then still had bound feet, but occasionally one would see the rare spectacle of a Chinese gentleman, in his long silk gown, cloth-soled shoes and silk pants neatly bound at the ankle, dancing with some foreign lady. These were usually embassy parties, for it was almost exclusively at this level that foreigners had the opportunity for any real social contact with Chinese, and this only in diplomatic circles in Peking. There were often Chinese couples in these parties, but rarely did they take part in the dancing.

Summer palace, Peking.

Even gayer than the tea dances were the polo games played regularly outside the Legation Quarter wall. These had all the air of a miniature Ascot, except that the ponies were playing polo instead of racing. Ladies appeared on the lawn in long dresses with pretty hats to match. Marquees were set up, one for the band provided by the Legation Guard and the other where tea was continually being served. On these occasions a few Chinese and Manchu ladies could be seen mixing with the other guests.

It was during one of these parties that I met Miss Carroll, an elderly American lady who had been one of the ladies-in-waiting of the old Empress Dowager, Tzu Hsi. Miss Carroll regaled us with fascinating stories of Manchu court life in days gone by, clearly for her a way of life that had only just passed. She gave me the impression of being not a little lost.

Treasures of the Forbidden City

Because we both enjoyed riding, Bill managed to borrow two ponies so that we could ride to the dramatic Temple and Altar of Heaven. There have been many pictures taken of the Temple of Heaven, with its beautiful roof of azure-blue porcelain tiles, standing in the center of three carved white marble terraces. But to me, of all Peking's many wondrous sights, more even than the Temple of Heaven, the pure simplicity of the Altar of Heaven was the loveliest. Standing quietly and alone in the very center of this beautiful monument was a most inspiring moment.

A Peking memorial archway built of wood, in a photo from about 1920.
Photograph by Donald Mennie, from The Pageant of Peking *(1920). Image courtesy of Historical Photographs of China, University of Bristol.*

The Altar of Heaven, in the Temple of Heaven complex.

This altar consists of three round, pure-white marble terraces encompassed by intricately carved balustrades, also of white marble, laid out in tiers one on top of the other, each tier about nine feet smaller than the one below, the whole rising about 18 feet from the ground. The top tier is an expanse of pure white marble, about 50 feet in diameter. The symmetry of the altar, with its carved steps and matching balustrades ascending at four cardinal points under a cloudless blue sky, is perfection itself. A truly fitting memorial to Heaven.

To be allowed inside the gates of the Forbidden City, special passes had to be obtained. Even then we were accompanied everywhere by one and sometimes two palace guards, courteous and gracious but always there. And no wonder, for room after room was filled with priceless treasures, fabulous gifts from tributary states and rich spoils of war. I recall a saddle made entirely of fine gold mesh studded with pearls, with stirrups of beaten silver inlaid with semi-precious stones. I recall, too, seeing a full-sized woven bed-mat made of thinly shaved strips of ivory, a replica of the fine reed mats that the privileged classes slept on during the hot summers.

Never had I ever seen or even dreamed of such priceless things: exquisitely carved jades and ivories and crystals, ancient bronzes, fine porcelains, dainty paintings on scrolls, silks and brocades and *k'e-ssu* (cut silk tapestry), and exquisite calligraphy everywhere. Alongside these were gifts from European countries: bulky porcelain clocks, huge ornate soup tureens, and washbasins with jugs to match. One thing from Europe that fascinated me (the guards, too) was a music box from Switzerland. It was a realistic replica of a canary in a golden cage; the guard wound it up for us, and it sang a most lovely song.

During the following years a great many of these priceless things found their way through the back doors of the palaces, sold by unscrupulous eunuchs who after all were no longer being supported by a government that was itself falling apart. I believe many of these treasures, sold no doubt for a mere song, are now in private collections all over the West. Hopefully they may one day find their way back into museums for all to enjoy.

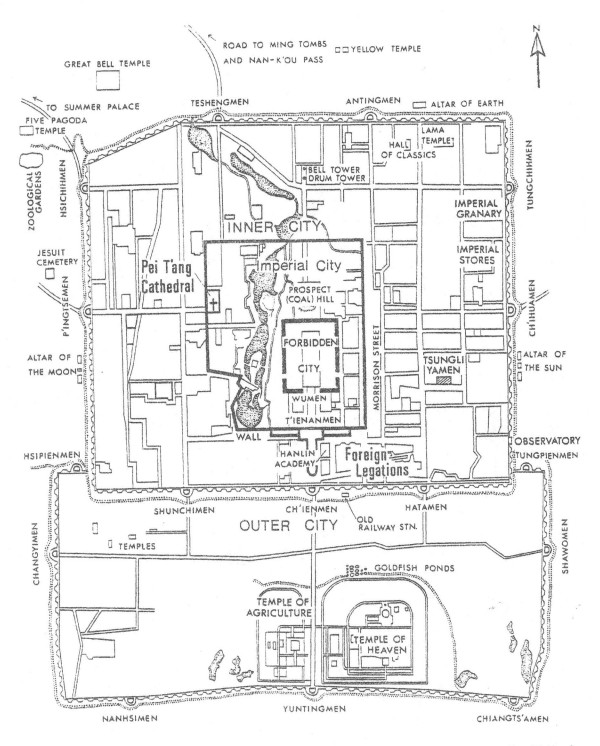

Map of Peking, from Claire's collection.

Ch'ien Men Gate and Ch'ien Men Street, Peking.
Image courtesy of Billie Love Historical Collection and Historical Photographs of China, University of Bristol.

Street Scenes and Camel Caravans

But the most fascinating side of Peking was the kaleidoscope of colorful street scenes, especially in the bazaars and marketplaces just outside *Ch'ien Men*, the main Tartar City gate. We'd join the jostling crowds, almost entirely men, in their long gowns of blue cloth or rich brocades. We would still see some queues, handsomely groomed and worn now only by Manchus. The men all around would either be bent on business, or they'd just be strolling around or sitting in open-front tea shops watching the world go by. You never saw women on the street, except servant women who went to the markets.

This was the main shopping area. There was the street that sold nothing but silver; there were Jade Street, Fan Street and Lantern Street; there were streets for porcelain and brass and rosewood, and streets that sold herbs and strange medicinal roots and brews. In Coffin Street, shop after open-front shop was piled high with coffins, from plain wooden boxes to highly polished, intricately carved ones.

Inside the coffin shops, the ceilings were festooned with strings of paper money, both silver and gold, red candles of all sizes, and incense. Farther back in the store, made of bamboo, covered with paper and realistically painted, were life-size replicas of maids and manservants, horses and carts and sedan chairs, foods of all kinds and more. All the necessities and comforts of life had been duplicated in paper, to be burned at the grave site to accompany the spirit of the deceased on its long journey to heaven.

Street traffic here consisted mainly of sedan chairs, wheelbarrows and peddlers with poles over their shoulders carrying anything and everything, including huge baskets of live chickens at one end, with their heads and long necks stretching comically through the holes in the baskets, and ducks on the other. Water-carriers with pails slung from the ends of poles maneuvered their way through the jostling crowds without spilling a drop, each carrier calling and shouting for others to make way.

Then there was the Peking cart with its blue, cloth-covered top and huge wooden brass-studded wheels, pulled by a thickset Mongolian pony. The carter sat on the shaft in front. These carts, heavily curtained, were usually the object of some curiosity, for they were known to be transporting women from the carefully guarded women's courts of one home to another. If you watched closely you could usually see the slight

A Peking cart. These were often used to transport women, as Claire explains, "from the carefully guarded women's courts of one home to another."

movement of a curtain as the women inside peeked out to catch a glimpse of the outside world as they passed by.

Then suddenly in the midst of all this could be heard the loud cries of the forerunner of some high-ranking official, shouting "*Chieh-kwang, chieh-kwang,*" to make way for the passage of His Excellency's official sedan chair, carried high on the shoulders of four or even eight fleet-footed bearers. They traveled fast, always with spare bearers running alongside. To watch the skill with which they changed bearers without slacking speed or losing a step was a delight. A few years later, these same officials traveled in newly acquired Model T Fords. With klaxon horns blaring and soldiers standing on the running boards, they would scream their way down these crowded streets while pedestrians scattered frantically in all directions.

But to me the most colorful sights of all were the long strings of camel caravans and horses, the Mongolian ponies, just arriving with their wares from across the Gobi and from faraway places across the desert. Accompanying them were many strange types, quite un-Chinese in appearance. Dusty from long travel but richly dressed in rough but colorful purples and gold and scarlet, these bold characters swung along beside their animals.

A shopping street in Peking, about 1920.
Photograph by Donald Mennie, from The Pageant of Peking *(1920). Image courtesy of Historical Photographs of China, University of Bristol.*

Sometimes stripped to the waist, with faces wrinkled and torsos tanned by wind and sand, Uyghurs, Mongols and Tibetans, traders from Inner and Outer Mongolia and from the steppes of Siberia strode through the streets with their long fur-pelt garments tossed nonchalantly over one shoulder or worn with the fur next to the skin, depending on the weather. Exposed to view were their enormous silver belt buckles, studded with semiprecious stones of all colors and supporting their money pouches in front. Hanging over one hip was a scabbard encasing a long knife. Attached to this belt at the back was a case containing a pair of chopsticks and knife, for these men lived and ate in their saddles.

Some caravan characters wore tall fur hats, others had fur-lined caps with large ear flaps that could be tied under the chin, and still others with shaved pates wore no hat at all. All of them strode about the marketplace, boldly seeking both business and pleasure. The noise and smells added their own dimensions to the scene.

Like all Chinese walled cities, Peking is symmetrically laid out with the streets, or *hutungs*, running north, south, east and west. Everybody lived behind high walls, and on the tops of the high walls was broken glass embedded in cement, to discourage intruders. You never saw inside these homes. Walking in these hutungs was like walking along endless blank corridors; the only breaks in the monotony were the front gates of the homes. Just inside each gate stood a spirit wall, a short wall that screened from view the court within, keeping its privacy while permitting the gate itself to be left conveniently open.

Everybody lived behind high walls

When I first came to the West to live, it was actually embarrassing to me, who had always lived behind walls, to walk along a street and catch myself looking right through a large picture window into a family's private life. At first this seemed unnatural — but as I became more familiar with the Western way of life, I sensed that this was almost a psychological need. A young mother who was alone all day, with only little children as companions, would die of loneliness behind walls, whereas inside a Chinese home were two and three generations of a family, all living together.

While it's true that a passerby couldn't see inside the gates of these homes, there was often a lot of activity outside around the gates. Peddlers of goods and services passed at regular intervals, offering to provide for every need. The itinerant barber, shoemaker and seamstress were always employed, as was the mender of broken bowls. With a handmade drill, this last artist would make a row of fine holes along each side of a crack, then cement in staples with a paste of porcelain powder.

Today when I see a neatly stitched surgical incision, I am always reminded of these bowl menders.

And there was always the beggar, going his rounds. Another familiar sight was that of a man standing close up to and facing a wall, calmly relieving himself. As far as I know, back then Chinese cities never provided public latrines.

Another everyday scene was of a woman sitting on the stoop beside the gate holding a baby, always a boy, over the cobblestones to do his "business," while at the same time she was ready, with her foot, to fend off scavenger dogs. Once while I was working at the mission hospital in Chefoo, a mother brought in her baby boy in a sad state. She said a dog had snapped off the child's testicles. I knew only too well how this had happened.

Lives in Nurses' Hands

Back in Shanghai, the training we got in the Victoria Nursing Home left much to be desired in the field of theory, but we more than made up for it in very sound practical training and experience, in a day when real bedside nursing was vitally important. The recovery of typhoid and pneumonia patients depended largely on the quality of nursing the patient got, for there was no drug of any kind available for these illnesses in those days. The standard of asepsis, or preventing the spread of infection in a hospital, depended entirely on how conscientious a nurse was about scrubbing her hands.

Dysentery in all its forms was endemic, reaching epidemic proportions in the hot humid summers. This was the season for the dread cholera, too, for flies were everywhere. The hospital was small and there were no interns; so outside of actual operations, the nurses did everything for the patient.

Most of the sisters had a great deal of experience — not only in England where they had received their training, but on active service in France and in the Middle East (Mesopotamia), for the First World War had just barely ended. And there were more sisters than there were probationers, so we had the good experience of working side by side with highly qualified nurses all the time.

Always required to do 12-hour duty, we were always in close touch with the patients, too. This stood me in good stead for the kind of 24-hour duty that I would do in years to come. In addition to our regular duty, we took our turn at emergency "theatre" or operating-room duty, and emergency ambulance duty; and, of course, we had a thorough training in maternity nursing.

Although I finished my training in October 1921, the matron asked me if I would stay on for a while longer to help out, for many of the nurses had been sick with dysentery and typhoid and were still convalescing. I agreed, with the understanding that I could go home in time for Christmas.

I arrived back in Chefoo on December 20, 1921. Holiday festivities were in full swing, and in spite of being very tired I was filled with enthusiasm. My mother was wonderful; day after day she let me sleep the clock round. Regularly at 4 p.m. there would be a gentle knock at my door, and in would come Mother followed by Yuantasao, our beloved amah, carrying the tea tray.

Over cups of tea, Mother and I would sit and visit. We talked and talked while Yuantasao sat on the foot of my bed and listened. Without understanding a word of what we were saying, she knew mother and daughter were getting to know each other again. This is the same in any language, and it really matters little what is actually said.

A Baby's Eyes

I think it was sometime in March. I had come in late from a party and was beginning to undress when I heard a man's voice calling me from downstairs outside my window.

I opened the louvers of the shutters just enough to peek through. In the circle of light cast by a lantern, I could make out a pair of feet. When I asked who was calling, the voice said he was the man from the coal yard down by the jetty. He said his wife was in labor and was in trouble, and would I please come quickly.

Coming down to earth with a thud, I asked the man to wait a minute. I didn't own so much as a pair of scissors, much less equipment to cope with some complicated delivery. I decided I had better ask my father. Tiptoeing into his room, I apologetically wakened him. Explaining the circumstances, I asked what I should do.

"Go," he said.

"But I don't have anything to work with," I pleaded.

Practical as always, Father told me where I could find the few things I might need down in his office. But he cautioned me not to bite off more than I could chew, adding that if I needed any help, I had better send for him. I knew he had enough to do, though, caring for his regular practice and all the ships that came in.

> *I asked him what I should do. "Go," he said*

I went back to my room and, calling to the man to wait, I got out of my party dress and into something more practical. I went down to Father's office and collected what I needed — then I went out into the night.

I could see only a bare outline of the man and his bulkily clad feet as I followed him down the narrow, steep path that led from our garden, a shortcut to the jetty. All I could see in the lantern's dim light was a pair of receding heels. Down, down we went and then along the waterfront. Finally we arrived at a gate in the high brick wall that enclosed the coal yard. At the far end of the yard was a little hut.

In the dim light of a little oil lamp, I could make out three little children standing quietly by, and I heard the cry of a newborn baby. The mother was moaning. She said the pains had got worse just after her husband left. Suddenly the baby's head had come down, but not the body. With one desperate effort, she had managed to deliver the baby herself.

Urging the mother to relax and rest a little, I examined the baby. I saw that in her frantic effort to deliver the baby, the mother, clutching at the head, had gouged out the baby's eyes.

Withholding comment for the moment, I prepared to deliver the afterbirth. First tying off the cord, I started to cut it with my sterile scissors. But the husband, holding back my hand, picked up a rice bowl and cracked it on the edge of the *k'ang*, or brick bed. He handed me one of the broken pieces, the sharp edge of which he asked me to use to cut the cord, explaining that it was bad luck to use scissors.

Chinese people knew from experience that to cut a cord with scissors was indeed "bad luck" — but they didn't know that the bad luck came from dirty scissors. I realized that under the circumstances, it was as well to do as the husband asked. If I used my scissors and the baby died, I knew my scissors would be blamed.

After getting the mother settled, I examined the baby again, then handed her to the father. He looked at her closely.

"Do you think she will live?" he asked.

I told him that if he took her to the mission hospital up on Temple Hill on the far side of the city, then maybe, *maybe* they could save the baby's life.

"Can they save the baby's eyes?" he asked.

"Nobody can save the baby's eyes," I said. He nodded.

After a moment, the father said calmly that it was out of the question for him to leave his wife and children for the doubtful advantage of having a blind baby live. He handed the little bundle to the mother.

I came down frequently to visit her. She recovered well, but the baby lived only a few days. There would be more babies. The mother knew, and I knew too, that for a blind baby in such a poor home, life would have been grim indeed.

My Guardian Angels

In my spare time I had many calls on my modest efforts to help, but often conditions were so extreme that it was too late to do much. Even so, I did what I could for rickshaw coolies, servants and their families, and for friends who had no one else to turn to for any kind of help.

My next S.O.S. was from a beggar woman who lived in a converted cave, dug out of the side of the hill that we lived on. She came to the back door and appealed to Yuantasao to call me. She had brought her little three-year-old son who had been bitten by a dog. She explained that he had "fire" (fever) inside, and would I please do something for him.

The child was sick indeed. His leg was swollen red and hard and he was burning with fever. Fortunately, the place where she lived wasn't far from our house, so I was able to treat the leg, visiting the child twice a day. We had no drugs in those days, only local treatment — but the boy got well. My guardian angels were working overtime in those days. I never had anything go seriously wrong.

My conservative friends constantly warned me that I was unwise to take on these stray cases; just let something go wrong and I could be in serious trouble. What they said was, of course, true, but that didn't seem to be a good enough reason not to try to help if I could. A beggar woman couldn't ride in rickshaws, nor with her little bound feet could she walk three miles with a sick child over cobblestoned city streets.

Looking back on it now, although I loved my official nursing, I know these were the things I loved best. Even though many times there was so little I could do, I sensed instinctively that there are more kinds of help than just the physical.

Forty Destroyers in Chefoo Bay

The summer after World War I ended in 1918, the American Asiatic Fleet destroyer squadrons, whose winter base was in the Philippines, arrived in Chefoo for the first time. From then on, every year through 1937, Chefoo became their regular summer base.

For five months of every summer, as many as 40 U.S. destroyers lay offshore in our little bay, along with their mothership the *Black Hawk*, plus a minelayer and a minesweeper towing a huge target for gunnery practice. As much as we enjoyed many aspects of this "invasion," the waters of our little bay were never clear and clean again.

The American submarines summered in Tsingtao [Qingdao], on the other side of the Shangtung promontory, while the British Royal Navy, whose winter base was Hong Kong, spent their summer at Weihaiwei, about 100 miles southeast of Chefoo.

Liberty boats would come in every afternoon at four o'clock, bringing hundreds of sailors on shore leave. For the first year or two they seemed to overrun Chefoo, but in time the Navy YMCA and other organizations arranged all kinds of entertainments and services for these men. In time, too, the whole of our small port learned to brace itself every spring for the arrival of the fleet.

Cafes, cabarets, beer halls and bordellos by the score sprang up everywhere, and local prices soared. All along the Bund, hanging over the low garden walls of the cabarets would appear the gradually familiar faces of the "girls" and their madams, beckoning to the sailors. These faces became so familiar that I found myself greeting them like old friends as they reappeared year after year.

A view from Claire's canoe in Chefoo Bay, a summer headquarters between the world wars for the U.S. Navy's Asiatic Fleet. The large ship is the USS *Black Hawk*, a destroyer tender, with two U.S. destroyers.

What Was the U.S. Navy Doing in Chefoo?

It was between the first and second world wars that Chefoo, a large seaport and fishing harbor across the Korea Bay from North Korea, became the main summertime harbor for the U.S. Navy's Asiatic Fleet.

Why did American leaders station dozens of warships here for part of each year? The official reason was the Open Door Policy.

Declared at the outset of the 20th century, this was the guiding idea behind U.S. actions in China. It held that any country wanting to do business here should have that right — that no single foreign nation should be able to gain monopoly control over any Chinese region or city where that nation had developed a strong trade and business presence.

Treaty ports (see page 11) were the center of most foreign trade in the early 20th century. These waterfront cities often harbored traders and diplomats from a variety of nations. (Smaller treaty ports were often called *outports*.) In Chefoo, for example, some 17 different countries set up diplomatic missions during the early 20th century, to safeguard their trade activities here.

The U.S. developed its Open Door Policy for two key reasons. It aimed to keep China open to free trade by all; the policy was also designed to protect China's territorial integrity, in an era when many feared it might be carved up by the large foreign powers, as Africa had been divided.

Along with basing its Asiatic fleet in Chefoo, the U.S. Navy also sent gunboats onto the Yangtze River. These smaller warships ventured as far as 600 miles inland, to protect American citizens and business interests along China's longest waterway. *The Sand Pebbles*, a popular American film set in China between the wars, centers on a fictional U.S. Navy gunboat on the Yangtze, on which Chinese laborers do most of the actual work.

Among the coastal treaty ports, Chefoo became an international trade center. The treaty that ended World War I gave authority over Chefoo to Japan — and it was partly to counter Japan's efforts to gain still more power in China that the U.S. Navy stationed its Asiatic Fleet here, every summer from 1919 to 1937.

Japan finally invaded China in July 1937, and a few months later it captured Chefoo. The U.S. Navy stayed close by for a few more months, safeguarding the American and British citizens who remained in the city. After Japan attacked the U.S. at Pearl Harbor in December 1941, the U.S. and China became allies in the world war that finally ended in 1945.

Claire and "Captain Church," according to her handwritten caption, aboard the USS *Black Hawk*.

Summers in the Harbor, with the Navy

All that first summer I watched the Americans building a giant breakwater in Chefoo. I would go out in my canoe and lean way over, and I could see these fantastic men in great big diving suits — they looked like men from outer space, with huge big feet. Those were the leaded boots that kept them down as they walked around the bottom of the harbor.

Cranes would lower these enormous blocks of cement, and these men down at the bottom would be putting these blocks into place. I would lean over far to watch, so fascinated that I'd regularly tumble out of the canoe, then scramble back in again.

Gradually as summer went on, the breakwater grew higher and higher until it emerged from under the water. Then they built it up; I think it eventually was about 28 or 30 feet above the water at high tide. There was a passage for ships, then this long breakwater that made a lovely sheltered harbor for us. Later on, we used to go out onto the breakwater and I would dive off it. That was great fun.

As more summers came and the fleet came back, we got to know many of the officers, and what fun we'd have going on picnics with them in their motorboats. They would bring pork and beans. I got to know some of the Navy doctors, and I would take them up to the hospital and show them around. They were always interested in that, and they wanted to see a Chinese woman's bound foot.

Well this was a little hard to arrange but I would manage to show them. The women didn't like to have their feet seen by anybody, but on the pretext of something or other, I was able to occasionally do this for them.

In 1919, during the first summer that the U.S. Navy anchored its Asiatic Fleet destroyers in Chefoo, Navy engineers built this huge breakwater to shelter the city's harbor.

Diving from the Black Hawk

One summer between the wars, Claire was swimming near the U.S. Navy's summer anchorage in Chefoo when she was hailed by the crew of the USS *Black Hawk*. A destroyer tender, the *Black Hawk* was the largest of the Navy's vessels in the harbor. Having spotted her in the water, an officer whom Claire remembers as Captain Church invited her up on deck.

"I knew him," Claire recalled. "Mother had entertained them — she'd had them to dinner and all that sort of thing. In fact, the *Black Hawk* band used to come up to the house and play in our garden. We would have lanterns all over the place and sit out in the summerhouse overlooking the harbor."

This time, she said, "Captain Church said to me, 'If you'll dive off my top deck, I'll let you invite all your friends out to lunch [on the ship]. How's that?'

"I said, 'Fine, fine, I'll invite my friends and we'll all come out, then I'll dive.' This was all said laughingly. He said, 'Okay, I'll send the boat out for you next Sunday.'"

So it happened that, the following Sunday, Claire and a half-dozen friends were ferried in their bathing suits to the *Black Hawk*. "And boy, I got outside the railing up on the top deck and — I wear glasses, but without glasses I couldn't see the water. I knew it was down there, but it was so far away, I could hardly see it.

"I do know that I could look right down into the funnels of the destroyers that were tied up alongside. I think Captain Church said it was about 45 feet. Well, I had to do this dive, I had a promise to keep ... so I got outside the rail and hung on, and every time I started to let go, everything would go black. I just didn't quite have the courage.

"I stood there, I think for about ten minutes. It seemed like an eternity to me, because by that time there was a head sticking out of every porthole on the whole side of this enormous boat.

"Finally I let myself go. Down I went, in a jolly good swallow dive — and I scrambled back up this interminable gangway and went off again, quickly, while I still had the courage."

For the rest of that summer, Claire and her friends went to Sunday lunch on the *Black Hawk*, and waterskied behind the ship's motor launches. "And I would dive — every Sunday I would take two dives. And whenever I came up, the band would play. It was great."

Claire on the deck of a U.S. Navy warship in Chefoo.

A "Tramp Nurse" on 24-Hour Duty

I was the only private-duty nurse on the China coast for 14 years, excluding my training. My full-time nursing was among Westerners. In the summers I was kept busy right in Chefoo, looking after the families of American naval officers. In the winters I would be called to small ports along the China coast.

I called myself a tramp nurse — I went anywhere they called me. I got known by word of mouth, and having the language, I was unafraid to travel. To get from Chefoo to wherever I needed to go, I traveled on small Chinese cargo ships. Accommodation on those boats left a great deal to be desired — but as I spoke Chinese, I learned to take for granted the dirt and cockroaches and sharing the only toilet with the Chinese crew.

I would go to remote areas, and there was never another nurse so I did 24-hour duty. I went into foreign communities where they didn't have any hospital and, very often, didn't even have a doctor. I would do what I had to do, for pneumonia, cholera, typhoid fever, dysentery, baby cases, anything.

The cargo boats took me from Peking and Tientsin in the north, east to Dairen [Dalian] at the southernmost tip of Manchuria, then back north and farther east to Antung [Dandong] on the Yalu River, which divides Manchuria from Korea. Then due

A cargo ship, Shanghai.
Image courtesy of Felicity Somers Eve and Historical Photographs of China, University of Bristol.

south again to Tsingtao [Qingdao], where for two years I was matron of a small American boarding school, set up to accommodate the children of U.S. Navy submarine personnel. From Tsingtao my nursing took me as far south again as Shanghai.

In the outports, the smaller ports along the coast, the foreign homes to which I went always had more than enough "help" in the house, so a nurse was needed only for real sickbed nursing. I invariably found that by the time I arrived on a case, everybody in the house was already exhausted. With no hospital and never another nurse available, this meant round-the-clock care. It also meant sleeping in the room with the patient, whether man, woman or child, who was usually too sick to be left alone.

I do recall going out one day and lying on the side of a Chinese grave mound in the sun

If the patient happened to be a man, I stayed in my uniform and took catnaps if and when I could. If my patient was unconscious or perhaps delirious, I would draw a chair up to the side of the bed and, with my arm across the patient, allow myself to doze, always aware of the slightest movement. I did this only when there was no alternative, of course, but it happened all too often. The minute a case was well enough to be left to convalesce, I was on to another serious nursing case — and in those winters I was always tired.

The foreign business community in Chefoo consisted of about 60 families, with homes strung out along the bay, while the American missionary compound was on Temple Hill among the hills on the far side of the Chinese city. The foreign community included seven or eight homes, a church, a primary school, a college and a hospital, with a training school for male and female nurses and a home for the foreign nurses within the hospital compound.

One of my very first cases, in 1922, presented when the senior American doctor at the hospital telephoned to ask if I would come to his home and help look after his family, most of whom were sick. When I got there, I found that the baby of four months was very ill indeed with whooping cough, the two youngest children were down with measles, and the two older ones had both measles and whooping cough. One of these boys later developed pneumonia. The mother wasn't sick, but the doctor was suffering with acute lumbago. In order to save both time and material, I regularly transferred the same mustard plaster from son Joe's pneumonia-heavy chest to his dad's aching back.

Everybody was tired. Pretty soon I was tired too, for I was afraid to go to sleep lest one or other of the children take a turn for the worse. Little did I realize that this was the beginning of many years of 24-hour nursing. I was on this case exactly three weeks and don't remember taking any time off. I do recall going out one day and lying on the side of a Chinese grave mound in the sun, and how good it felt just to get away from the sickroom for a few moments.

When at last they were all better and the time came to leave, the doctor asked how much money he owed me. I was covered with confusion, for I had never before asked anybody for money and was embarrassed at the thought. I had no idea how much to ask, but the doctor insisted. In the end I suggested $5 a day (five Chinese dollars, worth about 50 cents apiece). When he handed me a check for $105, I felt rich as a king. I always found it awkward asking for money, with the result that I was chronically short of it.

In the years that followed, I got to know Temple Hill Hospital well. Because this was a mission hospital for the Chinese, its staff was at first reluctant and not equipped to take in foreign patients; but with more and more Navy families arriving each summer, and now with a foreign nurse available to provide care, they finally agreed to allocate one room for private foreign patients.

As English was used only for doctors' orders and nurses' charts, it fell to me to teach the Chinese student nurses to recognize the one and chart the other. It was all I could do to keep ahead of them; they were sharp as tacks, and most were older than me.

One of the hospital's big problems in those days was that the nurses were not always willing to perform the many services that nursing calls for. Even though nursing students came from mud-village homes, they considered it beneath their dignity to do what they regarded as menial tasks, especially handling bedpans. In a land of the ubiquitous intestinal parasite, the bedpan is an indispensable source of information for diagnosis. They learned in time to accept this, but it took a decade or more to overcome this inhibition and many others.

The Routines of Home

Our home in Chefoo had once been the French Consulate. A large house built of gray brick, it had enormously high ceilings and, like most houses in those days, no modern conveniences. Standing on a hillside, it overlooked the harbor that was busy with the comings and goings of ships of all kinds, including great seagoing trading junks with their colorful patched sails. There was always the sound of ships' bells in the distance.

View from the family home.

From Mother's upstairs dressing-room window, her "million-dollar-view," as she called it, gave us a kaleidoscope of fascinating activities from morning till night. On the far side of the harbor was West Beach, with its long stretch of sand where, at low tide, I regularly rode my pony early in the mornings — when I was home, that is.

"All water had to be carried in buckets from a well ... through the bedroom where the amah would have already turned back the rug ..."

Bathroom.

Water was a very precious commodity in North China. For household use, all water had to be carried in buckets from a well at the foot of the hill. When the prevailing wind was from the land, the water was passable; but when the wind blew from the direction of the nearby harbor, it was so brackish that no amount of soap could raise a lather. Every day this water had to be carried: first up the hill, then up the outside backstairs into the house, along the hall, through the bedroom where the amah would have already turned back the rug to escape the drips, and finally into the bathrooms where the geysers and gongs were waiting to be filled.

Toilets were something else again. They were of the movable variety, made of white glaze crockery. Twice a day or more, another coolie hustled these jars out of the house, down the same backstairs and out to a backyard container. From here the public *tao-ma-t, ung'ti* collected this precious commodity for sale as fertilizer.

Amah, Who Ran the House

Yuantasao, our amah, never did anything by halves. She ran the house and everybody in it, and we all loved her dearly. Even so, I often wished she had come from somewhere else, for she spoke the most obscure dialect in all of North China. At times even the other servants couldn't understand her and teased her about it. Humming over and over the first two lines of "Jesus Loves Me," she would shake the house as she went about her chores, stumping around on her little bound feet.

Yuantasao, the Malcolm family's amah, on the back stairs of the family home.

Nothing made Yuantasao madder than to be locked out of the bathroom/dressing room when one or another of us women was taking a bath. She would bang and thump and rattle the door handle till I got out of the tub and dripped across the room to let her in. Muttering and grumbling, she would pretend to be about something important. But it was nothing of the sort — she just didn't like being excluded.

She would insist on scrubbing my back. This was always done so vigorously that she never failed to wet my hair, which always made me mad. Next time I wouldn't let her do it, which made her mad. It never got any better because she thought she had prior right over all of us, which she did of course. I gave up in the end because it was less exhausting to be a little wet and mad myself than to have her mad, mumbling and complaining about locked doors. But we couldn't have lived without her. She was part of the family and lived with us for 25 years, until the war with Japan parted us in 1941.

Yuantasao taught me how to sew. Together we would sit

cross-legged for hours on my bed drawing threads and hemstitching, and sewing lovely fillet lace onto slips and "teddy-bears" of the purest silk, making my trousseau. I eventually gave this trousseau away, for it was outmoded long before I was ever to use it. But she taught me how to sew a fine seam, and we became close friends.

But Yuantasao's real charge and true love was my younger sister, Mary. Dorothy and I were away at school and nurses' training most of the time, while Mary was not yet ten. No matter what Mother did or said to try and stop her, our amah would wait on Mary hand and foot. I recall coming into Mary's room one day to find her lying across her bed, reading, while Yuantasao was pulling off her stockings.

"Mary," I snapped, "how can you be so lazy?"

Mary dropped her book and made a dive for her stockings. But she had no idea what move to make — she didn't know whether the stockings were supposed to be coming off or going on.

At night, if Mother and Father were going to be out, Yuantasao would sleep curled up on the foot of Mary's bed. They loved each other dearly, and no amount of awkward dialect came between those two.

Golden Sand from the Gobi Desert

It is so easy to make statements about China that are absolutely true of one part and just as untrue of another. In the south the climate is subtropical. Here the temperature of the three winter months is delightful, clear and cold but never freezing.

Taitze — on frozen canal.

Brilliant poinsettias and bougainvilleas grow wild on the hillsides. But while the winter is lovely, it is neither cold enough nor long enough to fortify one against the onslaught of hot, humid, rainy summer that lasts for nine long months.

In the summer, to take advantage of the rapidly flowering domestic plants, most of the gardening is done in an endless procession of flower pots. The instant one variety shows signs of wilting, it is whisked out of sight by the gardeners, to be immediately replaced by the next in bloom.

In North China, on the other hand, it rains all too seldom. Here the summers are short and, for about one month, very hot. And with the exception of a too-brief rainy season in July, summers are also very dry, with temperatures sometimes rising to well over 100 degrees.

When the rain did come, it poured down in torrents, turning the powdery dust of the roads into deep mud and, in the countryside, washing away the precious topsoil from the land — and at the same time often dissolving the little huddles of country villages, whose houses and walls were made entirely of dried mud, protected by only their inadequate thatched roofs.

The autumns here are long and glorious. For the same reason that it seldom rains, North China gets very little snow but has three months when it is bitterly cold, with the thermometer often dropping to zero. During these months in my day, all canal transport was done by *p'aitze*, a heavy wooden platform mounted on thick wooden runners and propelled over the ice by a boatman with a long pole.

The spring is abrupt and plagued by awful sand and dust storms, which combine the gray dust of the city streets with the fine golden sand from the all-too-near Gobi Desert, turning midday into dusk and the sun into a red ball in the sky. On these days, the wise mother kept her children indoors. When I went out on such a day, I would tie my whole head up in a fine silk scarf, which permitted me to see just enough to know where I was going, yet kept the swirling dirt and dust out of my eyes and hair.

...turning midday into dusk and the sun into a red ball in the sky

I have witnessed freak rainstorms arising in the midst of such a sandstorm. With perhaps one loud warning clap of thunder, suddenly huge raindrops, mixing with the dust in the air, would come down as mud. To be caught out in one of these storms would ruin whatever garment one happened to be wearing. No amount of washing or dry cleaning could remove the fine brown stain beaten into the fiber of the material.

This eternal dust was the despair of every housewife. In spite of double windows and double doors, it seeped in, leaving a thick layer over everything. This dust was more like powder than sand, and had to be handled with the greatest care so as not to raise it again. The procedure was to first remove the drifts from the corners of the windows and doors with a little shovel. Next the remainder was gently stroked into a dustpan, with a fine camel-hair brush specially designed for the purpose. Then, and not till then, could it be dusted with a cloth.

After the wind died down, slipcovers, rugs and curtains were taken outside, thrown across the clothesline and beaten with a bamboo carpet-beater. There were no such things as vacuum cleaners in my day.

During this season, hospital clinics were crowded with young and old, waiting their turn for the painful treatment of trachoma and many other stubborn eye infections carried in the dust by the winds.

Differing from both north and south, the climate in Shanghai, in central China, is a happy blend of both. Here the gentle rain and fertile soil produce flower gardens rarely surpassed anywhere, and nowhere else in the world is there grown such a variety of green vegetables. In the countryside in our time the market gardens were incomparably lush and abundant — all fertilized by noxious "night soil," the smell of which relentlessly pursued and revolted one throughout the lovely spring days.

Via the markets, these vegetables turned the most scrupulously clean kitchen into a constant source of infection from the ubiquitous intestinal parasites, the most common and pernicious of which was the dysentery amoeba. These diseases took a heavy toll of lives among foreign and natives alike, but especially among native children, among whom the death toll was unbelievably high. One of the causes of such a high death rate among infants was that when a mother could not breastfeed her child, she had no alternative but to chew food until it was soft enough for an infant to take, then spew it into the baby's mouth.

The Tailor's Wife

I wish I could remember his proper name but I can't. He had known me since I was a girl, and we always referred to him as "Gold Tooth" because he had one shiny, all-gold front tooth. He was the community tailor, with the aid of Butterick's pattern book. His things didn't always fit, but they were always beautifully sewn. Gold Tooth was also a very gracious gentleman. We addressed him simply as *t'sai-feng* (tailor).

One day Gold Tooth stopped me on the street and asked if I would come and visit his sick wife. We arranged a time. Although I had been to his shop hundreds of times, I had never seen his wife.

When I arrived, he was standing outside the door waiting for me. With a bow, he first asked if I had eaten (the traditional greeting), then thanked me for coming. We went in and through his large familiar workroom, where his tailors were sewing, some at sewing machines, others seated around cutting tables working by hand. There must have been at least 30 of them. As we entered the room, these men all stood and greeted me by name. They all knew me — but more importantly, they knew I had come to see their employer's sick wife.

They remained standing while we walked through the room to the back, where there was a narrow closed-in stair leading up to what looked like a huge loft at the top. Within this large area was a small, box-like room built quite independent of the rest of the loft. This room was about ten by 12 feet, and from the outside it looked indeed like a large box, standing in the middle of a wide floor. Gently parting a curtain of long strings of colored beads, Gold Tooth invited me to go in.

The room was spotless. It had two beds, one along each side of the room. Against the far wall between the two beds stood a square table, and at its back stood the family (or kitchen) god. Incense was smoldering at the god's feet, in a little brass urn. On the table was a teapot and two cups, the kind with lids as well as saucers but no handles. A wicker basket, quilted on the inside for insulation, held the teapot.

As I stood at the door, a frail little woman lying on one of the beds invited me to come in, at the same time attempting to rise. It was plain that she was in a lot of pain, so I gently helped her back onto her pillow. Her husband brought a chair and placed it by the bed for me, then poured a cup of tea and presented it to me. I thanked him, sipped it once, then set it down.

After a little polite conversation, I asked the wife to tell me what her trouble was. She was clearly very sick, probably in the advanced stages of some serious illness. In a small

The tailor's home altar.

voice that I could hardly hear, she tried to describe her many symptoms, but said the pain in her abdomen was the worst.

She pulled down her bed covers and lifted up her jacket, exposing her emaciated little body. From the middle of her hollow abdomen bulged an enormous lump.

I didn't have to examine her to know she was far beyond any help I could give. Even so, I examined her gently and asked about her history.

With her husband's help, she told me what she could. Explaining to them that I wasn't a doctor, I suggested that she let me take her to the mission hospital on Temple Hill to see the American doctor there. "Oh no," they both cried.

They were afraid he might want to cut her open. Couldn't I just give her something? I sat there holding her poor little wasted hand. All this time the smell of opium was strong in the room. Ignoring this, I asked if she was taking anything for the pain.

Gold Tooth replied that yes, she was smoking and taking a little opium. When I asked if this seemed to relieve the pain, she said it did. By her appearance, I doubted if any doctor would be willing to operate, for she was not young and her condition was far advanced. I sat there holding her hand and talking with them both. Presently, as I got up to go, she asked if I would come again to see her. I promised that I would.

When we were out of earshot, Gold Tooth admitted that he knew his wife was too ill to be moved. As she was not willing to go to the hospital, I simply suggested that she continue with her opium whenever she felt she couldn't bear the pain. He nodded. He said he had known this all along, but just to please her he had promised to ask me to come. He thanked me again for coming.

I went to see her as often as I could, and each time I stepped inside the shop, whether Gold Tooth was with me or not, the workmen would quietly rise and remain standing till I had either disappeared up the back stair or, returning, had made my way out. One of them always courteously opened the door and called a rickshaw for me, directing the puller where to take me. I need hardly say that the wife didn't live long.

Most country people in any land are friendly, hospitable and kind, but I am sure there are no people in all the world who can compare with the Chinese in natural grace and exquisite courtesy. Whether he is the highest in the land or the humblest, this quality is bred in his bone. Compared with this, the Westerner does indeed often seem like a crude "barbarian."

Jenny of Chefoo

Her mother was Japanese, and her father was the Scottish skipper of one of the early China-coast steamers. They say that as a girl she had been very lovely. Today she was the shape and size of a tent, but with a heart of gold. Not pure gold, perhaps; she was also a mixture of sentimentality and unscrupulousness.

The first time I saw Jenny, she was belaboring a Chinese policeman with his own baton. He had said something cheeky to her, and she didn't like it. The next time she was playing the organ in the little Episcopal chapel, with her long braid of graying hair twisted up on top of her head. In the summer, her hat for church was a creation of blond straw smothered with a mixture of bright paper flowers. In winter she wore what resembled, more than anything else, a fur muff on her head. All this in honor of Sunday.

Jenny had lived in Chefoo for so long that she had become almost a legend — although, come to think of it, she wasn't really that old. She was just the kind that makes a legend fast, I guess. Her husband, Will, was a quiet Englishman. At one time Will had been an alcoholic, but she fixed him once and for all with a horsewhip. He went on the wagon and stayed there.

Much of the credit for this "cure" went to a staunch mutual friend of theirs, Arthur by name, who from that time on came to live with them. He became a fixture, and part of that fixture was a regulation hospital bed, the kind that winds up and down at the head and at the knees.

Jenny of Chefoo: "She had become almost a legend."

While visiting a sick pal at the hospital one day, Jenny spotted one of these beds. As the best was always just barely good enough for her good friend Arthur, she could hardly wait to write to Montgomery Ward for just such a bed. After it came, on Sunday mornings Arthur always had his breakfast served to him in style, perched up in this bed.

Will and Arthur worked side by side in one of the local import-export firms and were inseparable friends. But they were only part of Jenny's assets. In her own name she owned a variety of things, including all the freshwater rights for every ship entering Chefoo harbor. She also owned a couple of islands off the mainland. These alone brought her quite a handsome revenue. As Chefoo was extremely busy every summer with as many as 40 ships of the U.S. Asiatic Fleet, there were great demands on Jenny's commodities. She hired out Kentucky Island to the Navy for rifle practice, and Long Island to the port health authorities for quarantine purposes. She also owned not a little property in the native city.

She was the first person in town to own a motor car, and she was very particular about who she let ride in it; she would spread newspapers on the floor before letting anyone in. One day Jenny took me for a lovely drive along the new Chefoo-Weishien motor road, following the coastline west to the water city of P'englai. To enter that city we had to first get out of the car and into a sampan on the beach. The boatman rowed us out from shore about 200 feet, then doubled back through the huge water gate in the wall, which was built right out into the sea.

water-gate

P'éng-Lai.

As we passed through this gate, we entered a junk harbor full of boats of all sizes. Except for a small back gate for pedestrian use, this was the only entrance to the city. At dusk these gates were closed.

We spent a few pleasant hours there visiting a Chinese friend of Jenny's. Most of her friends were Chinese, and she kept her Chinese and her European lives quite separate. I would drop in to see her on a summer morning and would find her in a long, white, shapeless and sleeveless cotton gown and homemade slipper-scuffs, with her long braid down her back. More often than not I would find her sitting with her amah, cross-legged on the amah's *kang*, or brick bed, playing mahjong or cards.

Jenny had adopted three Chinese children. The oldest was a girl, Chin-djen, now married. The next was Ta-ke, a young man of 21. The youngest, Hsaio-tze, was a boy of 12. As she related it, the daughter was the result of an indiscretion between her amah and her houseboy. Hsaio-tze was a foundling, a little bundle left on her doorstep. But Ta-ke, Jenny claimed, was well-born. She was especially proud of this. She told me the story of how she came by Ta-ke.

While out shopping one day, she saw a crowd by the side of the street. A man was standing on the curb with a child in his arms, a boy about a year old. The appearance of the child's clothes told Jenny that he belonged to some wealthy family; a single long straw sticking up out of the child's hat indicated that he was for sale. Jenny joined the crowd and the chorus of bidders, and finally got the child for 50 silver dollars.

The next day, so her story went, there was a notice in the paper saying that the baby son of one of the local officials had been kidnapped. The notices went on to describe this child to the last detail.

"What did you do then?" I asked.

"Nothing," Jenny replied.

"But didn't you take him back?" I asked.

"Don't be a fool," she said. "I paid 50 dollars for him!"

She knew full well that she could have got back more than her 50 dollars. But at long last she had her heart's desire, a well-born child, and she wasn't going to give him up. She hadn't, either. Ta-ke was now studying engineering at the mission school on Temple Hill.

Jenny was fond of young people, and often invited a bunch of us down to the most sumptuous Chinese suppers at her house. After we were all stuffed to repletion, she would insist that we dance. The rugs would be rolled back and the floor sprinkled with borax, to make it slippery. And slippery it certainly was. The house was goodness knows how old, and the floor of her living room sloped off in one direction. So by the time we had circled the room a couple of times, we would find ourselves on top of each other, all crowded into one corner. It got to be a joke, but it didn't stop the dancing.

"Don't be a fool," she said. "I paid 50 dollars for him!"

In her way, Jenny was a great benefactor to those around her and she had many friends, but rumor had it that she also had many enemies. Even though she played the organ in the little chapel, her life was largely compelled by superstitions and fears. She didn't trust anybody or anything. Her ways were devious and cunning — and just to be on the safe side, she never let her right hand know what her left hand was doing.

She was always a little scared that somebody would poison her. She had her coffin all ready. Some friend of hers had given her a special tree and she'd had it all cut down and made into a beautifully polished coffin. She showed it to me; it was stacked away in the back, ready any time she might need it.

In the spring, often the Chinese ladies would take themselves off to the country and eat fresh garlic, really eat their fill. They would stay there and play mahjong and smoke opium. Jenny and two or three Chinese ladies went into the country and spent two or three days, eating Chinese food and rice and this lovely fresh garlic. It was supposed to give them a good spring cleaning after a long winter of starches.

On a Cargo Ship to Antung

In spring 1923 I received a letter from Antung [Dendong], in Manchuria. Antung is on the west bank of the wide Yalu River that separates Manchuria from Korea.

The letter was from a Mr. Ferguson, commissioner of customs in Antung. He wrote that his wife was expecting her first baby in September, and would I be free to come and look after her. An old Danish missionary doctor there would be attending her, but there was no hospital. If I could come, would I let his wife know what she should get ready in preparation for a home delivery?

I replied that I would be glad to come and sent her a long list of things she would need for the event. With the return mail came a letter from the expecting mother, saying she could not get any of the things I had asked for in Antung. Chefoo wasn't much better for buying supplies of this kind, so I set about making by hand most of what I would need, and had them sent to her.

The day was August 11. I was on a surgical case at Temple Hill Hospital when I received a cable from Antung in Manchuria to come immediately. Luckily my current patient was convalescing nicely. I dashed home to repack my bag and catch the night's boat out of Chefoo.

"Toilets on these boats were for all comers."

Flush →

At 6 p.m. I boarded the little cargo ship and found my way to the "saloon," a dingy little room about 15 feet by ten. A coolie carrying my bags showed me to a tiny two-berth cabin, the only one on the boat. There were ants on the bed and cockroaches scuttling away from my feet. The place smelled as though it had been hermetically sealed for years.

I won't say I was disgusted, for I knew more or less what to expect, but the prospects for a much-needed night's sleep weren't all that good. This was to be the first of many such trips in years to come. More than once I have shared a six-bunk cabin with five Chinese men, which I preferred as there is safety in numbers. I always chose an upper berth and would climb up on the bunk, push my hat forward, leave my shoes on and go to sleep, for I was eternally tired.

But this was my first such trip. In the corner of this cabin was a tall brass jug standing in a brass basin set into a cabinet. Lifting the jug I found a hole in the bottom of the basin, leading into a pail underneath. Sticking to a dirty cake of soap was a cork for the basin, and hanging from a hook above it was a doubtful-looking towel. Living in China had long since taught me to always carry my own towel and my own little pillow and toilet paper. After all, this was only a cargo boat.

I went out into the saloon again. By now it was full of men sitting around the table, signing what were obviously ship's papers. The only ones in uniform were the two customs officers from shore. The rest were members of the Chinese crew and the Japanese skipper. On these little coast-wise boats the skipper was always Japanese.

Presently everybody left, and the sound of the anchor chain being hauled up told me we were about to sail. I went out on deck. Our house in Chefoo was high above, overlooking the harbor. I wondered if Mother would be at her window. Sure enough, there she was — she and dear old Yuantasao were waving a towel from Mother's dressing-room window. In years to come they never failed to wave to me till my boat was out of sight.

My next move was to locate the toilet. Toilets on these boats were for all comers. They consisted of a white porcelain bowl, about the shape and size of a bidet, set into and flush with the floor. This bowl was flanked on either side by two raised pedestals for the feet to stand on. On the wall in front was a handle bar, a necessary support in a rough sea.

When I got back to the saloon the table was being laid for dinner. I was the only passenger and, as always, the only foreigner as well as the only woman. I ate with the captain and others. The meal was a mixture of foreign and Chinese food. Here again I knew to eat only hot food, to lessen the chance that flies had lingered there. When the meal was over, everyone withdrew.

It was the middle of August. With the thermometer at 80 degrees, I couldn't face the airless cabin, so I sat in the saloon for a while, hoping for inspiration. None came. I went into the cabin and got into my kimono, then came back into the saloon where there was a little breeze. I started to lie down on the settee, but it was so greasy and dirty that I just couldn't.

Presently I found myself lying on the saloon table. Suddenly (it was now midnight), the saloon door opened and in burst the Japanese captain. I leapt off the table. He was shouting at me in Japanese and pointing an indignant finger at the cabin. I didn't understand what he was saying, but there was no mistaking what he meant. Vaguely wondering how I happened to be on the table in the first place, I bowed and apologized in my best Chinese and withdrew into the cabin. I shut the door and locked it.

From this point my memory is a blank. I must have fainted and then drifted off to sleep right where I had fallen, for the next thing I knew it was daylight and I was lying on the floor of the cabin. To make matters worse, I had fallen on my glasses and broken them.

I was upset, for I had broken my precious glasses, but otherwise I seemed to accept this sort of thing as part of the drawbacks of travel in those days. Luckily I always carried an extra pair of glasses. As quickly as possible I got myself reasonably tidy, if not particularly clean.

It was 6 a.m. We had arrived at the mouth of the Yalu. While this river is very wide, in places it is only about two feet deep, so it was necessary for the passengers to be transferred to shallow-draft barges to navigate the 12 miles upriver to Antung.

The Toll of a Typhoon

When we arrived at the landing, I looked eagerly among all the Chinese, Koreans and Japanese for some sign of a foreign face. With relief, I spotted what had to be Mr. Ferguson. He greeted me warmly, thanked me for coming so promptly, and said Mrs. Ferguson was far from well.

Off we set through the Japanese settlement in Antung. This section of the city, well laid-out with wide streets lined by shade trees on both sides, was on higher ground than the low-lying adjacent Chinese city, and was completely enclosed behind a solid mud dike.

The commissioner's house was large and surrounded by a wide veranda-terrace that commanded a panoramic view. The native Chinese city, of one-story mud and brick houses, lay to the left as far as the eye could see. The Japanese settlement lay below and to the right; straight ahead flowed the wide, muddy Yalu. Easily visible on its far side was Korea.

After I'd had a much-needed bath, Mr. Ferguson took me to meet his wife, who was in bed. A young woman, she coughed incessantly; she was very ill indeed. The next day, the doctor told me she had advanced tuberculosis and dysentery, and gave me a long list of treatment he wanted her to have. With her wracking cough, the wonder to me was that she had not miscarried long before.

During the night it started to blow and rain. Between violent coughing spells and bedpans, I was up with my patient much of the night. By morning a full-sized typhoon was raging.

We were about to have breakfast when we heard a pounding. When we opened the front door, there stood the American consul and his wife and two little girls, drenched to the skin. They had wakened to find their house swaying around them; they got out just in time to see it collapse.

The day that followed was violent and dramatic. The typhoon was at its height, and we could see the whole surrounding area as though it were a stage. We watched the river steadily rising. Suddenly it burst through the dikes. By noon the whole native city was underwater.

At this time of year the river was full of huge logs being floated down from the forests in Manchuria. With the river swelling, these logs had got loose and were crashing into the native city on the flood waters. They behaved like battering rams, whirling and plunging and destroying everything in their path. Trees and houses with people clinging to the roofs went swirling by our astonished eyes.

In spite of all this, the Japanese settlement remained intact. The Japanese were out by the hundreds manning their dykes. The dikes held.

Gradually the wind went down. My diary notes, "Thousands homeless. Strangely beautiful evening." I still clearly remember that sunset, beautiful in the midst of so much devastation. The native city was a swirling lake of mud.

By now my patient was so sick and nervous that I decided to sleep in the room with her. That night at 2 a.m. she called to me. She was in labor. Quoting my diary: "6:30 a.m., delivered of male child breech presentation, 6 ½ pounds."

Transporting logs on a river raft.

The minute labor started, I had dispatched the gardener with an SOS to the doctor. Two days later I heard from him by letter, saying he was overwhelmed with work among flood victims. In the two months that I was there, the doctor never came; he simply couldn't get away from his hospital on the far side of the flooded native city.

For the first few days after the baby was born, the mother was so happy that she actually seemed a little better. Eternally scrubbing my hands, I was kept busy running between mother and baby in a separate room. Although the house was fully staffed with servants, Mrs. Ferguson had never engaged a baby amah, so there was no one to lend me a hand. I was by now getting very short of sleep.

For a while all went smoothly, but the mother's wracking cough never ceased and she was growing weaker. Mr. Ferguson decided to resign from the service and take his wife to the south of France as soon as she was well enough to travel. He asked me if I would go with them, but I had other cases booked, and besides, I just didn't want to go. Instead I wrote to Shanghai to arrange for a nurse and a "traveling amah" to come to Antung and accompany them back to Shanghai on the first lap of their journey.

It was three weeks before the nurse and amah finally arrived. I saw them off on their boat to Shanghai, where Mrs. Ferguson was taken straight to the hospital. A month later she died.

In the Shops and Streets of Chefoo

Shopping for silk in Chefoo was a pastime I enjoyed. Usually two of us would go together into the city. As we entered a shop, we would be graciously greeted by three or four gentlemen in long gowns, their hands stuffed into the ends of their long sleeves to keep warm.

On the ground floor the shelves usually displayed dark silks for men's clothes. Explaining that we would like to see some silk for ladies' dresses, we would be escorted upstairs, where more gentlemen in long gowns with hands in their sleeves received us, more as though we were expected guests than shoppers. We were shown to a little table and chairs and invited to please be seated. Little cups of boiling hot tea were placed in front of us.

Not till all the courtesies had been observed were we asked what we wanted to see. From there on it was fairly clear sailing, as long as we didn't try to hurry. But who wanted to hurry? I loved the silk stores; the colors and textures of those pure silks were so exquisite, and we were encouraged to look at and feel everything. Time was no object.

The silk stores sold furs, too — mink and seal and squirrel, fox and wolf and unborn lamb, even dog and cat skins.

Once, out walking by myself, I stood watching some children playing in the street. They were skipping rope, and among them was a little girl about nine years old. She was knitting something, and strapped to her back was a large baby. Two children were turning the rope while all the others lined up to skip. Each one in turn would run in, skip until she tripped, then run out while the next ran in.

This went on till it came to the little girl with the baby on her back.

The colors and textures of the pure silks were so exquisite

To my surprise and delight, this child calmly put her knitting in one hand and, with the other supporting the baby's bottom, took her turn. The problem of babysitting is all relative.

One of the distressing and disturbing sights in China in those days, especially in the cities, was the presence everywhere of professional beggars. The crippled ones were stationed in the streets, while others went on their rounds to the shops, stopping at every doorstep and making their presence known with a loud whining wail. A clerk would toss out a cash or two, for which the beggar would scramble.

Occasionally the beggars would demand more money, and if it was not forthcoming, they would gang up and congregate on the doorstep. These wretched human beings were often so diseased and abhorrent in appearance, often decaying with such maladies as leprosy and syphilis, that no customer would risk going into the store for fear of being touched by one of them. This tactic soon had the desired effect of producing a little more money — but still very little.

A city street scene, from Claire's collection.

Some of the more aggressive beggars could be very threatening, running alongside a rickshaw with a restraining hand on the side, threatening to touch the passenger with an ugly sore. But if one succumbed to the urge to give them something, you were soon followed by yet another. A rickshaw man dared not protest lest he himself be ganged-up on later.

Never once did I give to any of them, for I had to go regularly through the city in Chefoo to get to the hospital on the other side. In the end I was rarely bothered, for they got to know me, and they knew as well as I did that I dared not give. These beggars existed in the foreign settlements too, though not so many as in the native cities. They were well-known to be part of an organized racket controlled by the underworld.

The Rickshaw Men and Me

A rickshaw puller. *Photograph by Hedda Morrison. Image courtesy of the President and Fellows of Harvard College.*

Rickshaws usually congregated at recognized stands. When their pullers saw a prospective passenger, they would almost mob that person to secure the fare. For strangers this could be a frightening ordeal.

During Chefoo's bitter winters, my usual mode of transport was walking, in the interest of both keeping warm and saving money. The winter rickshaw pullers were steady old-timers who knew me and had watched me grow up. It was common knowledge even among them that I had to count my pennies — so usually, when I got to the foot of our hill where the rickshaws were congregated, we would simply exchange greetings and I would strike out on foot. But occasionally when I was dressed for a party or in a big hurry, I would hail one of them. They would decide among themselves which one would take me.

Once while I was in training in Shanghai, between 1918 and 1921, thanks to a rickshaw puller I was saved from the rough clutches of a drunken American sailor.

The Shanghai hospital was on the outskirts of the crowded Hongkew district. To get to town from there, we nurses had to pass through a busy waterfront area. Nearby was the landing stage where sailors came ashore for their shore leave, and where later they gathered to await the launches that would take them back to their ships.

The streets were wide, so often one would find oneself riding along abreast with another rickshaw. In my case the person in the other rickshaw was a very drunk sailor. When he saw me, with a roar and a lunge he reached for the mudguard of my rickshaw and hung on, bellowing to the rickshaw pullers to stop.

Terrified, I pleaded with my puller to go faster, faster. But it wasn't easy to loosen the grip of the determined sailor. Gradually my puller pulled forward harder while, with mutual consent, the sailor's puller held back, with the result that the sailor was nearly pulled out of his rickshaw. Frustrated and angry, the sailor started kicking his puller in the spine with his hard leather boot. That was the thanks the puller got for his kind concern for me.

On not a few occasions when I set out to walk, I had one of the rickshaw pullers fall in step beside me, start up a casual conversation, then as casually ask where I was going. When I told him, he would reply, "*Oh, ch'i-kwai* (strange), that is just where I happen to be going — so why don't you get in and let me take you." When I protested that I hadn't brought any money, he would say, "Money! Who's talking about money. We're friends. You get in."

Only if I knew the coolie well did I accept such an offer, for this was his bread and butter. But these were my friends, and their friendly gestures my warm claim to fame.

The puller would get into a jog-trot, trailing a wake of garlic aroma and talking to me about this and that. Had I heard lately from *Hsiao-yeh*, my brother now in Canada? Did I know what day the U.S. fleet was arriving this year?

More than once when I had been working at the mission hospital without time to get down to the settlement, my foreign friends would ask if I didn't get lonely up there all alone. "Alone! What do you mean?" I would ask. They thought that because there were no foreigners at the hospital, I was somehow alone; but it never occurred to me that I could be lonely just because I wasn't among foreigners. Unlike my homesick little mother, my chickens didn't have to cluck in English.

The Spirits of the Drowned

Among the many colorful Chinese festivals, one of the most entrancing was their memorial celebration to the spirits of the drowned. This was held on the fifteenth day of the seventh moon, which corresponds approximately to about the end of August by the Western calendar. To ensure the right weather, it was held on either that day or the first perfectly calm day after.

In the evening at high water, just as the tide was about to turn, families who had lost relatives at sea would place lighted candles set in little boats on the water's edge. Some of these boats could be very elaborate and quite large, while others were simply halves of melons or anything that would float. As the tide went out, these thousands of little lights would drift out to sea, threading their way in and out among the junks in the harbor, twinkling on the surface of the calm water as though the stars in the heavens had fallen. The air was filled with the scent of burning incense and the plaintive notes of the flute and one-string violin, adding to the magic of the scene.

On this evening each year, Mother always arranged a dinner party. After dinner we would sit out in the garden on the wall overlooking the harbor, watching these little lights far into the night.

Curious to see the different kinds of floats, I often got into my canoe and paddled gently out among the lights. Never did I ever touch any of them. Most of the boats were like little rafts, made of lengths of bamboo tied together with a candle in the middle, impaled on a metal spike; but once I spotted a large boat made of reeds. It was about two feet long with a bracket of bamboo erected at either end. From each of these brackets hung a lighted paper lantern. Arranged in the middle of this boat was a "spirit offering" of cakes, fresh fruit and a bottle of wine.

In the Mission Hospital

I used to be called up to the Temple Hill Hospital. That was the Presbyterian mission hospital, up on the hill on the other side of the native city. Most ordinary nursing I did right down in the community, in the homes; but for surgical cases, I would go up to Temple Hill. In the daytime I could always get a rickshaw, but at night I would have to walk alone with my flashlight through the cobblestones — dark, not a light anywhere, except through the cracks.

They're all open-faced doors along the Chinese streets, and people lived right in their shops. At night they'd board the doors up and, walking along, I would look through the cracks of these boards and see them playing mahjong inside, or just having dinner. Most of the time it was pretty late, and if they weren't playing mahjong it was all quiet and dark.

Two American nurses were supervisors in the hospital. This year one of them was going home on leave, and I was asked to substitute. So I worked steadily at the hospital all that year.

The women's wards were interesting. You very rarely saw a Chinese woman's bound foot, unbound. You'd go into the women's wards before dawn, and you'd hear them bustling. They were bathing and powdering and rebinding their feet, and nobody could see — no lights at all, so even the women couldn't see each other. By dawn, you'd go back into the wards and they would all be combing their hair and chattering. Their feet would all be taken care of. They took very good care of their feet; they had to.

Every patient that came in, regardless what they came in for, they all had to take worm medicine. That was for round worms, ascariasis, and the results were absolutely staggering. One little child had come in with an enormous potbelly and distended abdomen. She was given castor oil and Santonin early, early in the morning, and pretty soon the castor oil started to work and the nurse sat the child on a little potty. When she got up that little chamber pot was absolutely full of nothing but worms. There were 83 worms (we recorded them, you know). And that was just the first sitting. She kept passing them.

But the most dramatic case I had was a little boy who was admitted in agony, unconscious. We rushed him up to the x-ray, then took him straight to the operating room and they removed this large bladder stone. Brought him back to the ward and put him in a private room. He started vomiting very badly, and couldn't stop. He vomited for 24 hours.

Those days we didn't have the wonderful equipment you have today. The routine was a rectal drip, and on the second day the foreign doctor and two or three Chinese doctors were doing their medical rounds, and this little boy

Nurses at the American Presbyterian hospital in Chefoo. Claire is second from left; on holidays she would sometimes relieve American nurses at the mission hospital.

was really in a very, very serious state, critically ill. He couldn't keep anything down and they decided it was back luck and he was on his last legs with this awful constant retching.

After the doctors left the room, as I tried to get the rectal drip to go, a live worm came up through the funnel. I pulled the worm out with a pair of forceps, and I walked up to the doctors and said, "I think this is why he is vomiting." They said, "Well, it's too late, I'm afraid he's dying, the Chinese doctors agreed that he is dying." I said, "May I have permission to give him castor oil and Santonin? We have nothing to lose." They said, "Sure, if you think you can get him to keep it down."

Well, I turned this little unconscious child over on his side, and I smacked his little bare bottom and said, "Open your eyes, open your eyes." His little eyes rolled back and I said, "Open your mouth — I want you to take this medicine." I had made it warm, so it would go down almost without swallowing.

I kept the spoon in his mouth and I could see him swallowing it. His chin started to drop as though he were going to vomit again and I smacked his bottom and said,

Operating room staff at the American Presbyterian hospital.

"Don't vomit. Swallow, swallow, don't vomit." I could see the nurses sort of elbowing each other, at me spanking this unconscious child who was dying. I said, "Swallow, swallow, don't vomit," and I stood there for eight hours without leaving the room.

After that, the boy passed hundreds and hundreds of worms. Then he vomited worms. Two weeks later he walked out of the hospital. Every month, the mother and father would bring him back and make him get down on his hands and knees and knock his head on the floor to me, because I'd saved his life. They always referred to him as "my little bladder stone."

We had to train the Chinese nurses. And it's a difficult thing — having graduated, they would no longer scrub a bedpan. They would no longer do any menial job. This is what present-day China is having to break. Anybody who was a graduate in letters or in some sort of profession, when they were training they knew they had to do these menial jobs — the foreigners insisted, it was part of the training. But after they were trained, there was this dignity that they wouldn't stoop beneath; there was this barrier that prevented your scholar from stooping to any menial job.

Old Men and a Funeral

While I was there, I'd get up early and look out onto the countryside. I'd see these old Chinese gentleman walking in the early, early morning with their birds in bird cages. They would talk to their birds and the birds would talk to them. They had different kinds of birds, but the myna bird was a great favorite and they'd teach them to talk.

One evening there was an enormous funeral next to the hospital. There was a Chinese band with all these cymbals and noises, and there was a parade headed by the coffin. In front of the coffin was an empty chair with an enormous enlargement, a photograph of the deceased, sitting in the chair — then came all the mourners, in order of seniority in the family, all dressed in white, wailing and mourning and slowly walking toward the graveyard.

In the procession were every conceivable kind of thing that a man would need in his life after death, done in paper. There were paper effigies of men and women servants, of a horse, a sedan chair, furniture, tables and chairs for the house, and all kinds of food on a table, most ingeniously made.

The family gathered around the grave-mound area, and there was a ceremony and incense burned. When that was over, the paper things were all brought together and burned. They went up in a tremendous flame — just one great flash. It was fascinating to watch. Then more of this unbelievable Chinese music, rather like bagpipes only more so.

Riding Kim, Visiting Villages

Outdoor sports played a large part in the life of all the small western outports. The most popular were tennis, golf and all kinds of water sports in the summer, and shooting, field hockey and skating in the winter. Riding of the very best could be had all year round. With the vast hinterland at our very doorstep, I rarely needed to cover the same ground twice, although I had my favorite haunts.

During the years between 1918 and 1924 there was very little anti-foreign feeling in our neighborhood of Chefoo, so it was quite safe for me, a girl, to go anywhere without anxiety. Growing up both speaking and loving Chinese had a lot to do with that, of course. I worked steadily at the mission hospital, relieving one of the regular nurses who had got married and gone on home leave. That year I decided to keep an animal.

My beloved Kim wasn't the run-of the-mill China pony. I think he was half mule. Certainly his temperament was, and his expressive ears; those would go backward and forward as I sang at the top of my voice while riding along those empty beaches.

Kim was big and strong and had a wonderful gait, but neither of us was proud of his manners. He had a cute little trick of rearing up and tripping backwards the minute I mounted. This was strictly show-off, for he didn't do it when we were alone out in the country. But many was the rickshaw shaft and disrupted fruit stall for which I had to apologize, and later compensate.

Sometimes I would set out in the morning with a sandwich in my pocket and stay out all day, riding up to a favorite mountain pass. Dismounting, I would lead Kim down the other side. Kim had never been shod, and for this reason he was more comfortable climbing rock than are most horses with iron shoes.

I think he enjoyed all this as much as I did. We roamed far and wide through many little villages and past isolated farmhouses, where old people were tending the babies while the young ones worked in the fields.

In North China one didn't very often see women doing the heavy work in the fields because of their bound feet, but they tended the kitchen gardens and did the threshing and all such chores around the house. My rides would take me through the center of these little villages, for the narrow footpaths led directly from one village right through the next.

At first everyone was curious but always courteous. I looked like a girl, but how short my hair was and I was out all alone! When I overheard their speculations about whether I was a man or a woman, I call out "*nu-ti*," female, then we would all have a little laugh and

Claire, on a stone horse, and Kim.

they would invite me to "come down" and have a cup of tea. I would usually smile and bow and thank them, at the same time apologize for trespassing over their threshing floor. This large, hard mud floor always formed the middle of any village. It was about the size of two tennis courts, and crossing it was the only way to reach the path beyond.

Instinct always guided me to smile and speak to only the women and children. Should I inconvenience a man by unavoidably passing his way, I would bow but without the familiarity of a smile, while at the same time asking his pardon.

At other times, responding to an invitation, I would get down at some lone farmhouse, a modest two-room mud hut, to share the only bench with some dear old woman with a kindly weatherbeaten face and pass the time of day with her. The first questions were always how old was I, and how many children, for they took for granted that at my obvious age I was married. (I was 25 then. I didn't marry till I was 36!)

Then I would ask how many sons she had, and if they were married and had any children. I didn't need to ask if the sons were at home, for this went without saying. It was of paramount importance in the Chinese social order to have sons, including their wives, to continue the family farm and to support and take care of parents in their old age. The Chinese loved their daughters just as much; but when girls married, of necessity they left their homes to become active members of their husband's homes, and there to take care of his parents.

My visits usually ended by the dear old people graciously cutting a stalk of sugarcane or picking a bunch of grapes off the vine and presenting it to me with an invitation to come back again sometime. I never dreamed of spoiling such a sincere gesture by offering them money — but this is also the reason I hesitated to accept such hospitality too often, because I didn't want them to part with their precious fruits.

Still, I loved them and I know they enjoyed our visits.

A Curse and a Chase

One day Nigel, one of the young men in the port, asked where I went when I rode. I said I just went where the spirit moved me, usually across country somewhere. He asked if he might come with me one day, for he had never been far afield on his own. I said sure, if he liked.

Nigel was about my age. He had been born and brought up in Chefoo. At ten he had been sent to England to school, which was the custom among English people. After finishing, he returned to Chefoo where he now had a job in his father's office, an import/export company. He spoke very little Chinese. It wasn't necessary for his work, because the office staff all spoke English.

Among the families of the foreign business communities, the theory was that children should be discouraged from speaking Chinese, for fear of hearing undesirable things from the streets and servants. The result was that the only Chinese these children learned was a conglomeration of vehement swear words, which they heard all around them on the streets. Rarely did they have the remotest idea of the meaning of these words. At best they knew them to be highly provocative.

Nigel joined me the next day. As this was to be his first ride into the country, I wanted it to be a really nice one — so I followed one of my favorite routes, south along the coast for quite a long way, then inland and back through a village I knew. As we were crossing the threshing floor of the village, out of the corner of my eye I noticed a group of men in uniform, sitting at a table sipping tea.

"You fool! Come on, let's get out of here"

These were the warlord years, and young men from the villages were being pressed into service. Growing up in an always potentially hostile land, caution becomes second nature, so I refrained from turning my head in their direction. But I heard one of them laughingly hurl some sort of profanity at us, followed by raucous laughter.

Unfortunately this was one of the handful of Chinese phrases Nigel understood. To my dismay, he turned and shouted back at them in the same vein. I looked just in time to see two of the soldiers jump up and disappear behind one of the houses. They were carrying riding whips.

"You fool!" I shouted at Nigel. "Come on, let's get out of here."

I put the whip to my surprised pony, and in no time we were out of the village and onto one of the narrow dikes that divided the low-lying grain fields. I could hear our pursuers gaining on us, for they were whipping their ponies hard. Soon they were right behind Nigel, belaboring his pony with their whips. Luckily it was impossible to pass on these very narrow paths.

Up ahead I could see a path leading to the top of the nearby hill. It crossed ours at right angles. I shouted to Nigel to be prepared to make this sharp turn and shake our pursuers.

It worked. The two soldiers shot past. By the time they had found a spot wide enough to turn and retrace their tracks, we had gained the top of the hill and were in full view of the foreign settlement below. The soldiers didn't attempt to follow us. I don't think they would have done anything to us if they had, but I couldn't be sure.

By now I was more angry than frightened. I was too out of breath to say much to Nigel, but he knew what he had done. It was hard for me to believe he hadn't had more sense.

The very next day I went straight back to the village. I rode quietly onto the threshing floor, hoping the soldiers wouldn't be there. Some children were playing around and an old woman was sitting on a bench, smoking. I smiled and she smiled back.

I dismounted, and led Kim over to where she was sitting. She motioned me to come and sit beside her on the bench, and called to one of the boys to take Kim. She offered some of her "white tea" (boiling water). I thanked her and sipped it. Then, taking her hand, I explained that I had returned to say how sorry I was for what had happened yesterday.

Patting my hand, she replied, "*Kuniang* (daughter), we're sorry too." With that, she went over to a sort of grape arbor. Each bunch of grapes was tied up inside a newspaper bag, to keep the birds from them; and she picked a bunch of grapes. I didn't have any money with me, I never carried money — so I wasn't able to pay her, but I doubt if she would have taken money anyway. She insisted that I take this goodwill gift.

I thanked her and stayed a little while, talking to the children. Then I mounted again and off I went back home.

A Baby Tower

On the way back, on a deserted, barren hill I passed, as I often did, a baby tower. It looked like a little pagoda, eight or ten feet tall. It was a brick structure — some were eight-cornered, some round — with a little opening near the top, just under the roof. You couldn't see into the opening, but it was as high as you could reach. This was where unwanted babies were dropped in.

They would be put in there: babies that were physically imperfect, babies that were illegitimate, and too many girl babies that the parents didn't want. The wealthy families usually did this sort of thing through the priests in the temples. They paid a certain amount and went through a certain ceremony to do it, but the poor just popped their babies into a tower. They didn't take their lives, they just popped them in.

More than once I remember, very distinctly, riding past the path that took me past this tower and hearing little noises coming out of it.

Baby tower, Chefoo.

A Dot on the Horizon

I recall another day going for a ride following the rocky coastline south. The footpath rose high above the pebbly beach. On my right stretched large fields of millet. The heavy heads of ripe grain were almost ready for harvesting. Beyond were the usual clusters of mud farmers' houses. On my left was the calm blue ocean. It was one of those clear days with the cloudless blue sky so characteristic of North China, where it rains all too seldom.

Both Kim and I were enjoying the day as he ambled along. As usual I was singing at the top of my voice, my thoughts ranging free, when my attention was caught by a small black dot on the far horizon above the water. It was noticeable only because there was no other spot marring that wide expanse of blue.

When I looked again the spot had grown bigger, but was still strangely black. As I watched, it grew larger and began to resemble a dark, unnatural-looking cloud. In such a clear sky this seemed peculiar. As I stopped and watched, the cloud drew nearer and grew bigger until it filled the sky above us.

Before I knew what was happening, I was surrounded by and covered with enormous, grasshopper-like locusts. They were in my hair and all over me. Kim, to protect his face, turned his back towards this onslaught. I dismounted, and without taking time to pull these things off my clothes or even out of my hair (for more were coming all the time), I buried my face in Kim's neck and waited.

I don't recall how long it took them to pass overhead, but they settled by the millions on the fields of ripe millet. Immediately the farmers — men, women and children — rushed into the fields, frantically beating on pots and pans and waving sticks and towels and shouting at the top of their voices, trying in vain to chase them away.

While I was pulling them out of my hair and off my clothes, I could actually hear these locusts devouring the millet. The sound was a little like that of rushing water. In a matter of minutes they had reduced those fields of grain to a stubble. These hard-working farmers had lost all their rich crop; their livelihood for the year was gone.

Disaster comes to countries in the Western world, too, but for the Chinese farmer there was no government relief, no Red Cross to bring help. Instead these people faced the age-old story of starvation.

Mystery on the Night Boat

On a Saturday afternoon in September 1923, we had been watching a soccer match and were having tea at a friend's house when the phone rang. It was Mother calling to say there was a telegram for me from Mr. Carney, Standard Oil, Dairen [Dalian]. A young man, "Red" Swan by name, of National City Bank, was very ill with pneumonia and would I come as soon as possible.

I knew there was the usual overnight boat out of Chefoo for Dairen, sailing at 6 p.m., but I didn't think I had time to catch it. One of the young men at tea was with the Customs Service, and he offered to hold up the ship's papers till I got on board. He did that and I made it. The boat weighed anchor at 7 p.m.

I found myself on the familiar, dirty old SS *Yunglee*. I knew the cabin had only two bunks and was curious to see who, if anyone, would be sharing it with me. To my surprise, a woman was in there.

She looked like a Russian refugee. With a white scarf tied around her head, she was dressed in a long, shapeless "Mother Hubbard" dress, black stockings and white tennis shoes. In spite of this she looked strangely familiar, but I couldn't place her.

Presently she started talking to me in Russian. I shrugged and responded in English. It was her turn to shrug. I tried Chinese. She beamed; we could communicate! But I was still puzzled, for I was reasonably sure I had seen her somewhere before.

Suddenly it dawned on me.

Each spring, just before the arrival of the destroyers, Chefoo would blossom with all the hangers-on that follow the fleet. Along the Bund, cafes, cabarets and dance halls opened to accommodate the thousands of sailors who would be flocking ashore every afternoon. Hanging over the walls of these places could be seen the "girls" and their madams, anticipating patronage for the evening. Year after year many of the same faces would reappear. In time they became so familiar that, as I passed by, I found myself smiling at them as though at some old friend.

This old gal sharing the cabin with me was one of the madams. She recognized me, too, and soon we went out on deck to watch the activities of getting underway. Deckhands were rushing to and fro, sometimes brushing against us for the deck was very narrow. With a protecting arm about me, my companion would fend them off if they got too close.

Soon we were out of sight of land. It was getting dark, so I went to the cabin. My companion was having a cup of coffee from a thermos. She offered me a cup. Not wanting to seem unfriendly, I accepted. With my head in my suitcase for the moment, out of the corner of my eye I noticed her drop something into my cup.

I couldn't help being a little puzzled. It could easily have been just a tablet of saccharine, but surely she would have first have asked if I wanted it. Stalling for time, I went on fumbling in my suitcase. Then she asked why I didn't drink my coffee. I made the excuse that I wanted first to locate the ship's toilet. She offered to go find it for me.

Customs jetty, Chefoo.

The minute she left, I stepped outside the cabin, which opened directly onto the narrow deck, and poured the coffee over the rail. When she returned, I was busily wiping my mouth.

Our destination is on the end of the Liaotung [Liaodong] Peninsula, the southernmost tip of Manchuria. It's across the Gulf of Chihli [Bohai Sea], a short overnight trip from Chefoo. I had never been to Dairen before, but I knew we would be arriving very early the next morning.

I awakened to find my companion completely dressed. She announced that we would be arriving soon — and it took my breath away to see what she was wearing. Instead of the shapeless garment and black stockings of the night before, Madam had blossomed forth in a becoming dress, silk stockings and high heels. She wore a very attractive turban, fashioned from pink and gold brocade.

I couldn't believe my eyes. Why the change? It left room for all kinds of speculation.

Soon I heard the anchor chain being let down. Looking out, I was puzzled to see a pebble beach instead of a proper dock. The Chinese passengers were clambering down into a sampan, then along a plank onto the beach. I asked my companion about this, and she insisted this was the place to get off.

So I followed her and the coolies onto the beach. Luckily, the main road wasn't far away. My companion hailed a passing *droshky* for me; I thanked her and bade her goodbye.

Soon we arrived at the gate of a large compound. The driver roused the gateman, for it was still not yet 7 a.m. When I asked if Mr. Carney lived here, the gateman said he did and directed the driver to take me to the house. I went up to the front door and rang the bell.

Soon the "boy" arrived at the door, hurriedly buttoning up his long white gown. He confirmed that Mr. Carney did indeed live here, but that "Master" wasn't up yet. I explained that Mr. Carney was expecting me and would he please tell him I had arrived.

Mr. Carney came down in his dressing gown. He was surprised — he asked if I hadn't got his telegram. I said that I had, and had caught the night boat out.

"But," he said, "I sent two telegrams, a second one saying that young Swan had died!" I had made such a quick getaway that I was gone before the second telegram arrived.

Dairen had for many years been a Russian settlement. It was not only a bustling seaport, but also the southern terminus of the South Manchurian Railway, which linked up with the Trans-Siberian Railway. This port was extremely important to Russia, for it was that nation's only warm-water, year-round ice-free port. Following the Russo-Japanese War of 1905, it had been taken over by Japan and was now a Japanese colony, but with a Russian flavor still remaining.

All this superimposed on a Chinese background.

"What in the World?"

It was May 1924. Father had been in Shanghai at some medical conference. When I met him at the jetty on his return, he stepped ashore with a big brown box under one arm and a huge horn under the other.

"What in the world have you got there?" I asked.

"Don't speak to me," he blustered. "I must get home and set this thing up before I forget how it goes together."

By dinnertime our unbelieving ears were hearing the sounds of music and laughter and the clink of glasses, and, in the background, "Boy, bring me a whiskey soda" — all coming, the announcer's voice said, from Farrand's nightclub in Shanghai. Father glowed with pride. The rest of us found it almost unbelievable.

The next night Father combed the radio dial for something more interesting, but the air was filled with nothing but the ubiquitous dot-dash of wireless operators talking with each other.

That settled it.

"Mary," said Father to my younger sister, "You're a Girl Guide, aren't you?"

"Yes ..."

"Well then, you must know the Morse code. I want you to teach it to me."

"All right," said Mary, not suspecting what she was letting herself in for.

"Come along then. There's no time like the present."

Picking up two chopsticks, he handed one to Mary and they started tapping out the letters of the alphabet on the dining room table.

A couple of days later, Father came in with a sheepish grin. In one hand he clutched a coil of electric wire, in the other two wireless transmitter keys. In no time he had the wire stretched from his work table in the dining room to behind the closed doors of his office. For days to come, Mary spent hours there, patiently buzzing the letters of the alphabet for Father to receive at the other end. It took lots of practice, but it wasn't long before Father began to recognize some of the fleeting things he was hearing on the air. Already he was beginning to make friends on the air among other ham radio operators up and down the coast.

In the spring, as soon as the American fleet arrived, Father went out to the flagship to pay his usual call on the admiral. After a

Mother, Claire, Father and Mary, in Chefoo.

decent interval, he asked if he might visit the ship's radio shack. The next day when I came home at noon, there was Father, flanked on either side by two young American sailors in spotless whites. This was to become a familiar scene, that summer and for many summers to come. After a few years of this, home just wasn't home without at least two American sailors in the house.

It wasn't long before Father's wireless grew into a very efficient set indeed, thanks to many good U.S. Navy spare parts. (Nothing of that sort could be purchased on the streets of Chefoo.) In time Father reached professional standards, and kept regular schedules with his favorite lighthouses and coast-wise steamers and his many Navy friends in Manila, gradually extending his range farther and farther afield.

"By George, the Antipodes!" he bellowed one day, for he was never without his earphones over his ears. This had the effect of making him treat the rest of us as though we were deaf.

"I've just been talking with Montevideo!" he shouted, grinning from ear to ear.

"And what did you have to say to Montevideo?" I asked archly at the top of my voice. (It's difficult to be "arch" at the top of one's voice.)

"Were you speaking to me?" asked Father, beaming and not bothering to wait for my reply.

Visiting with the Junks

In the summer of 1925 I fell heir to two more boats. One was my brother's canoe, and the other was a long, narrow racing shell or skull with a single sliding seat and outriggers for the long feather oars. This was my pride and joy. Che-che Che-che Bang Bang, I called her. I jokingly claimed that I had to part my hair in the middle to keep from capsizing.

I would take Che-che out in the early mornings, when the sea was usually a flat calm. Threading my way among the destroyers, I would head toward the horizon. When they spotted me, sailors in their powerboats would go out of their way to cross my bows. I lay flat on my back, holding the handles of the oars firmly together to ride out the tidal wave of their heavy wake. Never once did they manage to capsize me, though the rascals never ceased trying.

Alone in my canoe that summer, I spent many hours exploring. One of my favorite excursions was to paddle around to the harbor to visit with some of the great seagoing junks that arrived each spring from the south, bringing cargoes of bowls of all kinds and cloth in exchange for peanuts, soybeans and huge "cartwheels" of bean cake, the residue of the soybean after it had been hand-pressed to extract the oil. This cake, still rich in oil, was valuable as fodder as well as fertilizer.

I never went aboard these junks, but would come alongside and call up to them. The lowest part of the deck, amidships, was about eight feet above water, while the bow and stern towered high above that. As I called, the first greeting was always the barking of a watchdog. Then, to see what the commotion was about, first one head then another would appear over the side.

In time they got to know me and we cheerfully greeted each other. From year to year I would renew their acquaintances. It wasn't easy to carry on a conversation, for they came from faraway places like Foochow and Swatow and Canton in the south where the dialect was so very different. But they always knew me, and I numbered them among my friends.

One time I was out early and there was a British submarine in the bay. I came up fairly close, and I could see that they were having breakfast out on the rounded deck of the submarine. There was a woman and a gentleman — it was Helen and Guy Herbert; he was the British consul general in Chefoo at the time. They hailed me and I tied up, got onboard and had breakfast with the officers and the Herberts. They were eating what they called "submarine comforts" — tinned sausages, delicious. I had such fun, then we sat for a while and I went on my way.

One summer one of the big junks was wrecked in a storm off Lighthouse Island, one of the three islands about seven miles offshore. Carrying a cargo of bowls from Foochow, the junk was caught in a storm too close to shore, and was dashed onto a rock that stove a jagged hole in her bow. Towed later into shallow water, she was unloaded and left there.

A breakfast of "submarine comforts" aboard the HMS *Osiris*, a Royal Navy sub built in 1928. Claire is second from right, between Guy Herbert, British consul general in Chefoo, and Helen Herbert.

Whenever we went to Lighthouse Island that year, I would spend most of my time exploring in, around and through this wreck. My greatest thrill was to take a deep breath, dive down into the dark hold, squirm under a partition and out into a shaft of light on the far side where, with luck, I knew I could then follow the light to the surface — if my breath lasted long enough, that is. The first time I did this it took all the daredevil courage I had, for by then there were sharp barnacles to be avoided as well. Even now I shudder when I think of some of the chances I took, for it was a long and tricky plunge and allowed for little or no miscalculation.

I'd also go to the other end of the bay and watch the fisherman fish for sea slugs. They would jump out of the sampans and lean with

their arms over inflated pig's bladders. Attached to the pigs' bladder would be a rope, and the rope would go down to a stone on the bottom. The divers would rest on the inflated bladder — and when they got their breath, they would pull themselves down by this rope. At the bottom they would collect these sea slugs. [Also known as sea cucumbers, these marine invertebrates are widely used in Chinese cooking, both in fresh and dried forms.]

They would come to the surface with one in their mouth, one under each arm and one in each hand, and up they would jump. They'd push themselves up and throw these things into the sampan, then rest again on these inflated bladders. The men in the boat would cut open the sea slugs, disembowel them and wash them there.

Warlords and Gunboats

During the 1920s there was a constant undercurrent of political unrest. Warlords were vying with each other for control of the cities, from which they could levy taxes on the surrounding countryside. Who were these warlords?

After the Manchu government was overthrown in the Revolution of 1911, there followed a long period of struggle to create a new national government. In the meantime there was no central control of China's large, isolated remote areas, where there were neither adequate roads nor means of communication. So it fell to the local governors or strongmen of the provinces to administer these territories.

Peasants from the villages were indiscriminately pressed into service to provide personal armies for these warlords. Without any thought for who was left to till the land, these men, often tied together with ropes around their necks, were marched off, then transported far enough from familiar surroundings so as to discourage defection. Armed but not paid, these rabble armies soon became bandits and the scourge of the land, preying on the helpless countryside.

Although these civil wars were not directed against foreigners, anti-foreign feeling was never far beneath the surface, and it could turn angry without much warning. If an emergency of this kind arose, the large treaty ports had volunteer corps that could be called up — but in the small ports there was no such thing. Instead, each consul was responsible for his own nationals. So for mutual security, suitable locations were established as concentration points in different parts of the settlement.

We all knew to keep cases of tinned foods in readiness for such emergencies. Alarms were arranged. At the first alarm, each case of food was sent to its assigned concentration point. At the second alarm, in theory we followed our boxes, carrying with us only what we ourselves could handle. But in practice it was more often than not too dangerous to be on the streets — so we usually stayed in our homes and hoped for the best. Each home had a flag of its own nationality, and people would run them up.

During these years, for months after trouble was rumored, a foreign gunboat could be seen lying offshore in Chefoo. Sometimes this ship was Japanese, sometimes American or French; but more often it was British, for the larger proportion of the foreign community in Chefoo was British.

The British gunboat HMS *Bree*, about 1924.
Photograph by G. Warren Swire. Image courtesy of John Swire & Sons Ltd. and Historical Photographs of China, University of Bristol.

China's Warlord Years

Inside China, the 1920s were a time of turmoil and violent struggles for power.

After the Nationalist Revolution of 1911, Dr. Sun Yat-sen served just three months as the new Republic of China's first president. An army general replaced him in 1912, held onto power through military force, and declared himself emperor in 1915. But an anti-monarchy rebellion forced the general to give up his would-be throne — and across the country from 1916 until the late 1920s, dozens of warlords fought each other for control of regions, cities, even neighborhoods.

In this section, Claire describes some of the uncertainties and tragedies of this time, when it could be hard to tell the soldiers of one force from another and control of a city could change overnight. The country had a Republican government during this time, but it held no real power outside Beijing.

After Dr. Sun failed to regain the presidency through a military campaign, he joined the forces of his Kuomintang, or Nationalist Party, with the young but growing Chinese Communist Party and its backer, the Soviet Union. Sun sent his top general, Chiang Kai-shek [Jiang Jieshi], to Russia for military training, and Chiang built a much stronger Nationalist army. The growing Soviet influence within the Kuomintang sparked controversy, even as a Russian emissary, Mikhail Borodin — whom Claire encounters during her travels — became a key advisor.

Dr. Sun died in 1925, and General Chiang took over the Kuomintang's leadership. Chiang led a Nationalist-Communist military expedition that was on the verge of overthrowing the Beijing government when, in 1927, the general ordered some 5,000 of his Communist allies massacred in Shanghai. The 1,000 survivors formed a new force, the Red Army, that attacked the Nationalists, were defeated by them, and then retreated to a mountain region in southeastern China.

Through the rest of the 1920s, the Kuomintang held onto power from its newly declared capital, Nanking, while the Red Army gradually built its numbers and struck the Nationalists wherever they could. This Chinese Civil War would continue well into the 1930s, until both sides turned toward a new enemy: the invading forces of the Empire of Japan.

Dark Night of a Civil War

During the winters of 1927 and 1928 there was just such a conflict clashing back and forth around Chefoo. It was a wealthy city, a wealthy district, and the warlords wanted it to secure the taxes they could impose from the city on the surrounding countryside. Han Fuju and Peifu, I think, were the two contending warlords at that time.

The first alarm was in effect all the time. We lived under a six o'clock curfew, imposed by whichever general was in control at the time. In theory foreigners were exempted from this curfew and passes could be had, but the town changed hands so frequently that we often didn't know which pass was in effect.

The change in power usually took place at night, with little fighting around the foreign residential areas, so there was no way of knowing who was in control from one day to the next. And as the uniforms of the soldiers were so casual and so much alike, those were no help in identifying them either.

If we happened to be out after curfew, our first warning would be a loud shout from a group of three sentries at the nearest street corner. Our reply was always to first identify ourselves as foreigners, then to give, in Chinese, the name of the *hong* or company we represented. Coming up to the sentries we would present our passes, often to be told that they belonged to the retreating army and were no longer valid. With a caution to have these changed before nightfall, we would then be allowed to proceed, only to be met with the same challenge every few blocks.

This was sometimes serious, for we learned that sentries in a hostile area were nervous people and did not hesitate to shoot if they didn't get a satisfactory response. So in spite of the privilege of a pass, we hesitated more and more to be on the street after six o'clock. During those two long winters we planned our lives accordingly.

The change in power usually took place at night

As the foreign homes were spread out along the bay, we didn't see much of the fighting, which took place around and within the native city. But one night it came very close indeed.

I was staying at the time with my sister Dorothy. Her husband was in the Chinese government salt administration; he did a lot of traveling upcountry with the salt police, to inspect the stations where they levied their taxes. Dorothy had her three children and a houseful of servants. The oldest child was only five and the youngest just six months. Dor herself was not well and was confined to bed.

This night we had gone to bed as usual, but we could hear gunfire in the distance coming closer all the time. I went to the phone to ask our consul what we should do, but it was dead. The first thing the warlords did was always to cut the international cables and the telephone wires. Before long we heard the whine of bullets close by, and the scuffle of feet around the garden wall.

There was nothing we could do but wait and hope for the best. I dressed and packed a small suitcase with a few things — though who was going to carry it, if we had to make a run for it, I didn't know. With three children and a sick sister, my hands would be more than full.

The baby slept in the room with me. I tiptoed into Dor's room. Her other children were in there asleep, but she was wide awake. We looked at each other. What to do? Nothing, of course. Without the telephone, it was impossible to know what was happening. After what seemed an interminable time, the sound of the gunfire gradually receded.

Daylight came at last and all was quiet. My sister's three amahs came trembling in from their courtyard at the back of the house. They begged to be allowed to hoist our

Union Jack — for, sure enough, lying at anchor in the bay was a British gunboat. Every residence had a flagpole in the garden.

All the next day a stream of frightened women and children kept arriving at our back gate, begging for asylum within our walls and under the well-known protection of the foreign flag. These terrified women described the panic in the native city, where soldiers were looting right and left and fathers were reported to be selling their daughters on the open market. They knew the girls were going to be taken anyway.

The amahs told us the wells and trees were full of women. They meant that the men and boys had taken to the hills — but the women, with their little bound feet, couldn't hope to follow, so they were drowning themselves in the wells and hanging themselves from the trees.

"*Mei-yu fa-tzu*," they said. "Nothing can be done about it." In those days, this was one of the commonest phrases on every tongue. If you couldn't solve your problems yourself, there was no hope of getting help from any other source, least of all from the government.

The day that followed was quiet and sunny. The fighting had moved on, and the memory of the night before seemed almost like a dream, but as a reminder we found a bullet lodged in the front door. Later when the children went out to play, they found a bundle in the corner of the garden. Luckily they didn't touch it, for it turned out to be a hand grenade wrapped inside a discarded uniform.

The state of emergency continued for quite some time. The mob had overrun the telephone exchange and laid it to waste. It had also entered the foreign telegraph offices and cut the overseas cables. Business was at a standstill, and not only for foreigners; the whole native city was cut off from the outside world.

Once again Father's wireless came to the rescue. The British consul had earlier asked him to send out the alarm for a gunboat; now he was inundated with requests to send and receive business messages to Shanghai, and generally to keep in touch with the outside world. In the end he got so tired that the consul arranged with the gunboat, HMS *Concord*, to send three radiomen to live in the house and stand duty around the clock.

Trudging to a Siege

About 15 miles south along the coast from Chefoo was the small walled city of Muping. Most cities in China were originally encompassed by high walls; but as time went on and the cities spread in every direction, it was almost forgotten that they had once been confined behind the wall that still remained in the heart of the city. Muping was one exception. It was like a rural fortress, the model of a walled city still.

Its one gate was approached by a drawbridge spanning a moat that encircled the city, about ten feet beyond the base of the wall. This large gate was additionally secured by a portcullis, a heavy, vertically closing door — and above it were holes in the wall, through which, once upon a time no doubt, molten lead or oil or something similar could be poured down onto the heads of unwelcome visitors. The city itself was on a headland overlooking the sea to the east and south, and was bounded on the other sides by cultivated fields.

A few weeks after Chefoo was occupied, rumor had it that the current army in control was about to lay siege to Muping. One day while walking along Chefoo's main street, I was held up by a band of men straggling along the road. As they shuffled by, as shabby-looking as you can imagine, I concluded that they were the remnants of an army. There wasn't a whole uniform among them: one would have the cap, another would have a jacket and another would have just the uniform pants. Along with their various war scars, I noticed that many had only one eye.

Chinese people were lined up alongside the streets. I was standing among them and I said, "Where are these people going?" Someone said, "They're going to Muping. They are going to lay siege to the city."

Wherever I had been going, I never got there. Instead I stood for hours watching this scene go by.

Following the "army" came a stream of civilians who had been temporarily pressed into service. Men and animals; more men and more animals, all carrying the great variety of things needed to sustain an army while laying siege to a city.

First came long wooden ladders on the shoulders of men. Next were enormous bales of fluffy cotton wool, swinging from either end of bamboo poles over the shoulders of men. Then came men with five-gallon tins of kerosene hanging from the ends of their poles, then mules with huge crocks or gongs balanced on either side of their saddles.

I stood for hours watching this scene go by

These were followed by little donkeys staggering under the weight of cases of ammunition; men walking in pairs, each pair with a heavy weight of ammunition suspended from a pole they carried from one man's shoulder to the other's; and scrawny ponies loaded down with great bags of fodder for themselves, and flour and millet for the men.

All these and more filed by.

I looked at the impassive faces of still more men carrying ropes and saws and axes. Those were implements of their own livelihood, precious tools inherited from their forebears and belonging to their families. When they had delivered those things to their destination, these civilians would be dismissed to return to their homes, for the army didn't want extra mouths to feed. The men knew only too well that they would never see their equipment again, so they'd be robbed of their one means of support for themselves and for their families.

Straggling by came more, and still more. I watched them till the last, all on their way to Muping. I asked another bystander what could possibly be wanted with so many bales of cotton wool. He explained that the cotton was to be soaked in kerosene, then set on fire in an attempt to smoke out the defenders from behind their walls. Then the soldiers would scale the walls with the ladders. The large gongs or crocks were to contain fresh water for them.

I shook my head.

"*Mei-yu-fa-tsu*," everybody said. "There's nothing that can be done about it."

Visiting the Siege City

One morning about two weeks later, the amah announced that the siege of Muping was over and the besieging army had withdrawn. The little city had held out; apparently the siege force, in a hostile countryside, had run out of both food and water.

The next day I heard that some of the foreign men in the community were planning to visit Muping, to congratulate its people and take them a few supplies. Asking if I might go along, I offered my services as interpreter. I knew none of the men spoke more than a few words of Chinese.

We had to apply for a pass. I can't recall where it came from, but we got it. The following day, five men and I piled into a Model T Ford and off we went. After rattling our way along 15 miles of rutted roads, we finally arrived.

As we approached, the drawbridge began to lower. It was a crude-looking thing, but not as crude as the portcullis above it. As I passed under, I got the feeling that if this vertical gate fell at just the right moment, it might do quite a job on us. Presently the big gate behind it swung slowly open to let us in, then closed again.

As we approached, the drawbridge began to lower

The cobblestoned streets were deserted. Not a soul was to be seen except the soldier who had let us in. He beckoned us to follow him. The city was so small that it had only two real streets. They crossed in the middle at right angles, one going east and west, the other north and south. Standing where they crossed in the middle, we could see the city wall at the end of each street.

Shortly we came to a large red gate. On each of its two doors as they come together was a brass plate in the shape of a lion's head, with a brass-ring knocker hanging from each lion's mouth. Cut into this big gate was a small door, just big enough to admit a man. Here the soldier stopped. With the flat of his hand he pounded on the door and called:

"*K'ai men.*" (Open the door.)

"*Shei?*" (Who?) asked a voice from within.

"*Wo*" (Me), replied our escort.

"*Lai-le-ma?*" (Have they come?)

"*Lai-le.*" (They've come.)

This unhurried conversation was followed by the sound of a heavy wooden bar being withdrawn.

The small door opened, and one by one we entered a courtyard and were welcomed by the officer in charge. He smiled and showed us into a small, rather dark reception room, where we were formally seated in straight-back chairs around the room.

I made the introductions while each of us was presented with the usual cup of boiling hot tea. Then one of our party presented the "general" with the provisions we had brought, including 12 cartons of cigarettes. He accepted these with a bow, then handed one of the cartons to an orderly, who opened it and took out one cigarette.

Holding this cigarette in two hands, the orderly courteously offered it to me. I accepted. In this same manner he presented each guest with a cigarette, followed closely by another orderly who lit each cigarette with a separate match. I apologized that I didn't smoke, but continued to hold my cigarette in my hand.

Next the "general" opened a little bottle of wine. When he poured this out into tiny, thimble-like cups, it looked startlingly like red ink. I accepted the cup but declined to drink, in spite of the general's assurance that it was quite harmless.

On the ramparts,
Muping.

Gradually our stiff little party began to unbend. We were asked if we would like to walk around the top of the wall to see how they had defended the city — for, he explained, they had long since run out of ammunition.

We filed out along the cobblestoned street until we reached the embankment. This had been honeycombed with tunnels, where the men had taken turns sleeping and watching. When we reached the top where the wall rose above the embankment, I asked in surprise why the wall was so broken.

The general reminded me that they had run out of ammunition. Leaning well out over the wall, he pointed to a litter of broken bricks far below. He said they had allowed the attackers to scale their ladders to within reach of the top, then hurled pieces of broken brick down on their heads till they were forced to withdraw.

"Our wall was not only our defense but our ammunition too," he said proudly.

Opium on the Night Train

By 1926, China was being torn apart by civil wars. That autumn my sister Dorothy and her husband, Gordon Pearson, were transferred from Peking to Tsinan [Jinan]. The capital of Shangtung province, Tsinan is about 200 miles inland from Tsingtao on the North China coast.

Early in November, I received a letter from Dorothy saying that her two boys, ages three and four, were both very sick with bronchitis and could I possibly come and be with her for a while, as Gordon would be traveling upcountry and she would be alone. There were servants, but the responsibility was hers.

To get to Tsinan from Chefoo was first a 24-hour boat trip to Tsingtao, then an overnight train journey. I caught the night boat on November 19. My diary tells me I shared a cabin with a woman suffering from severe asthma, and that I was up most of the night looking after her.

The boat arrived at Tsingtao the next evening, just in time for me to catch the night train. The train service was good, and I had been fortunate enough to get a lower berth in a Pullman car. We left promptly at six in the evening, and I wasted no time in getting to bed and to sleep.

Early the next morning, as I lay half awake, I slowly became aware of a sickly-sweet smell pervading the air. It gradually dawned on me that I was smelling opium. For the smell to be so strong, I knew the smoker must be very close. I found myself listening to a whispered conversation just outside my curtain.

The smoking was clearly being done right across the aisle. Filled with curiosity, I opened my curtain a crack and looked out.

There, lying on his bunk with his curtains drawn wide apart, was a Chinese gentleman enjoying a pipe. In the corridor squatting on his heels was a soldier in uniform; in one hand he held a small alcohol lamp, in the other a three-inch metal pin. As I had never before seen opium being smoked at such close quarters, I decided to have a good look. Clearly the general — for so he turned out to be — wouldn't mind, or he would be doing it more privately in the first place.

Acknowledging his greeting, I wished him good morning. He proffered me his pipe. The gesture was meant only as a courtesy, I knew.

The stem of this pipe was about 15 inches long, made of bamboo. The mouthpiece was of colored glass. (They were also made of silver or amber, even jade.) On one side of the stem, about three inches from the other end, was a small brass bowl that held a pellet of opium. As the smoker was usually reclining, this end could be rested on the couch or supported by an attendant.

With one hand the orderly was holding the bowl of the pipe over the alcohol flame, while with the other he was "playing" the opium pellet with the metal pin. Opium is sticky and it does not burn readily; to make it smolder, a live flame has to be applied.

I watched the smoker slowly inhale till his lungs were filled. After holding his breath for what seemed a long time, with his eyes closed, he began to slowly exhale.

I had seen enough, and repaired to the washroom to dress. By the time we reached Tsinan, the general — by now dressed in his smart uniform — and I were sitting in our seats looking out of opposite windows. It was weeks before I could get the sickly smell of that opium out of my coat.

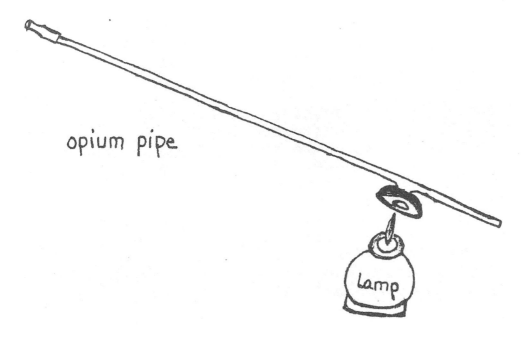

opium pipe

lamp

Street Fighting and Sunken Roads

Tsinan was large, extending far outside and beyond the original old walled city. It was commercially and politically important: it was not only the capital of the province but also was the headquarters of the ruthless, unscrupulous northern warlord Chang Tsung-Ch'ang. Rumor had it that, among other things, Chang had 16 Russian concubines.

Having attended a large official dinner given by Chang later that month, my brother-in-law Gordon described how his host had sat throughout the meal with one of these girls on his lap, considering this the modern thing to do. Chinese have always regarded with distaste and embarrassment the Western habit of embracing in public, but this was Chang's chance to demonstrate that he too could be modern.

At this time, Tsinan was full of Russian cavalry officers, among whom was Mikhail Borodin, the well-known Russian adviser to the Kuomintang, the Chinese Nationalist Party. My one encounter with him came one day while I was out riding with the American consul.

On a narrow street we passed a file of mounted Russians, almost brushing shoulders. They recognized the consul and saluted smartly. As they came abreast of me, I too got a salute. Afterward the consul explained that the officer in the lead had been Borodin.

A couple of weeks later, while riding alone in the country one morning, I passed through a mud-hut village occupied entirely by Russian mercenaries, all in the traditional tall fur hats, fur-lined knee-high boots, and long ankle-length topcoats belted in at the waist. As I rode by I was conscious of menacing looks and remarks, cast in my direction by some of these rough-looking characters. Instinct told me to return home by some other route.

Another time while riding along on a wide road between fields, I heard rifle fire. I looked all around but couldn't see anyone. As I rode on, the shots sounded closer, then just ahead. Suddenly I saw where the shooting was coming from.

In a deep trench up to their armpits along the side of the road stood a row of six soldiers. With their rifles resting on the surface of the road, they were practice-shooting across the road, into a wooded graveyard beyond.

Having grown up in this always unsettled land, I took this kind of thing for granted, as I did my role of a privileged foreigner. So without a moment's hesitation, I called out that I would like to pass, please.

The shooting ceased and I rode by. But as I passed, I heard the men cursing and swearing. Again I decided to find another route home. As I neared a rather large, unfamiliar village, I discovered that what seemed to be an army was bivouacked there. Soldiers, not much older than boys, were sprawled all along the sides of the roads, resting. They were armed with nothing more than long bamboo poles with knives lashed to the ends. I asked where they were going.

"South," was the reply. "To fight southerners." That was all they knew.

As I neared the middle of the village, I saw there was a street fight going on. Being mounted, I could see over the heads of the crowd. Two men seemed to be at each other's throats, but were being held apart by groups of onlookers.

How does one describe the drama of a Chinese street fight? Clearly someone's family honor had been besmirched, and it was up to one of these two men to expunge the insult. To a Chinese man at that time, saving face was even more important than the fight itself — and achieving this end required an enormous public display of high indignation, accompanied by all kinds of noisy histrionics. All the world must know that an insult is not going to be taken lying down.

These two men were going through the motions of wanting to tear each other apart. With their queues wound around their heads, their sleeves rolled up and the veins in their necks standing out, they were cursing each other's families and ancestors for generations back. Straining to get at each other, at the same time they were extending one arm for the crowd to hold them back. (A few years ago when China was "sabre-rattling" her nuclear weapons at the United States, I was somehow reminded of this street scene.)

All this was such a familiar sight that I wanted to laugh, but at the same time I was anxious to get through and away, for I knew I couldn't turn back. So here again I called out, "*Chieh-kwang, chieh-kwang*" (Clear the way, clear the way. May I pass, please). Everything paused and the crowd parted while I passed through.

I didn't look back. I got home safely, but I got a scolding from both the American and British consuls, with orders not to ride that far afield again.

Riding over the dry, plowed winter fields, I would sometimes come upon the curious spectacle of a little cloud of yellow dust in the distance, traveling across the field by itself as if moved by some unseen hand. On getting closer, I could see a small red spot,

Peking carts on a sunken road.

moving along just ahead of this cloud of dust. Drawing closer, I could see the blue cloth top of a Peking cart. Here was a sunken road.

After thousands of years of travel on the bone-dry loess topsoil so characteristic of this part of North China, these roads had been gradually worn down until they were sometimes eight feet or more below the surrounding fields. A cart plodding along one of these sunken roads would stir up that powdery dust, which would float up in the cart's

wake. The red spot was a piece of braid attached to the tip of the carter's whip, where it was held on the front of the cart.

During the short but torrential rainy season in July, these roads became practically impassable — for along with the rain, water from the surrounding fields drained into the roads, turning the deep dust into thick mud. This was the season when travelers were often waylaid by bandits.

Once during this season, our cart met an oncoming cart. In trying to pass, we capsized. Everybody was covered with mud and fury, including the poor floundering horse between the shafts. Pandemonium followed.

The Boy Emperor's Tutor

It was at this time that Sir Reginald Johnston passed through Tsinan. Returning from London to Tientsin, he spent a long weekend with us. From 1919 to 1924, Sir Reginald had been the English tutor in Peking to P'u Yi, the Manchu "Boy Emperor." P'u Yi and his bride, both only 16 when they were married in 1922, now found asylum within the British Concession in Tientsin.

After years in China, Sir Reginald had returned to England with the intention of retiring there — but he found England so peaceful and uneventful after his stirring years of political involvement, between the collapse of Manchu rule and the emergence of China's struggling so-called Republican government, that he had come back. He brought with him two large autographed photographs of England's king and queen, to be presented to P'u Yi.

During his visit with us he described how, when he first arrived in Peking to assume his role as tutor, he was shown into the *yu-ch'ing king*, the imperial schoolroom. In the middle of this large room stood a table and three chairs — one for the imperial pupil, one for the tutor and one for a palace administrator, there to make sure this foreigner didn't attempt to convert the young pupil to Christianity.

One of a series of eunuchs stood motionless against the wall, to be relieved every half hour lest he fall asleep. The administrator, on the other hand, went to sleep regularly, sitting at the table, and the young pupil never made a move to awaken him.

Sir Reginald Johnston, at right, presenting a portrait of King Edward VII.
Image courtesy of the UK National Archives.

Far from trying to convert P'u Yi to Christianity, Sir Reginald had long been a practicing Buddhist himself. He was full of stories of the inhibited but decadent court life inside the Forbidden City, where this young boy lived surrounded by corrupt and servile eunuchs, and by the other idle, mischievous sycophants that infested the Forbidden City. The intrigue and corruption defied description, he said. The Boy Emperor was never permitted any normal exercise; he was not even allowed to walk, but was instead carried everywhere in an elaborate palanquin. Sometimes he would escape, and could be found clambering over the rooftops.

P'u Yi, who as a boy became China's last emperor.
Image courtesy of Historical Photographs of China, University of Bristol.

One day, despite much opposition, Sir Reginald got permission to take the boy, now 18, outside the Forbidden City for the first time in his life. This was a trip to the Summer Palace, about eight miles from Peking. The expedition was accompanied by a retinue of all kinds of eunuchs, escorts and officials. P'u Yi was fascinated by his first glimpse of the Summer Palace Lake. Eventually his tutor taught him to row on the lake, gradually insisting on many other physical activities for the boy.

P'u Yi was devoted to his English tutor, just as the tutor was to his pupil. Eventually Sir Reginald was to save the lives of the young emperor and his bride: in 1924, to escape the revolutionary mobs around the palace, he smuggled them out of Peking to the relative safety of the British Concession in Tientsin. P'u Yi was eventually to become a tool of the Japanese, acting as puppet emperor of Manchuria during the Japanese occupation.

Suspicion, Fear and Executions

The atmosphere in Tsinan at this time was charged with suspicion and fear. Chang Tsung-Chang's press gangs were draining the outlying villages of their military-age men, leaving no one to protect the homes and till the fields.

The Shantung peasant is a big man. As late as 1926 he still wore the traditional queue and small black brimless hat. His dress in winter was a long, gray, thickly padded cotton gown, whose sleeves extended beyond the tips of the fingers to keep the hands warm. Around the waist was wound a long cloth sash, and his shoes were homemade of cotton cloth with thick cloth soles.

Every day on the fields of winter wheat, we could see these peasant recruits being drilled by some strutting young boy, smartly turned out in an officer's uniform. It was a pitiful sight to see these bewildered, ungainly farmers, when they failed to goose-step in the approved fashion or to distinguish left from right, being lashed across the face with a Sam Browne belt by one of these arrogant "boy officers," obviously sons of some government official.

Local conditions were so distressing at this time that I even hesitate to describe them, lest it seem like gross exaggeration. All hotels were being systematically searched for anyone suspected of being a southerner. When found, these unfortunates were taken out and shot.

Immediately behind my sister's house was a small village with a large threshing floor, which had been turned into a parade ground where these suspects were brought. As a prisoner arrived with his hands tied behind his back, he would be ordered to kneel. A soldier would put his revolver to the back of the man's head and pull the trigger. As the body fell, it was kicked into a nearby trench prepared for this purpose. Many times my sister and I, both horrified and fascinated, witnessed these nightmarish scenes from an upstairs bedroom window.

One day Dor's two children, who had been out for a walk with their amah, came in breathless, describing how they had seen two heads hanging up in a tree. "Their faces were black and their tongues were sticking out," one child said excitedly.

Another day, sitting on the curb outside the front gate of our compound was a well-dressed, middle-aged man with his hands tied behind him. On either side of him stood a soldier. As I came through the gate, the man looked up at me.

"Good morning," I said instinctively. He returned my greeting. When I casually asked him where he was going, with his chin he indicated the back of our house. When I asked what was wrong, he simply shrugged his shoulders.

The day came when I had to go back home to Chefoo. It was no longer possible for my pony to return overland the way we had come, so before I left I gave him to my friend the American consul, who promised he would have the pony shot rather than let him fall into the local military's hands. This he did a month later, when the consul and all the other foreigners were evacuated.

Soon after that, all farm animals were commandeered by the soldiers, and the poor farm families were left even more destitute and helpless.

My journey out of Tsinan was very different from the one three months earlier, when I first arrived. Local unrest had disrupted everything; all who could leave were trying to. The trains were not running on any schedule. For hours after dark I waited on the freezing, crowded station platform for "yesterday's" train.

Soldiers with blindfolded prisoners.
Image courtesy of Dr Elizabeth Hensel and Historical Photographs of China, University of Bristol.

Many of the Chinese had come from far away. Tired of waiting, some of them unrolled their bedding on the station platform and went to sleep under their padded quilts. It started to snow. Pretty soon these sleeping bundles looked like mounds of snow.

Towards morning a train arrived. I found myself in a compartment with two others, who occupied the two berths. I sat in a corner for the rest of the night. While I dozed, a rat bit me on the toe. I wakened with a shout just in time to see the thing scurry out of sight.

So ended my visit to the capitol of Shantung.

Losing Bill

My closest friend in all the world in those days was my brother Bill. He was just 15 months younger; we spoke the same language and had few secrets from each other. Bill and I spent long evenings together while he read aloud to me and I knitted. Those were treasured times.

Going back to 1923, Bill had a job then with Casey and Dent Company, a local silk firm. Just too young at the time of the first World War, he had chafed at having been denied the adventure of joining up. I was at the Mission Hospital at the time, on emergency duty. The Chinese nurses had all walked out on strike because of some complaint about one of the Chinese doctors. So I was standing by round the clock in one of the mens' wards, catching snatches of sleep on a camp bed. I was especially distressed about a case that had just been brought in, a soldier who had been "flayed for insubordination" — 200 strokes with a split bamboo.

This was a traditional form of punishment. The weapon consisted of a two-inch-thick bamboo pole, split into narrow strips down half of the pole to form dozens of sharp knife edges. From his neck to the end of his spine, the flesh of the man's back had been reduced to a pulp that had all sloughed away, leaving his ribs and spine exposed. His whole back was by now crawling with maggots, for he had been left for three days on the floor of his cell.

The phone rang. It was Bill saying that he was fed up with sitting at a desk and had decided to leave. "Leave for where?" I asked. He was going to Shanghai, he said, and would take the first boat out to either Australia or Canada, it didn't matter which.

Bill Malcolm and Rex, a family pet, in Chefoo, 1927.

Depressed beyond words, I hurried back to the ward. Everything was being done to make the poor soldier as comfortable as possible. I can still see him lying there on his stomach, moaning quietly. Every time I came near his bed with a drink or a pill, he would try to thank me for "helping" him. It nearly choked me to see his uncomplaining gratitude when there was so little I could do for him. There were no antibiotics in those days.

A couple of weeks later we received a cablegram from Bill in mid-Pacific, saying he was on the *Empress of Australia* headed for Canada. Then one day a letter arrived to say he had passed his exam for the Royal Canadian Mounted Police. Eventually he found himself up somewhere in the far northern part of Quebec, complete with dog team. He loved the life and stayed for three years. Then he returned to China, for he was engaged to be married and his fiance felt she couldn't face life as the wife of a Mountie.

One day in 1928, when Bill had been back in Chefoo about a year, I was nursing the American consul; he'd had one too many and had fallen down the stairs at three o'clock in the morning, breaking his collarbone. I couldn't stand the guy, but there I was. He said to me, "Don't you want to go out there and have a swim before lunch? I'm not in any hurry, I'll wait until you get back."

So I went out to the raft, and Bill was there and all the chaps, great fun. Bill said to me, "I've got a funny spot on my foot." On his instep. It looked like a mosquito bite, but there was a wide circle of red around the bite, about the size of a silver dollar. It was very, very hot.

I said, "When you go home, show it to father." He said, "Oh, nonsense." I said, "Don't be silly. What's the use of having a doctor in the family if you can't make use of him?"

It looked like a mosquito bite

I went home the next morning and there was Bill, lying in bed with his foot raised up on the chair. I said, "What are you doing here?" and he said, "Well, this is what you did. I showed that thing on my foot to Father and he insisted on lancing and opening it and putting in a little drain, and I've got to keep it up in the air."

Father called me into his office and said, "I am worried about Bill's foot. It doesn't seem to be responding." The red lymphatics were beginning to show threads up the leg, to his groin. In those days, we didn't have any miracle drugs; we didn't have sulfa, we didn't have penicillin. Bill's gland in his groin was enlarged, and this worried Father.

He said, "I want you to change that dressing every hour, on the hour, night and day." I said "Right. I will."

So I did. He was under a mosquito net all evening and I would set my alarm; every hour on the hour, I would get up and change the hot fomentation that I was putting on it.

The next day, Bill started to run a temperature. Father said, "I'm going to take him up to the hospital." I said, "I'm coming too."

So we put him on a long bamboo chair (no stretchers in those days), and four coolies walked him through the native city, with me in a rickshaw, up to the Temple Hill Hospital.

They took him straight into the operating room, and made three or four incisions up the leg to drain this obvious infection. I remember saying to Father, "I didn't know Bill was so tired. He looks absolutely exhausted."

He was only there, I think, five days. I never left his side night or day, didn't close my eyes for one moment. His temperature went higher and higher and this poison got up to his lungs. His temperature was 107 and we were giving him, intravenously, this, that and the other — all sorts of things. He had this excruciating headache, "ten thousand headaches" he described it, and he wouldn't let me leave his side. "Don't leave me, don't leave me."

Father gave him every drop of blood that he could spare. I had the same blood type, wanted to give my blood, but they wouldn't take it because I was already overtired and they needed me to look after him. By then his leg was like a tree trunk. Everything was unbelievable. The pain was so excruciating that they gave him morphine.

What we didn't know, weren't able to know, was that he had an allergy to morphine. It drove him absolutely wild and it took seven of us to hold him on the bed. At the end and he was delirious, terribly delirious, and he kept calling to me, "Jump! Jump, jump!" His dog team: He was calling the dogs by name, and calling me to get on or get off or something like that.

At the age of 26, Bill died. He was buried in the little community cemetery there in Chefoo.

Francis "Lin" Lintilhac

Just seven years later my sister Dorothy's youngest son Billie, age seven, succumbed to an attack of flu. He was buried right beside his namesake Bill. Their graves are still there.

A Meeting in Tstingtao

In 1929-30 I worked for a year as a matron for a boarding school for children of the American fleet in Tsingtao [Qingdao], the U.S. Navy's Asiatic submarine summer base. In the autumn of 1929, I was invited to a small dinner party at the home of Mr. and Mrs. King, the British consul and his wife.

Two young Englishmen were there. I recognized one as a Tsingtao resident; the other, a stranger to me, I concluded to be one of the officers from HMS *Hermes*, a British aircraft carrier that was in the harbor. [Launched in 1919, the *Hermes* was the world's first ship designed as an aircraft carrier. It was sunk by Japanese dive bombers off the coast of Sri Lanka in April 1942.]

Lin - Tsingtao - 1929

Claire in Tsingtao, 1930.

At the end of the evening, that gentleman, whose name was Lin, walked with me the short distance back to where I was staying. As we parted, he asked if I would go riding with him over the weekend. He suggested the following Monday, as that was a bank holiday. Neither of us owned a mount, so we arranged to meet at the Russian Riding School where there were ponies for hire.

Monday turned out to be a beautiful day, and we had the most heavenly ride along the firm sands of Long Beach at low tide. Before the morning was over, Lin tried, without much success, to arrange a time for another ride. I enquired how much longer his ship was going to be in port.

"What ship?" he asked.

"The *Hermes*," I replied.

"I'm not on the *Hermes*," said Lin. "I'm stationed here with the I.C.I." (That was Imperial Chemical Industries, the British equivalent to DuPont.)

It was arranged that Lin would come with me on a Saturday morning picnic with my 12 young boarders. That turned out to be great fun. The following Saturday he turned up again, this time with a huge open "touring car'" of ancient vintage, complete with driver, that he had hired for the day. With my 12 boarders and numerous baskets of sandwiches, we piled into this old bus, and off we went for another lovely picnic.

For Lin it must have been rather like courting "The Old Woman Who Lived in a Shoe." For their part, the children were beginning to sense that they weren't getting as much of my attention as they had come to expect. So when the next Saturday rolled around, there were wails of "Aw, M's Malcolm, don't invite THAT MAN again, because when he comes you don't play games with us!"

That was how Lin's and my friendship began, but it was a long time before it got much farther. That winter of 1930-31 he was transferred to Tsinanfu, where at the age of 23 he was in charge of his first I.C.I. office, which he ran entirely in Chinese.

A little bit of Lin's history: His grandfather, P.E. Lintilhac, was an Englishman of French descent who established a silk company that traded with China. When his son, Lin's dad, completed his schooling, he was sent to Shanghai to represent P.E. Lintilhac and Company.

Lin's dad, Charles Eugene Lintilhac — Chussie, we called him — was more interested in sailing than in the silk business. He built three schooners in Shanghai and sailed them out to the blue water. The Yangtze River delta was all muddy water until you got about 15 miles out to sea, when you ran into the blue water of the East China Sea.

Lin was born in Shanghai, but when he was young he was sent to Tunbridge Boarding School in England, and went five years without seeing his family. After he came back out from school, the bottom fell out for many small companies in China, and P.E. Lintilhac had to merge with one of the big silk firms. So Lin joined Imperial Chemical Industries.

Occasionally that winter he came down to Tsingtao for the weekend. We would go dancing at the Tsingtao Cafe and dine on scrambled eggs and sparkling burgundy. The year passed smoothly enough — but I was eager to get back to my nursing, so I turned down the board's offer of another year at the school. I decided to go back to Shanghai, where I knew there were other nurses and I could get private-duty nursing with only 12-hour duty.

Claire and school
children, Tsingtao.

PART 3

Love and Invasion

1931 – 1939

I'd been saving all my pennies to buy a ticket to Vancouver to visit my sister Mary in Seattle, who was living there and had not been well. I got to Shanghai, bought a second-class passage to Yokohama, then got a ticket on a Japanese cargo boat to Vancouver. It took 15 days or something like that. I was very tired; I got on board, and just went to bed and slept the clock 'round. I'd waken, ring the bell, have a cup of tea and some toast, and roll over and go to sleep again.

At the end of three days I was beginning to surface, feeling better, when I heard a shuffle of feet outside the cabin door and a sharp knock on the door. I was the only woman on the boat, as usual, and the only foreigner. I said, "Come in" — and in filed the captain, the purser, the doctor and two stewards, all Japanese.

The doctor said, "Oh, very sorry but we haven't seen you, are you well?" I thought, they think I'm dying of some unmentionable disease or something, and they can't stand it any longer. And quite rightly.

Japanese are awful sticklers about quarantine and all that sort of thing — so I jumped up and said, "No, I am not sick, just very tired. I will come out to lunch."

"Yes, oh yes, very sorry," they said, and they all trooped away.

I finally arrived in Vancouver, then went by boat along the coast to Seattle. Mary was far from well; she'd put on weight, and she was nervous and upset. I was convinced that she had better come home. I didn't have any money because I had spent it all on my passage. I went back on the same kind of boat — to Japan and then from Japan to Dairen in China.

Facing page, above: Sandbags outside Capitol Theatre, Shanghai, 1937. *Photograph by Malcolm Rosholt. Image courtesy of Mei-Fei Elrick, Tess Johnston and Historical Photographs of China, University of Bristol.* Below: Claire outside her room in Shanghai.

Red Cross launch, with Japanese cruiser.

Image courtesy of Joanna Dunn, Philippa Lamb and Historical Photographs of China, University of Bristol.

When I got to Dairen, I had exactly five dollars left in my pocket and I just had to get home. They said, "There's no boat today to Chefoo." I said, "There has to be — there's a boat every night out of Dairen for Chefoo." I had lived up over the harbor, and I'd seen this boat arrive every morning. They said, "No, just a launch." I said, "That's what I'm talking about. That's what I want to go on."

They had a cargo of laborers on board. I said, "I want to go on this boat." It had a cabin with six bunks, one for me — but the cabin was hot and stifling, so I thought, "I think I'll go out on the deck."

The coolies were everywhere on deck, packed like sardines. I couldn't sit down anywhere, there were so many bodies lying around. I went up on the bridge, but the boat was rocking, there was a storm a-blowing, and I thought, "Well, I can't stay up here." So I decided I better go down to the cabin and try to stick it out.

In the dark, I felt my way down.

There were 700 men on the deck, and they were all seasick — every one of them. I squirmed my way down, stepping on ears and fingers and things. I couldn't open the door to the saloon, which led to the cabin, because the coolies had crawled into the saloon to get in out of the weather. On deck, they had nothing over them in the rain.

I found my way back up to the bridge. There was a coolie up there and I said to him, "Have you got a chair, or something for me to sit down on? I can't get back into the cabin."

He said, "I'll get you a bed" — and he produced a very dirty cat bed. I thanked him and pushed it up against the bulkhead. I sat on that and he said, "I'll get you a blanket." I said "never mind," but he did; he got me a really filthy blanket. I thanked him for it and gave him one of my dollars, and put the blanket down on the floor. I wasn't going to sleep under that thing, but before the night was out I was glad of it, because it was pouring rain and there was nothing else to protect me. I was seasick, everybody was seasick, and I was sick into the wind because I couldn't get to the other side of the boat.

These boats were capsizing all the time

In the night the storm got very bad. The boat rolled over far enough that I swear I thought the funnel was going to dip water. These boats were capsizing all the time, because they always took on too many people and too much cargo. I calculated that if this one did capsize, I would throw off my coat very fast and jump clear of it. I was a very strong swimmer in those days, five miles I'd often done. I thought, I'll jump clear and keep afloat long enough for them to know this boat is missing. I had that all worked out.

We were due to arrive at about five in the morning, but it was ten o'clock before we got in. The storm had gone down a bit by then — but there were a lot of Navy power boats, whale boats I think they called them. I thought, "What's going on? There must be some sort of a maneuver." But they all seemed to come out, circle this launch that I was on, and go away.

Father met me when I got in. I said, "Don't touch me — I've been sick, everybody has been sick." He said "Mercy — I had the Navy alerted. They were all out looking for you." I said, "Is *that* what all those boats were out there for?" He said, "Yes, they identified the boat and came back and told me it was still right side up."

Shanghai and a Nurse's Pay

I spent a peaceful summer in Chefoo. How good it is to know that one is always welcome at home, even if one doesn't often have the chance to *go* home.

Lin and I had seen a lot of each other and he wanted to become engaged, but I would not. He was nearly eight years younger than me. I said, "You've got to marry somebody more nearly your own age." He said no, he didn't want to, and I said well, I wouldn't agree.

He was going on home leave, on a long trip round to Australia, New Zealand and

Francis "Lin" Lintilhac, mid-1930s.

then England; then he was going to come back via Canada. I said, "I think you should be fancy-free and footloose for that wonderful trip, not be tied down, not be writing letters." He was very reluctant to agree to this, but I couldn't think of tying myself down, and I wasn't totally sure this should be. So that was the arrangement when I went back to Chefoo.

In September, refreshed and rested, I set out to try my luck in Shanghai. The International Settlement there was a very large, cosmopolitan community. It was exciting to be in a big city again after so many years in small outports. For the first two weeks I stayed with friends till I found a room with an elderly Russian couple in their apartment on Bubbling Well Road. These were White Russians, so many of whom had flocked to the China coast in the wake of the Bolshevik Revolution.

As soon as I was settled, I went to call on Miss Rice, the matron at the Country Hospital, to ask if I might have the privilege of joining her private-duty nursing staff. She surprised me by offering me a job on the hospital staff. I was flattered, but reluctant to tie myself down to a permanent job. I still wanted to be a private nurse, free to come and go, but doing only 12-hour duty for a change.

Miss Rice said I was welcome to join her private staff on one condition. She had been given to understand that I was in the habit of under-quoting the regular nursing rates. Surprised, I said if I had been undercharging, it was because I had no idea what the rates were. Apparently the rates in Shanghai were eleven *taels* for 12-hour duty and 15 taels for 24 hours. (Maternity nursing was always 24 hours.)

A tael is a given weight of silver. At that rate, nurses were getting about 15 Chinese dollars for 12-hour duty. I gasped — I had been charging only five dollars for 24-hour duty! No wonder I was chronically short of cash and couldn't make ends meet. I was thrilled that I would now have the authority of the hospital behind me to ask a reasonable fee. Miss Rice agreed, and I left the matron's office walking on air.

A state of emergency was in effect during this winter in the International Settlement, for in January 1932 the Japanese commenced an attack on the Chinese city of Shanghai. Martial law was imposed, and we were under war conditions — but it hardly affected me that winter, because most of my time was spent on my nursing duty.

1932: The First Fight for Shanghai

The conflict between nations that became World War II first ignited in battle with the Shanghai Incident — an assault by Japanese forces that began at midnight on January 28, 1932.

Having pushed for years to expand its business and political influence in northern China, in late 1931 Japan took over China's three northeastern provinces, which together make up Manchuria. The Japanese could then easily move troops and supplies deeper into North China. Shanghai's International Settlement contained a sizable Japanese community; in the first weeks of 1932, claiming it needed to protect its citizens there, Japan sent several thousand troops, plus dozens of ships and warplanes, to the city's shoreline. A large Chinese force had meanwhile taken positions outside Shanghai.

Warplanes from Japanese aircraft carriers began bombing the city at midnight on January 28, and Japanese troops attacked the next day. The air assault has been called the world's first terror bombing of civilian targets. It was also the first carrier-launched

attack in the Pacific region, almost nine years before Japan's 1941 raid on Pearl Harbor.

The U.S., Great Britain and France tried but failed to bring about a ceasefire, and in February, both the Japanese and Chinese Nationalist leader Chiang Kai-shek greatly expanded their forces fighting for the city. But the Chinese forces were outnumbered, outgunned and unable to stop Japan's air and naval bombardments.

Chinese troops pulled back on March 2, and both nations soon agreed to a ceasefire. Shanghai's International Settlement had been spared most of the battle and bomb damage. Its residents, like Claire and her sister Molly, could do little but watch in horror as the fighting raged and thousands of Chinese people were forced from their homes as refugees.

For the next five years, tensions simmered between China and Japan. Shanghai stayed mostly quiet until July 1937, when Japan launched a full-scale invasion of China. Soon after began the second, even more terrible battle for Shanghai.

Chinese poster showing Japanese planes dropping bombs on a hospital. *Image courtesy of Historical Photographs of China, University of Bristol.*

A Political Refugee

My first call came asking me to report to the hospital for day duty at eight o'clock the next morning. My patient was a young Englishman who had been thrown from his pony and was suffering from a severe concussion. I was on the case for two weeks. When he recovered, he invited me to the French Club for a tea dance, but he never got around to paying his bill.

A few days later the hospital called me again, this time for night duty. There was increased fighting around the Settlement. The volunteer corps, all foreigners, were called up to man the perimeter. There was heavy shooting in the native city, where long-range Japanese guns caused panic and a lot of destruction. But I reported to the hospital at 8:00 p.m.

My patient hadn't come in yet. Puzzled, I asked who my patient was. The day staff said he was a Chinese gentleman, not sick at all, but he had requested a room in the hospital and wanted a night nurse on duty. His room was the biggest and best on the floor. I turned down the bed and waited. At a quarter to ten the door opened, and in came two Chinese gentlemen dressed in long gowns.

"Good evening," said one. "You must be my night nurse." Pointing to the telephone, he requested that if it rang, would I please answer it for him and take any message. I asked if there was anything else I could do. He said that all he asked was that I not leave his room on any account. Indicating a large chair in the corner of the room, he suggested that I make myself comfortable there for the night.

The sound of heavy gunfire rattled the windows from time to time, which helped to keep me awake, but my patient slept peacefully through it all. Twelve hours of hard duty is simple compared with trying to stay awake all night in a comfortable armchair in a dark room. Each night it was the same: Mr. Chen came in at a quarter to ten accompanied by the same gentleman, until the last three nights when a lovely-looking Chinese lady came with him. She seemed to be his wife, although he didn't say and I didn't ask. As she left, she would hold the door open for me to go in.

> *The sound of heavy gunfire rattled the windows, which helped to keep me awake*

This went on for two weeks. In all that time he told me nothing, and I asked no questions. He was obviously a political refugee. Kidnapping and assassinations were common in those days. At the end of the two weeks, he explained that he was leaving, and paid me in cash. His lady companion presented me with a lovely black leather handbag and thanked me for being so patient and understanding. Whatever the emergency had been, it was apparently over.

"Don't You Know the War Is On?"

We had a ten o'clock curfew, but I had to be on at eight o'clock so it didn't affect me, to the point where I almost forgot about the curfew. Except one time.

I was off for two or three days between cases and I was with Kay Jones. Her husband Frank was the private pilot for Zhang Xueliang, the son of a northern warlord who was in charge of Chiang Kai-shek's Manchurian troops. So Frank was away, and Kay invited me to join her and her party for dinner at the Columbia Club, out in the suburbs of the settlement. Three young men were with her; one was the private secretary for Ronald Colman, the actor, who was in Shanghai for some reason. They were all volunteers in the settlement's defense, taking time from their duties.

Well, after dinner, somebody said, "Gosh, we better get cracking and get back before ten o'clock." So we jumped into the car. We were at the race course when all of a sudden in front of the car was this burly British policeman with his arms outstretched. He said, "My orders are to stop all cars after ten o'clock. It's five minutes past ten."

So I said to one of the young chaps, "Show him your pass, you said you had a pass." Well, it turned out his pass had expired — and it was a French Town pass, not for the International Settlement at all. These boys had all been having "one over the eight," I'm

Members of the Shanghai Volunteer Corps, on the race course in the early 30s. From its creation in 1853 to its disbanding in 1942, the Corps included volunteers of many nationalities, including Americans, Europeans, Filipinos, White Russians, Chinese, Japanese, and the Scots volunteers shown here. Lin Lintilhac (who was actually English, rather than Scottish) is second from right.

afraid. In those days I never drank, not one drop, or smoked or any of those things while I was nursing.

The policeman said, "I'm sorry but I'm going to have to take you into the police station." He got on the running board and took us into the station, where a police officer gave us a really good dressing down. "It's irresponsible people like you that give us all the trouble," he said. "Don't you know the war is on? What are you doing?"

We couldn't wait to get out of that station. "I'm serious when I say this is serious business," the officer said. "I will see that you get home." He gave us a policeman on the running board again.

I went home with Kay, and she was so thankful to get back with her babies. The boys went on with their police escort to the Columbia Club, where they were staying — and we found out afterward that they had had more champagne, or whatever they were drinking, and finished up by touring the frontline trenches with a police escort. Anyway, that's another story.

It was actually quite exciting for me to be living among the bright lights of Shanghai and Bubbling Well Road, right amid all this. I found Shanghai very, very exciting and interesting. I had spent all these years upcountry in remote outposts, where everything was sort of makeshift; what a thrill it was to come home after dark and wander up and down the streets, with all the shops and bright lights.

The Morphinist

It was seven o'clock on a Tuesday morning in January 1932. There was fighting going on all around the settlement, and the noise of machine-gun fire was rattling the windows. The telephone rang: would I report to the hospital for duty as soon as possible. An hour later I was standing by the night nurse's desk, idly listening to bellowing noises coming from the next room.

"That's a noisy character you seem to have on your hands," I remarked.

"That's your patient," she replied.

The elderly gentleman, Muller by name, was a morphine addict. He had taken to sleeping at his office downtown, to free his two young nephews to do their volunteer defense duty. On Saturday night he had dined alone at the Cathay Hotel. He recalled ordering oysters for dinner, and that Ronald Colman was dining at the table next to him. How he had later got back to his offices, he couldn't seem to remember.

At six o'clock on Monday morning the office coolie, who had come in early as usual to clean, found Mr. Muller on the floor in a state of collapse and in an appalling condition. From what must have been food poisoning, he had been helplessly vomiting and purging, all alone since Saturday night. He was rushed to the hospital. By the time I arrived on Tuesday morning, he was like a roaring lion demanding morphine.

It was hard to believe so thin and wasted a figure could make so much noise. My orders were to try and clean him up — but he angrily refused to let me touch him. He was getting one full grain of morphine every three hours. That didn't seem to be the amount he was used to taking, yet the doctor was afraid to give him more. Although he had been taking care of Mr. Muller for many years, the doctor had never been able to find out from him how much morphine he was taking.

I spent the day driving bargains with him. If he would allow me to wash his face, I would give him an injection. Then, unless he would let me wash his back, I would not give him his next shot. With the hypodermic needle in my hand, I would stand at the foot of his bed and drive my bargain hard. Later, when he was a little stronger, the doctor and the orderly together were able to give him a tub bath. At last he was clean.

After a week of this, he gained enough strength to demand to go home. The doctor finally consented, on the condition that he take a nurse home with him. "In that case," he said, "I'll take Miss Canada." (That was what he called me, as I was born of Canadian parents.) The next day, fortified by what seemed an enormous dose in his poor thin arm, we set out for his home in French Town. Along with a long list of treatments, the doctor asked me to try and find out just how much morphine Mr. Muller actually took every day.

At the door of his house we were met by his cadaverously thin cook-boy, reeking of opium. Together we helped Mr. Muller up the stairs and into bed. While the boy unpacked his things, I went out to the car to collect my bag. By the time I got back the front door was shut and locked.

Race course and Grand Theatre, Bubbling Well Road, Shanghai. *Image courtesy of Historical Photographs of China, University of Bristol.*

I knocked. No answer. I knocked again. A voice from upstairs called down saying that he wasn't going to let me in, that he hadn't wanted me to come in the first place.

"I promised the doctor to take care of you, so I have no choice but to stay," I said. "However, if you want to be quiet for a little while, I'll wait out here till you decide to let me in." I knew he was desperate to get at his morphine.

I stayed till quite late that night. The next morning I arrived back at ten, only to be told by the "cook-boy" that his master was sleeping. Not knowing quite what to do, I settled myself on the porch to wait. Presently a querulous voice from upstairs asked if I was there. I said I was and I was getting cold. Presently the front door opened. The boy had been told to let me into the living room and to give me a cup of hot coffee.

I spent the rest of the day arguing through the locked bedroom door. By evening I was actually allowed into the room, but just for a visit, not for any treatment. This return of his good nature indicated to me that at last he was getting his accustomed dose of morphine. At his suggestion, I shifted my hours of duty, coming to the house at midday and staying till midnight, for he never stirred till noon and never closed his eyes till midnight.

"Fifty thousand taels," he said, fondly caressing one of the tins

I was with Mr. Muller for two months. Before I left we had become good friends and he learned to trust me, even to the point of permitting me to watch him prepare and administer the massive doses of morphine that he took. It came in little white cubes, looking for all the world like after-dinner-mints. He even showed me two large tins in which he kept his supply, and disclosed the hole in the wall behind a picture where he hid one of the boxes.

"Fifteen thousand taels," he said, fondly caressing one of the tins in his arms. (One tael roughly equaled 40 grams of silver.)

Watching carefully, I finally worked it out that he took 16 grains — just under 65 milligrams — of morphine a day! It didn't seem possible, but he confirmed it. His first two grains he took when he wakened at noon, repeating this dose every two hours till midnight when he doubled it. After that he slept.

Bit by bit the story came out. He told how he had started the habit 30 years ago, claiming that he was given it by his doctor for health reasons. He had begun his career as a young civil engineer, right here in Shanghai. He had made a fortune twice over, but he had gone through it all buying this expensive stuff. At one point he had tried using Japanese morphine because it was cheaper, but it gave him boils. Now he bought it from German sailors who smuggled it in from Switzerland. It was devilish expensive but it was pure.

In the early days he had married a lovely Norwegian bride. When their baby daughter was born, he insisted, against all his wife's entreaties, that Shanghai was no place for a daughter of his to be brought up in. He sent them both back to Norway to live.

"Fool that I was," he said — "in time my lovely wife ran off with a young naval officer. What did I expect? My daughter, a beautiful woman now, is happily married and living in Norway."

Years later, in 1920, he was married again, this time to his English secretary. "She was wonderful to me, and bore me two fine sons," he said. "She stuck it out as long as she could, but in the end she couldn't keep my condition from the children, nor could she tolerate it any longer herself. They live in a lovely home in Norway that I have provided for them. The desire of my heart now is to see them once more before I die."

"Have you never tried to break yourself of this habit?" I asked.

"My dear Miss Canada, you don't know what you're talking about. I have read everything that has ever been written on the subject of morphinists," as he called himself. "Out of every ten attempted cures, one dies, two go off their heads. The other seven go right back to it once the restraining hand is removed."

I couldn't argue. I knew nothing about redeeming morphinists.

"As long as my money holds out, I might as well carry on the way I am," he said. "They say that morphinists are dirty and slatternly. Am I?" He was spotless, so fastidious about his person. "It is also said that morphinists are given to committing crimes of all kinds. Do you think I am capable of such things?"

"Ah," said I, "but if I were to withhold your morphine for any length of time, I think you would as soon stick a knife in my back as not!"

He sighed. "Maybe you're right."

He was a courtly old gentleman and a great reader. We would have long discussions far into the night, which he enjoyed. But his life must have become intolerably lonely. At the end of two months, he was strong enough again to go down to his office in town. I went with him once or twice and met the two young engineers, nephews of his, who worked with him. They seemed to regard him with great respect as well as affection, and they admitted that in spite of his handicap, he could still work circles around any one of them. In his private office he showed me his safe, which he opened. There was another large tin of morphine.

"Twenty thousand taels," he said, patting the tin. With the machine-gun fire still rattling windows, he lived in constant fear of being separated from it as he had been that first dreadful weekend.

Eight years later, after I was married and back in Shanghai, while walking along the Bund one day I passed a thin figure of a man. There was something familiar about him that made me turn. He was older, of course, and thinner and looking even more transparent, but it was Mr. Muller. To think that he was still alive staggered me. As he drew near, I said, "Mr. Muller, do you remember Miss Canada?"

He swept off his hat and bowed. After I had asked how he was and wished him well, it seemed kinder to move on. I've often wondered with apprehension what happened to him after Pearl Harbor shattered the world.

An Unexpected Visit

Still on night duty, I was asleep in the day when there was a knock at the door. Mrs. Goldberg said, "There's a lady here to see you." When she came in, who should it be but Dolly Lintilhac, Lin's mother.

I was a little taken aback, but she sat down and we talked. She asked what I was doing. I told her and said, "Have you heard from Lin?" She said yes, he was in Australia. Then she said, "I want to ask you something. Why won't you marry my son?"

I felt, actually, that this was not anybody's business except Lin's and mine. I said, "Well, I have my reasons." She said, "But if you don't marry him, he'll never get married." I said, "I may not know your son as well as you do, but I think in time he will forget me and get married — and I have to do what I have to do. I'm older than Lin and I think he should find someone his own age. That's why I've asked him not to write to me, so he will feel free to meet and get to know other girls."

"No," she said, "you don't know." She opened a parcel and presented me with a picture of Lin at 17, when he'd just come out to China from school in England. It has always been my favorite of him. This sort of touched me; I thanked her, and she invited me to go to a tea dance.

I went to the French Club, it was a lovely party. Awfully friendly everybody was. There was never any shortage of parties. It was just a matter of getting to them, if I was not on duty.

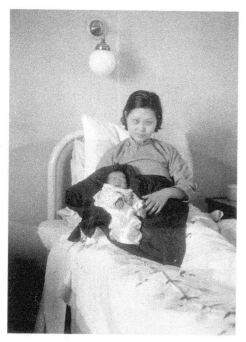

Concubine, 15 years old, with her baby at the Wellington Nursing Home in Tientsin.

Delivering Babies in Tientsin

For the rest of the year in Shanghai I was kept busy with routine nursing, most of which was at the hospital. I don't remember Christmas — I think I was out on duty.

But my first choice of nursing had always been maternity, and I was beginning to miss it. The drawback was that it entailed living night and day in someone else's home, which allowed me no life of my own. As a young girl I would put up with anything — but now I was getting older.

I was beginning to feel I should try to get maternity work in a hospital, where there would be other nurses and a reasonable chance of having some time to myself. The big maternity wing of the Country Hospital in Shanghai didn't appeal to me, so I wrote to the British Municipal Council in Tientsin. They offered me a temporary

Claire in her room at the Wellington Nursing Home.

position at the Victoria Hospital for three months, after which I could get a transfer to the Wellington Nursing Home, the small maternity hospital there. The contract was for four-year terms, with pension and home-leave benefits.

This seemed to be the job I had been hoping for — and I felt I had had enough "tramping." So I became one of two nurses in charge at the Wellington Nursing Home.

I doubt if any nurse anywhere has ever been happier than I was there for the next four years. I was able to do my favorite nursing and, at the same time get some sleep. With a full capacity of only eight beds, Grace and I shared the duty turn-about. The staff also included a trained night amah, a day amah, two houseboy-orderlies, two coolies, a cook and two laundry men. We only had eight rooms, eight beds — but even so, eight mothers with eight babies is quite a lot of work for just two nurses, night and day.

The two-story nursing home was contained in its own compound, about a mile from the Victoria General Hospital, all within the British Concession. The ground floor consisted of the two nurse's rooms and baths, with a common living room between, plus kitchen, laundry and men-servants' rooms. Upstairs were the patients' rooms, all single, the delivery room, nursery, a tiny nurses' dining room, and two amah's rooms. The whole place was not much bigger than a large home. Most of our patients were the young wives in the foreign community; this made the atmosphere more like a home than a hospital.

Although Grace and I were both on call at all times, we otherwise divided the work evenly with 24 hours on and 24 off. In four years I never had a weekend off. Usually patients phoned to say they were on their way, but sometimes they arrived unannounced. Once I rushed upstairs in my dressing gown just in time to deliver the baby.

Nothing could pry me loose from my now happy position. Almost nothing, that is — for it was towards the end of my four years here that Lin's path crossed mine again.

Tientsin lies about 60 miles southeast of Peking. Geographically it is drab to look at, on the dry, barren North China plain, but the community life there was exceptionally warm and friendly. Tientsin was big enough to allow for a diversity of interests and activities not possible in smaller communities, yet it was small enough for all to get to know each other.

The foreign community consisted of five foreign concessions and other settlements: British, Italian, French, German, Russian and Japanese. While these were considered privileged areas with their extraterritorial rights, they were also sort of ghettos. The average foreigner didn't stray far outside the concessions. For the most part our social activities centered on the race and country clubs on the outskirts of the concession. Riding was a favorite sport the year round.

Grief and Vision

The only change in the nursing home staff during the four years I was there was when Lee-ta-sao, the darling old mother of our trained day amah Ma-nai-nai, died. Lee-ta-sao had been our night amah, but she suddenly complained of pain and redness on her face and back. The isolation hospital dianosed erysipelas, an acute skin infection. In spite of every care, she got steadily worse.

Ma-nai-nai now took over her mother's night duty, and we got another amah, Chang-ta-sao, to do the day work. After about six days we were told that Lee-ta-sao was sinking fast. I urged Ma-nai-nai to go to her mother but she refused, saying that her son was there.

Night came. Ma-nai-nai insisted on coming on duty as usual, but I stayed with her. It worried me that she wouldn't talk or communicate in any way. I was afraid she might go to pieces when the final word came that her mother had died.

At three o'clock in the morning the phone rang. I picked up the receiver and heard the son's voice saying that Lee-ta-sao had died. He asked to speak to his mother, but she refused to come to the phone. With my arm around her, she stood for a moment, silent tears running down her cheeks. Then, without a word, she turned on her heel and started down the corridor. Not knowing what she had in mind, I followed her. On the way, I roused Chang-ta-sao and asked her to go on duty.

When Ma-nai-nai got to her room, she picked up a *pan teng*, a narrow wooden bench, and without a word of explanation she started down the stairs with it. I followed. She opened the hospital's front door and went straight out into the silent night street and

Ma-nai-nai and Claire.

placed her bench right across the middle of the road. Seating herself on one end, she began to wail in a loud voice for all to hear.

I sat down beside her and put my arm around her. Pretty soon the policeman on point duty came up and asked what had happened. Ma-nai-nai kept right on wailing, so I explained that her mother had died. He offered his condolences. As though out of nowhere, a crowd of a dozen or so people collected around us. Each new person wanted to know what was wrong, and I explained.

This went on for over half an hour. Then all at once, as abruptly as it had started, the wailing stopped. Wiping her eyes, Ma-nai-nai got up, picked up the bench and stomped back into the house and up to her room. Putting the bench down, she then went back on duty, all without a spoken word.

A few months later, Grace remarked that Ma-nai-nai was getting a bit careless. She said when she came to bathe the babies in the mornings, their bottoms were always dirty. I had noticed this, too — and I had also noticed that by morning, Ma-nai-nai's eyes were always very red. It turned out she was having difficulty seeing at night. I suggested that we send her to have her eyes examined.

Ma-nai-nai refused to go. I suspected she didn't want to spend the money, so I offered her a pair of old frames of mine. This she couldn't resist, and off she went with her son to the oculist. A few days later she appeared on duty wearing my old horn-rims. She was thrilled beyond words, for the whole world looked new.

She started to thank me. In the middle of it she stopped, and stared. Pointing to my face, she said, "You aren't nearly as young as I thought you were!"

A Funk Hole

The foreign concessions were very often used by Chinese officials as asylums during political emergencies. These officials acquired for themselves large foreign-style houses within the concessions — and there were many such residences in Tientsin, all surrounded by high brick walls with vicious pieces of broken glass embedded in cement along the top. Above the glass was stretched a tangle of barbed wire, and topping all that was a single strand of electrified wire, connected to a network of alarms around the house. There was also a night-and-day watchman, usually accompanied by a savage dog that barked aggressively at the sound of a footstep.

Such a wall separated the Wellington Nursing Home from the elaborate premises next door. That place belonged to a Peking official — his "funk hole," we called it. Our upstairs windows overlooked his courtyard garden. Most of the time the huge house was shut up tight, with only the watchman doing his rounds by day and the sound of his bamboo alarm being struck at regular intervals through the night. But there were times when, without any warning, this place would spring to life and become a hive of activity.

XU3MA Foils the Bias Bay Pirates

Margaret Holder was eight years old, the daughter of British missionary parents, in January 1935 when she boarded the China Navigation Company's coastal steamship *Tungchow* in Shanghai. On board were some 70 schoolchildren and half a dozen teachers, all bound northward for the China Inland Mission School in Chefoo.

"Suddenly there was a huge cry and a shout and a firing of weapons, firing of guns and pistols, and some nasty-looking men came up the steps," Margaret told BBC Radio in 2016.

About a dozen Chinese pirates had boarded the ship, posing as passengers with pistols hidden in the sleeves of their robes. They shot dead a Russian guard, wounded a British officer, and headed the ship south toward their island hideout.

"When the ship failed to arrive at Chefoo, piracy was immediately suspected," the BBC's Kate Silverton reported. "It was rife in those waters."

Dr. Malcolm, amateur radio operator XU3MA, "was at his wireless, listening in," Claire recalled — "and quite by chance he picked up an SOS signal from farther south. It was from the *Tungchow*, saying they had been pirated and they were heading south, not north, and then the thing went off the air."

Dr. Malcolm with his wireless set, shown at right. Claire's father was one of the world's earliest — and at the time one of China's only — amateur radio operators.

"Father had a standing schedule at the time with the British legation in Peking, and he told them he had picked up this message. Peking Legation immediately got in touch with the Royal Navy in Hong Kong."

When a Royal Air Force search plane flew overhead, the kids, who had been confined in their cabins, ran out on deck and signaled — and the pirates escaped by boarding a nearby Chinese junk.

"The last I saw of these pirates was in the distance," Margaret Holder said. "Quite a beautiful scene — the sun about to set and the pirates being rowed to a distant island." They were in Bias [Daya] Bay, a notorious pirate haunt.

For Chefoo and its Shantung province during the turbulent 1920s and '30s, Dr. Malcolm was often the only local radio operator, providing a vital link to the outside world. "His station XU3MA was, for that matter, one of the few consistently active in all of China," writes Clinton B. DeSoto in his 1941 book *Calling CQ — Adventures of Short-Wave Operators*. "The service he rendered more nearly resembled that of a communication center for an entire city than of an amateur station."

Chinese officials occasionally banned private radio communications, forcing XU3MA off the air, DeSoto writes. "But always the inhabitants of the Shantung Peninsula protested so loudly that his authority to operate was restored."

In 1938, the invading Japanese cut the cable link between Shanghai and Chefoo. Dr. Malcolm, then in his late 70s, responded by transmitting hundreds of messages for the cable operators.

The SS *Tungchow*. *Photograph by G. Warren Swire. Image courtesy of John Swire & Sons Ltd and Historical Photographs of China, University of Bristol.*

On these occasions, Ma-nai-nai would point with her chin toward the window, saying, with a knowing smile, "*Hwei-lai-la.*" (They've returned.) By this we knew that for some reason, Peking had turned on the "heat" again.

As she walked away from the window, Ma-nai-nai would give my sleeve a tug and point with her thumb over her shoulder. This meant the Old Boy himself was out in the garden, doing his *t'ai ch'i ch'üan,* a cross between fencing and shadow-boxing that was always done with such deliberation and grace.

With his long silk gown wound around his waist and both arms outstretched, he would strike an attitude, holding it poised for a moment; then, slapping a thigh, he would pivot, take a couple of quick steps, then freeze in another dramatic pose. These movements were repeated with slight variations until he had had enough exercise. Then, pulling a folded fan from the collar at the back of his neck, he would withdraw to a wooden bench that circled the trunk of a weeping-willow tree, and quietly fan himself.

After resting here awhile, he would disappear into the house, then reappear with his pet mynah bird in its cage. This he placed on the bench beside him under the tree; and without opening the cage door, he would clean out the cage little by little with a pair of long metal chopsticks, talking all the while to his chatty companion.

As the evening wore on, there would be the sound of eating and drinking and merry-making. This went on far into the night, accompanied by the music of a flute or a one-string violin and sometimes the high falsetto note of a theatrical entertainer. Always in the background was the ubiquitous clatter of mahjong tiles and sometimes the sickly sweet smell of opium. At dawn all became quiet again. After a few weeks of this, as suddenly as it had begun all would return to silence, broken only by the clack-clack of the faithful night watchman's bamboo alarm.

We never really knew just who our neighbor was, just that he was one of Peking's high-ranking officials. That Chinese sought refuge in the foreign concessions was one of the reasons for resentment toward the concessions, among Chinese students.

A Life Decision that Changed

As I said before, no one has ever been happier than I was during those four years in the Maternity Home in Tientsin. I had a permanent job in my favorite branch of nursing, with three weeks annual holiday and home-leave privileges every four years — which meant passage to England and back, with six months' leave on full pay — and a pension. These were benefits not often available to a woman in those days. So I decided the time had come for me to settle down.

I had so many lovely friends in Tientsin. It was bitterly cold; we used to have about three months of skating weather, but very little snow. It's north, you see, and there's very little precipitation in that part of the world. It was drab and flat. People often said to me, "How can you stand this place?" And I said, "I just adore Tientsin, all my dear friends."

But the fact was, I just hadn't found someone I couldn't live without. I recall vividly the night when, at age 35, I made the final decision to forego marriage and devote myself to my work. I knew full well what I would be giving up; it's a woman's natural desire to have a home, family and babies of her own. I cried a little as I consciously burned that bridge. But when morning came, I knew that, for me, I had made the right decision.

Then in the spring of 1935 a patient was admitted to the hospital. She had come all the way from Swatow [Shantou], in South China, to have her baby here. Discussing small outports with her, I said I understood that Swatow was a real hole in the ground to be stationed in. She defended the place, saying there were so many nice people there. And in the course of our conversation she mentioned the name Lintilhac.

"Lintilhac!" I exclaimed.

"Yes," she said, looking surprised. "Do you know Lin?"

"Well ... I used to. But I haven't seen him since 1931. I didn't even know where he was stationed, till now."

Marguerite returned to Swatow and told Lin who had nursed her in Tientsin. A few weeks later I received a letter from Lin, saying that in October he was planning to take his mother for a holiday to Peking.

"She has been in China all these years and has never been to Peking," Lin wrote. "I'm getting my holiday in October and taking her, and we pass through Tientsin. Would you be willing to come down to the train station and see us as we pass through?"

I thought long and hard about this because I realized how solemn my reply just had to be. I wrote back and said, "Yes, I'd love to see you." He wrote back and I replied, and all summer we corresponded. By October I had arranged to save four days of my three weeks' holiday to spend with Lin and his mother in Peking.

They came in October. They spent four days in Tientsin and I went with them to Peking. When we came back, I think there was one more day in Tientsin. We'd had very serious talks, but I said, "Lin, let's just — this is too serious to take lightly. Let's wait until you get back to the broad light of day in Swatow before you make any firm moves."

But when I said goodbye to Lin at that time — he had to catch his boat in Shanghai, back to Swatow — I knew that I loved him more than anything in the world. I thought, "I don't know whether he's going to ask me to marry me or not;

Dollie and Lin Lintilhac and Claire in Peking, 1935.

Above: On shipboard leaving Chefoo for Shanghai to be married, July 1936. Below: Lin and Claire at their wedding.

but even if he doesn't, I now know that I loved somebody with all my heart. Whether I marry him is something else altogether." There was no mention of getting married or even of being engaged. When the moment came to part, the train pulled out and we waved goodbye.

I had been engaged two or three times, during this time that I hadn't seen Lin — but I had broken them off, because I just felt I didn't want to give up my nursing to get married. In those times, you couldn't do both the way you can today. They were nice chaps, those men I was engaged to; and when I say "engaged," they were very formal affairs. But I broke them.

Lin hadn't gotten all the way back to Shanghai when he sent a cable asking me to marry him. I cabled back, accepting. We corresponded regularly but didn't see each other again till the day before we were married, nine months later.

Lin and I were married on July 21, 1936. Mother had naturally wanted to have the wedding at home in Chefoo, but there were reasons why I didn't want this. It would have taken up all of Lin's too-short leave just to get that far north and back; and because I had stayed on my job right up till the last minute, I was so tired that I just couldn't face a big wedding. So I met Lin halfway, and we were married quietly in Shanghai.

We spent our wedding night in the elegant bridal suite at the Cathay Hotel, on the corner of Nanking Road and the Bund, with a lovely view overlooking the river. Adjoining the bedroom there were two bathrooms, no less: the bride's was a pretty pale blue, while the groom's was in handsome black onyx. All very "swish."

The next day we sailed for Swatow on a cargo boat not unlike the kind I was so accustomed to. It was a three-day trip, and there was one bathroom to share with the other eight passengers. The only bathtub was full of live fish swimming gaily about. Lin apologized, but I just laughed, for it was all so familiar.

Gracious Living in Swatow

Next to Canton, Swatow is the largest and busiest city in Kwangtung province and just an overnight boat trip from Hong Kong. It was from here in the south, as from Chefoo in the north, that thousands of men were shipped to France as laborers during the First World War.

It was sub-tropical here. The crops were largely tobacco, sugar, tea, rice and tropical fruits of all kinds. In our garden we had banana and papaya trees and the huge, delicious, loose-skinned honey-oranges of South China. Gosh, but they were good!

Also in our garden were so many, to me, unfamiliar forms of vegetation, most conspicuous among them being the huge banyan tree with its tremendous gnarled, exposed roots that rooted and re-rooted themselves, eventually covering wide areas. Then there was the kapok tree, rising straight as a mast to an enormous height. The branches grew straight out at right angles from the trunk, beginning well out of reach and rising in a spiral like a winding staircase. The blossom of this tree was large, fleshy and brilliant orange in color.

my first home on island of Kakchiao — Swatow South China.

It was fascinating to watch the birds eat the blossom, tearing it apart as though it was made of flesh. The seed-pods of the kapok tree look like fat cucumbers — and when they ripen and burst, the air is filled with their silky, fluffy down, the stuff that pillows and lifebelts used to be filled with. Kapok seed oil is used for making soap.

In the winter poinsettias grew wild on the hillsides. Their blossoms were not the large handsome ones that florists produce here, but they were colorful and gay. Bougainvillea grew everywhere, adding their lush color to the scene. Garden flowers were grown mostly in pots, for the flowering seasons followed each other in such rapid succession that before one lot of flowers began to fade, the next would be in full bloom. This kept the gardeners busy, whisking one set of pots away and instantly replacing it with the next. This endless procession was all so new to me, who had lived all my life in barren North China, where it was so hard to coax a garden of any kind to grow.

The I.C.I. house, a large bungalow with lofty ceilings and wide verandas — it had been built way back in the clipper ship days — was on Kakchow, a little island in the wide river delta that separated it from the mainland. There'd been five bachelors in there before I got married. Lin had turned them all out, saying, "Out you go, chaps, I'm going to get married and bring my bride home."

The view from the I.C.I. bungalow in Kakchow, toward Swatow city and Lin's office.

The house had huge rooms, with polished wood floors and ceilings about 15 feet high. There was a wide veranda all the way around the house and long, French windows everywhere. Through our telescope, from our garden on the top of the hill that

overlooked the jetty and the river, I could see Lin's office on the mainland near the waterfront, with the sprawling city of Swatow all around.

Kakchiao [Queshi], a sort of island where we lived across the river from Swatow, was about three miles in diameter in all directions. It had no electricity or running water. On it was a small clubhouse for the community, plus the homes of most of the foreign residents of Swatow: the consular officials, the commissioner of customs (who had a huge house), and the executives of shipping companies and import/export firms, such as the shipping company Butterfield & Swire, British American Tobacco, and the trading firm Jardine Matheson & Co. These were old *hong* homes, dating back to the opium, silk and tea trade days. The most colossal house, popularly known as the Princely Hong, belonged to Jardine Matheson. (A *hong* was a 19th century trading company in China. Jardine Matheson & Co. was one of the earliest foreign hongs, established in 1841.)

All the houses were spacious, high-ceilinged things — because the only compensation, I think, for living in the tropics is to have space. Today, you go to Hong Kong and Singapore and you have little regulation-size houses because you can air-condition them. But to me, to live in air conditioning defeats whatever pleasure there is in living in the tropics. All the houses had *punkas*, fans that drop from the ceiling with a cord that runs through one wall, with little pulley set into the wall, to be pulled by a coolie outside.

Social life in China in those days was very gracious indeed, made possible by the easy availability of domestic help. But help alone wouldn't have done it; what made life gracious was the quality of help rendered by the impeccable Chinese servant. Every home had a "number one boy," who was responsible for the smooth running of the household. The other servants were all answerable to him, and he took responsibility for their work and conduct. All knew their role as they moved noiselessly about in their soft, cloth-soled slippers.

Tiffin (lunch) parties and tea parties seemed to go on all the time, usually in one's own home except on Saturdays, when there were always gala dinners and dances at the elegant clubs. The dance floors in the ballrooms of these clubs were fabulous things, laid on spring coils or slung. How the huge floor of the Tientsin Country Club was slung, I don't know — but when one walked just normally across, it would swing and sway almost like you were on a trampoline. One could dance all night on those floors and never tire.

But most dinners were given in one's own home, quiet and elegant, followed by lots of good conversation. The communities in all those places were always very cosmopolitan, representing firms and banks and consulates of all the different nationalities. The gentlemen were always in dinner jackets, the ladies in extravagant evening gowns. In those days I wore a monocle in the evening — what ho! — especially if I was attending some formal occasion. But today I wouldn't swap any of it for my lovely, clean, functional, modern American home here in Stowe.

The Village at Home

I had always considered that I knew my China well, but now I was discovering that South China was a different world. It wasn't just the vegetation and the climate, but also the mode of living and travel and the dialect. In the north, travel was by cart and mule-litter and wheelbarrow; but the south was networked with canals, so travel was everywhere by boat. In many ways this was delightful, especially for us — the company owned a lovely motor yacht, named *Dreamland* no less. It was roomy and comfortable, with a permanent crew of four: two sailors, a coxswain and an engineer, all with quarters of their own on board.

Among its many uses, the *Dreamland* carried Lin's lunch across the river to his office every day. Every day, I sent a little note with his lunch. He had also shown me how to blow on one of his huge conch shells; this was part of our communication system. I would blow a couple of loud blasts sharp at noon from our front terrace, after first focusing the telescope on the office across the river. Lin immediately appeared on his office veranda, waving my note in his hand.

But the biggest difference was the dialect. I could hardly understand a word of Swatowese; it had eight tones as opposed to north China's five tones. It seemed so strange to be among Chinese yet not be able to talk freely with them. If I spoke slowly, pointing at things, I could put my meaning across well enough, but there could be no such thing as conversation. And there were so many to have conversations with — servants in the house, I mean. The only one who spoke any English, and that was "pigeon English," was the number one boy, Wong. "Gentleman Wong," we called him, for I was soon to discover that he considered himself almost too much of a gentleman to do a useful job of work around the house.

Dreamland, I.C.I.'s motor yacht.

One day I asked Lin if he had any idea how many *mouths* he was feeding in the quarters at the back. He said he knew there were a goodly number, but he hadn't actually counted. So I set out to take a tally.

First was Gentleman Wong. It turned out he had a wife and five children, complete with an amah to look after his children. Next was "my" amah — the wash-amah, a nice woman who moved quietly about on her big bare feet, such a contrast to the bound feet of women in the north. Then there was the cook and his grown son, apprenticed to him as second cook. Next came the indoor coolie; then the outdoor coolie, who was the water carrier, for every drop had to be carried in pails from a well at the far end of the garden, back across the lawn, up a flight of 66 steps into the house and to the kitchen quarters.

Last but by no means least was the gardener and his son, a sort of assistant gardener whose main function was to empty the "dubs" twice a day. (The term *dub* being short for W.C. or water-closet, a luxury we definitely did not have.) I invariably ran into this fellow as he was hustling one or other of these containers out through the side door, and he always insisted on saluting me with one hand as we passed each other. I couldn't help wishing he'd skip the salute and keep both hands on what he was doing, but I hadn't the heart to stop him.

With all these people, including the five children running around all day laughing and crying, I sometimes felt as though I had inherited a whole village.

On the river delta we'd watch the boats coming in, the fishermen calling on their great big conches. There were fisherman of all kinds in Swatow. They would be standing on long, narrow rafts made of three or four big bamboos lashed together, with oars and high rowlocks on each side. They would go out in pairs with a net between them, trolling, and they'd catch millions of little shrimp, about a half an inch long. Plankton I suppose is what they really were.

I remember the first time we bought a whole basketful from these men, straight out of the sea. We had scrambled eggs for supper that night, and the cook scrambled these little shrimps in with the egg. He brought this dish onto the table and it was absolutely glowing with phosphorus. I said, "We clearly can't eat that!" and he said "Yes you can, it's all right." We ate it and it was a delicious dish.

We would anchor the *Dreamland* among all of the fishing junks — and one night we had a big storm. The junks were all calling to each other on their conches all night long, to keep from crashing into each other. We had to man the decks all night long, too.

The crew of the *Dreamland*.

The Cost of a Bride

One afternoon the following spring, I was languishing in bed with the beginnings of the awful amoebic dysentery that was to lay me low soon after. As I lay there, Lin came into the room. Hesitating to disturb me, he said he was worried about the water coolie, Ah-foong, who was lying on the floor in the servants' courtyard apparently having some kind of seizure. His eyes were rolled back and his limbs were twitching, and he was frothing at the mouth.

Lin didn't know what to do. I asked if Ah-foong was alone at the time. On the contrary, Lin said, all the servants were gathered around, wringing their hands. After pondering for a bit, I suggested there was nothing wrong with Ah-foong — he was only 22 — but that he might be staging a fit of hysterics for some reason.

Slightly surprised, Lin said, "All right, if it's hysterics, what shall I do about it?" I told him to go to the ice-box, get a glass of ice water, then go out and speak sharply and directly to Ah-foong, ordering him to get up off the floor and explain what was wrong. If the lad didn't respond, then dash the ice water in his face. Lin agreed to give it a try.

A while later, he appeared again in the doorway with a broad smile. He had followed my directions, got no response from Ah-foong, and pitched the cold water into his face. Ah-foong leapt up off the floor, clutched Lin about the knees and began begging for "mercy."

Slowly the story came out. It turned out he had taken to visiting the "teahouse" in the city with Gentleman Wong, and had fallen in love with one of the "sing-song" girls there. Determined to marry her, he had had to borrow money from all his friends, including my amah, to buy the girl out of the teahouse. He finally had married her — and now his friends were clamoring for their money. But Ah-foong was spending it as fast as he earned it.

In the end, Lin arranged to hold back five dollars from his wages each month to help meet his commitments. It took a little time, but we finally got his wife paid for.

A member of the Swatow household staff, with his family.

Marriage and the Movies

Traditionally, a Chinese girl was betrothed very young, sometimes even in infancy, as a mutual arrangement was often made between two congenial families. When the girl came of age, at 15 or 16, she was married. Usually she didn't see, much less get to know, her husband-to-be until her wedding night.

To the average western girl who thinks of marriage in terms of *romance*, this custom seems unbearable. But a Chinese girl at that time knew from early childhood that her role in life was to be a wife and mother — and even more importantly, to be a dutiful and respectful daughter-in-law to her husband's mother, for therein lay her only hope of happiness in her new home. She was taught the skills needed to fulfill these duties. She was under no illusions about romance; she understood she must earn her husband's respect, and then perchance his love. Hopefully the same applied to him. But in a home where seniority had first priority, the role of a young bride could be very hard indeed.

But Julia and Judith Wong were not conventional Chinese girls. The march of time had catapulted them out of their traditional role, into the world of Western movies! Their father, Mr. Wong, was *compradore* (a local manager for a foreign business) for one of the large foreign lace and embroidery companies in Swatow. He was a man of property in the city, where he had a large, impressive home. The girls had been sent to Shanghai to attend high school at the elite McTyeire School for Girls. This was founded and directed by the Methodist Church to accommodate the daughters of Shanghai's wealthy families. Among its graduates were the three Soong sisters, who became Mrs. Sun Yat-sen, Mrs. Chiang Kai-shek, and the wife of H. H. Kung [Kung Xiangxi], China's Nationalist minister of finance.

Through business, Lin had gotten to know Mr. Wong, who one day asked him if Julia and Judith might come to call on me. Julia was engaged to be married soon, he explained, and was eager to meet a "Western" bride. So a day was set for them to come to tea, and the *Dreamland* was sent to bring them across the river.

Traditionally … when a girl came of age, at 15 or 16, she was married

When the girls arrived there were four of them, for Julia and Judith had each brought a friend. They were darling girls, bubbling over with enthusiasm and curiosity to see everything I had and did in my Western-style home. Later in the evening Lin arrived, bringing with him the two bridegrooms-to-be, who had come to escort the girls back to their homes. Julia's fiancee, Harry, had a job with the telegraph company in Swatow.

The day for Julia's wedding was finally set. A messenger arrived at Lin's office to inquire if he and I would accept an invitation to the wedding. Assured that we would be delighted, they sent us a gorgeous red-and-gold invitation.

We saw the girls and their young men a number of times before the wedding, for they enjoyed the informality of coming with us on the *Dreamland* for picnics. Julia confided to me that 500 guests had been invited to the wedding — and that although the invitation said seven o'clock dinner, we should not come before nine, as our table wouldn't be eating till nearly eleven. All the poor friends and relations, she explained, had to be served early.

She surprised me by saying she was planning to have the wedding ceremony itself in the morning at a Christian church in the city. I questioned her about this, knowing she was not a Christian. Now it was her turn to be surprised; she answered, "But this is the modern way!"

I asked her where she got that idea. "From the movies," she replied.

At the church Julia looked lovely in a long white satin dress and veil and orange blossoms. As she came out on the bridegroom's arm, the groom's friends threw quantities of rice at them. Looking back as our rickshaws swept us away, I couldn't help noticing beggars gathering up the rice off the church steps.

Julia mentioned that, far from the traditional custom of her having to go and live in her husband's home in Canton, Harry was going to be living in her home here in Swatow, where his job was. Mr. Wong had had a modern second-floor apartment built over his and Mrs. Wong's personal section of the house, with its own separate entrance.

A bride and groom in a "Western-style" wedding.
Photograph by King's Studio, Hong Kong. Image courtesy of C.H. Foo, Y.W. Foo and Historical Photographs of China, University of Bristol.

At 9 p.m. Lin and I arrived at the residence. We were met at the gate and piloted through courtyard after courtyard, where guests were eating and drinking amid a maximum of revelry. Improvised kitchens had been set up in the open courts under temporary cloth awnings. Gradually leaving the noise behind, we arrived at a quiet inner court and from there were led upstairs to the bride and groom's apartment. Here the immediate family was gathered together with a few close friends. They were serving martinis!

Julia looked elegant in a long, sleek *cheongsam*, a one-piece dress of scarlet and gold lamé. Over this she wore a red satin jacket, beautifully embroidered in all colors. She apologized for it, saying it was part of her mother's wedding dress that she had agreed to wear just to please her mother. I glanced at little Mrs. Wong, who was sitting there looking lost and bewildered.

I sat down beside Mrs. Wong and took her hand in mine. She complained wistfully that Julia was very tired, that she had wanted to help with the wedding preparations, but that she didn't know what to do for it was all so strange and foreign to her.

Every half hour or so a servant appeared at the door, to announce that another table had been filled and the guests were calling for the bride and groom to come and drink to their health. Julia and Harry would disappear for a little while, soon returning to the family gathering. Finally, at about 11 o'clock, Lin and I, the mother and father, and a few others were invited to come down to dinner. In the middle of dinner Julia and Harry appeared at our table and we formally drank to their health, with the bridegroom doing the drinking for them both while the bride simply put the cup to her lips.

Normally at a Chinese dinner, when the meal is over the guests depart. But Julia whispered in my ear to please come up to her apartment again before leaving. When we got upstairs, we found the bride sitting, with her eyes appropriately lowered, beside the groom on a traditional narrow wooden bench (not unlike an ordinary sawhorse) in their bedroom. Lounging around on the beds and chairs in the room were a dozen young men in various stages of inebriation, eating oranges and throwing the skins all over the lovely new carpets, at the same time baiting the newlyweds with ribald remarks calculated to make a "blushing bride" blush.

When Julia looked up and saw me, she patted the end of the bench they were sitting on. I hesitated, but she insisted. With her eyes still modestly cast down, she murmured that, according to old Chinese custom, these young men were entitled to follow the bridal couple around, taunting them and denying them any privacy, for as long as three days.

"What they don't know," she added, "is that Harry and I are going off on a honeymoon tomorrow."

Illness and Attack

In March 1937, I suddenly broke down with a severe attack of amoebic dysentery and was taken to Hong Kong, where I languished in the War Memorial Hospital for the next six weeks. Lin had to return to Swatow, where it was not easy for him to receive news of me during that time. I was too sick to write myself — so Father, away north in Chefoo, established a schedule with a ham radio pal in the Royal Navy in Hong Kong, who was able to give him daily reports from the hospital.

My progress was discouragingly slow. At the end of six weeks the hot weather was beginning to set in, so the doctor advised that I be sent north to convalesce. He reluctantly gave me permission to return to Swatow to collect some clothes. Lin came for me.

Three days later, in Swatow, I collapsed again. This time they didn't move me, but sent to Hong Kong for nurses. As soon as I could be moved, the doctors urged Lin to get me out of the heat of Swatow. So Lin took me north to Shanghai, where Mother met me and took me north again to Chefoo. All this time I "lived" on my indispensable rubber bedpan.

Such is amoebic dysentery.

I failed to improve after two months of Chefoo's invigorating climate, so at Father's request the hospital there put me through a course of tests (and I volunteered to serve as Exhibit A for a class of student nurses). One day Father came in with a sheaf of papers in his hands and tears rolling down his face. I said, "What's wrong?" He said, "I've just got the reports from Temple Hill Hospital."

He read the diagnosis: cancer of the pylorus, which connects the stomach to the duodenum. The hospital recommended that I go immediately to Shanghai, for another checkup and possible exploratory surgery.

Just at this time, Mary and her second husband, Neil Starr, were passing through Chefoo on their way to Peking. (They had been married in San Francisco that year.) Mary unselfishly stayed behind and accompanied me back to Shanghai, where Lin had arrived just in time to meet us. After 24 hours in Mary's and Neil's lovely penthouse apartment in the Broadway Mansions overlooking the river, I was admitted to the Red Cross Hospital in Hongkew [Hongkao], about six blocks from Mary's apartment.

The Japanese attacked Shanghai the next day, while I was in the middle of tests and X-rays. They shelled the Hongkew district from gunboats anchored at the mouth of the river. Instantly the whole hospital was evacuated. Luckily for me, Lin was beside me at the time. I didn't think I could walk — but I discovered I could run, with Lin pulling me along by the hand.

Refugees waiting at a steel gate, Shanghai, 1937. *Photograph by Malcolm Rosholt. Image courtesy of Mei-Fei Elrick, Tess Johnston and Historical Photographs of China, University of Bristol.*

1937: The Battle of Shanghai

One of the most terrible battles of the mid-20th century unfolded months before World War II had even begun. Japan invaded North China in July 1937, and from August through November of that year, over one million Chinese and Japanese forces fought closely and hard for control of China's largest, richest city.

Just as in 1932, China's Nationalist army — on foot with mostly hand-held weapons, and virtually no air or naval forces — was ill-equipped to counter Japan's mechanized, highly mobile land, sea and air power. But the Chinese were desperate to slow down the Japanese advance, and they fought far more fiercely than the Japanese military expected.

The three-month battle churned in stages through the central native city, its outlying districts, and the shoreline along the Yangtze River and Hangzhou Bay. Soldiers fought from house to house in the city; the combat and the Japanese bombardments wrought huge destruction. In late November, the Chinese finally retreated and the Japanese took control of the Chinese portions of Shanghai. They left alone most of the city's International Settlement and its French Concession, where some 70,000 foreigners had been living, though many were evacuated or fled the city before, during and after the battle.

Japan seized the International Settlement on December 8, 1941, the day after its attack on the U.S. at Pearl Harbor. Its forces would hold the entire city, and much of North China, until the end of World War II in 1945.

"Bloody Saturday": a baby in the ruins of the old Shanghai South Railway Station after Japanese bombing in August 1937.
Photograph by H. S. Wong.

Bombs and Cabbages

When we got into the street, we found that buses and streetcars had all been abandoned. The crowds were running toward the bridge into the International Settlement. When we reached the Broadway Mansions, we were surprised to find that Japanese soldiers had already sandbagged the entrance. They refused at bayonet point to let us in until Mary came down to identify us.

The Chinese Nationalist troops had fled with the approach of the Japanese. In the meantime, the International Settlement was being flooded with thousands of refugees from the outlying areas, now huddling in every doorway. From Mary's penthouse atop the twentieth floor, we looked not only over the wide Huangpu River but also down on the Japanese consulate, which was right below us on the river's edge. Anchored alongside the consulate was the Japanese Navy flagship *Izumo*.

The next day Nationalist planes attacked, one after another. Their main target was the Japanese consulate and the flagship. From Mary's terrace we had a dramatic view: we could see the Japanese sailors manning the antiaircraft guns down on the decks of the *Izumo*, firing these shells that burst with puffs in the air. The Nationalist planes were trying to stay well out of reach, flying so high that the bombs were dropping indiscriminately into the river.

Chinese refugees streaming over Garden Bridge onto the Bund, Shanghai. Photo taken from Broadway Mansions, where Neil and Mary Starr had a penthouse apartment. *Image courtesy of Historical Photographs of China, University of Bristol.*

The Huangpu River was crowded with all kinds of crafts, large and small — mainly great flat-bottom lighters, or barges, from upcountry, laden with vegetables, cabbages and things for Shanghai's hungry market. These big barges were breaking in two; people, cabbages, oars and things were flying in all directions into the river. The bombs were playing absolute havoc. Some hit the Bund, killing hundreds, but they never did hit the Japanese consulate or the *Izumo*.

Also on the river were little *yuloh* boats, one-oar boats that were sort of water taxis. This great river opposite Shanghai had no bridge across it; you had to get into these little yulohs and the oarsman would taxi you across. Well, as the bombardment continued these yulohs would dart out from the side of the river and duck in and out among the wreckage, picking up the cabbages and avoiding the heads of people. Each oarsman would fill his boat, unload and then back they'd come, picking up more things that they could use.

It's hard for a Westerner to understand how any human being could possibly pick up cabbages and not attempt to rescue people. But the Western human being has never been at such a narrow margin of survival. When you've got more mouths in your family than you can feed, you don't take on more mouths. And if they had rescued the drowning people and taken them home, those people could claim support from their rescuer for the rest of their lives. The superstitions were such that if you snatched those drowning souls from the river gods, you were going to set in motion some jealous spirits that would come and haunt you. So you didn't interfere in that fate, and those people were left to drown.

In the meantime — this was after we'd been evacuated — thousands of refugees were pouring from the outlying districts into the International Settlement. Pretty soon there were families in every little doorway. This was the downtown district, the business area; there were families on every little back street, and starving people on the doorsteps.

Catastrophe and Survival

Ultimately the Red Cross collected money and one of the big tobacco companies offered their big warehouses and compound as a refugee camp. I think something like 20,000 people were taken over there. The Red Cross cooked rice, but it's a big undertaking to distribute cooked rice to 20,000 people. So they broke it down into family units of about 20 people each. Every unit was then told to select their own spokesman, who would take delivery of the rice and bring it back to their own unit.

That seemed to be working all right, but after two months we thought there was an epidemic of some kind in the camp. On investigation, the Red Cross discovered that people were dying of starvation. They found that the heads of the family units — the fathers, the uncles, whoever they were — had been holding out among their own families. They were holding out for money, for one copper or whatever they thought they could get. Or for rings, for any valuables. If you didn't come across, you didn't get your bowl of free Red Cross rice.

Again, it's quite impossible to imagine such a thing from a Westerner's position of security and safety. But China has been through so many catastrophes — natural calamities, wars — and each head of these families knew full well that the Red Cross wasn't going to take care of them forever, and whoever survived with the most money was the one who was probably going to live. Their alternatives have always been on that level. It's just impossible for a Westerner to think of it.

After a while, the Japanese took full command of the International Settlement and the refugees were relocated out around the outskirts. One of those refugee camps was right around the Imperial Chemical Industries compound, where our home was. (We had been evacuated by then.) Right outside our compound was reclaimed marshland. It was Shanghai's mud flat; you'd scratch the surface and come to water. Refugees were settled there, and they scraped together bits of mat and stuff and made crawl-in shelters, to sleep in at night.

They had no water, no light, no nothing. Out on the main road, the municipal council would open the water hydrants twice a day, in the morning at eight and in the evening at five. People with their pots and pails would go out there, collect water and trail back. A boy and a woman would carry a pole between them, sagging with a pail of water in the middle; or a man would carry a pole and two pails, one at either end. This went on for the duration of the war.

Children and adults queuing with rice bowls, Shanghai.
Photograph by Malcolm Rosholt. Image courtesy of Mei-Fei Elrick, Tess Johnston and Historical Photographs of China, University of Bristol.

All Colors, Clutching Passports

As the bombardment continued, we received a message from the Japanese consulate with orders to evacuate the penthouse immediately, warning that they couldn't be responsible for the possible bombing of the building.

Grabbing a few things, we went downstairs to the lobby. But of course, no cars or taxis were anywhere to be seen. Eventually a large truck came by with a Russian driver. Where he came from we never knew, but he agreed to take us to Lin's sister's house in the French Concession on the far side of the city. We stayed here for the next three days, as gunfire vibrated the windows and shook the chandeliers down from the ceilings.

The bombing got worse, and more and more indiscriminate. On the third day the British consulate radio station announced that all British women and children were to be evacuated to Hong Kong, and to gather immediately at the Metropol Hotel near the river, to be ferried to British destroyers lying at anchor in the middle of the river.

The Nationalist planes had agreed to a moratorium on bombing while we were being taken on board — but not surprisingly, they failed to observe it. Bombs fell all around us as we were herded aboard and below deck. Poor Lin had to let me go, not knowing when he was going to see me again, if ever.

So there we were below decks on these destroyers. I looked around the wardroom and there were all colors of the rainbow. There were Chinese, there were Indians, there were Eurasians and white people — all colors, all clutching British passports, as was I. We were not hit by a shell, but they were falling all around. We went down the river and were taken out to the ocean liner SS *Rajputana*, of the famous P&O line (the Peninsular & Oriental Steam Naviation Co.).

When we finally got on the *Rajputana*, thousands of us, there were two or three hundred sleeping on the deck. Because of my being sick, Lin had applied for a cabin; so Mary and I, luckily, had a cabin and, better still, a bathroom. But there were many people sleeping on deck for three days and three nights to Hong Kong. Luckily it was warm weather and calm, so it wasn't too bad. The food was awful, but I had this tin of powdered milk that I lived on.

Evacuees on the Bund, waiting to leave Shanghai. *Photograph by Malcolm Rosholt. Image courtesy of Mei-Fei Elrick, Tess Johnston and Historical Photographs of China, University of Bristol.*

Bombs on an Ocean Liner

Three days later at nine o'clock at night, the *Rajputana* steamed into Hong Kong harbor in a pouring rain. Lin had cabled I.C.I.'s Hong Kong office to book a room for us at the Peninsula Hotel, which was within walking distance of the dock. But unbeknownst to us, during those three days Shanghai had been declared in quarantine for cholera — so when we docked, no one was allowed near the boat to meet the passengers.

A telephone message confirmed that we had a room at the Peninsula. So in the rain with our heads tied up in kerchiefs, Mary and I set out, she with a small overnight bag and me with my tin of powdered milk, to walk to the hotel. We arrived drenched — and I will never forget walking into that enormous hotel lobby, with all the people sitting around having their after-dinner coffee, watching the refugees arrive.

We went up to the desk, only to be told that before we could have a room we must report to the infirmary, to be innoculated against cholera. Then we were shown our room. But in the middle of the night, Mary awakened, absolutely tied in knots with stomach cramps. She said, "Gosh, don't tell me I've got cholera!"

I didn't think she did, but I didn't want to tell the authorities, for fear they would send

The SS *Rajputana* carried Claire and Mary to Hong Kong from battle-torn Shanghai.

P. & O. S.S. RAJPUTANA, 16,600 TONS GROSS.
India Mail and Passenger Service.

us away somewhere. She was really tied up in knots; I suspected it was food poisoning. In the morning I phoned the switchboard and said, "Is there a pharmacy open?" They said, "Why?" I said, "Well, I need some medicine." Well, what medicine did I want? There was a doctor; did I want to see the doctor? I said, "Well, no, never mind."

I was really scared that they would separate us, take her away or something like that. You're always afraid of that. Mary said, "I'm not going to the doctor, skip it."

So we skipped it and took a chance. She drank a lot of warm water — we didn't have a thing — and after a while she was better. Then I phoned the I.C.I. office, and they came over with some money. Hong Kong wouldn't take Shanghai money, because the bottom was dropping out of

"Gosh, don't tell me I've got cholera!"

that market. The minute there is an emergency, the local currency is suspect.

Two days later the office received a cable from Lin saying he was leaving Shanghai that day by freighter. Five days after we'd arrived, Mary and I staggered down to the waterfront to meet this cargo boat. I was sitting on the running board of somebody's Model T Ford, and Mary said she would go farther along and see if she could find Lin.

She had wandered far afield, and somebody was walking toward me. I kept trying to look around this person, to keep track of Mary. Finally I looked up to see in front of me this man, all dirty with his face black. It was Lin! He'd been quartered for three days below the steel decks of the freighter, sustained by only three sandwiches.

After he'd had a good scrub, Lin went to the I.C.I. office in Hong Kong and applied for permission to take his home leave immediately, to take me to the Mayo Clinic in the United States. They agreed to let him take his leave six months early, but he had to go back to Swatow to hand over the office there to his relief, and to pack up all our belongings. My doctor wouldn't let me go with him.

While Lin was away, Mary received a cable from Neil saying he had succeeded in returning to Shanghai. She resolved to join him there, come what may. Now married to an American, she no longer officially came under British jurisdiction. So in the face of much opposition, she booked a passage to Shanghai on the SS *President Hoover* of the Dollar Steamship Lines. On the third day after she had left, I heard a rumor that the *Hoover* had been bombed.

What happened was that as the *Hoover* approached the mouth of the river at Shanghai, Nationalist planes flew over, dropping bombs on the ship. The radio reported that the ship had been badly damaged but not disabled, and that as far as they knew only one passenger had been killed. It was days before there was any other news of her, so I had no idea how or where Mary was.

A week later, Lin arrived back in Hong Kong from Swatow. Typhoon signals were out, so he wasted no time getting our boxes off the ship and into the I.C.I. godown, or warehouse. The typhoon struck at six that night. By morning we learned that no less than ten large seagoing vessels, including the ship Lin had arrived on, had gone to the bottom of Hong Kong harbor. The big Dutch vessel he'd been on had broken from her moorings, gone careening down the shoreline, and bashed into something. There was awful destruction.

It wasn't till we returned to Shanghai, a year later, that we found that the godown where we had stored our boxes had been under saltwater for a full week. Everything was ruined — everything, save one small box that happened to contain our photograph albums!

War and More

Two or three days after Lin arrived we got aboard the *Empress of Canada*, heading for Vancouver. When we arrived in Kobe, Japan, who should be waving at us from the dock but Mary! It turned out the *Hoover* had never made it to Shanghai. They'd had six direct hits, all the glass on board had been broken, and the ship had been diverted to Japan.

Mary told us she had applied for passage on a Japanese troop ship bound for Shanghai. No other ships were being allowed up the river. She was even more determined to join Neil there — and she did. But we didn't hear that till three months later in London, when they phoned us from Manila. Mary was then also able to give us news of Mother and Father, about whom we had had no word since we left. (Nor had they heard how we were.)

We landed in Vancouver, then hurried on by train to Rochester and the Mayo Clinic. I recall Dr. Willie Mayo asking to meet us, not because of any concern about my health but to question Lin about what the Japanese were up to in China.

Faced with the prospect of heavy medical expenses, I began to realize that for the first time in my life I could no longer take doctor and hospital care for granted. Our company health insurance covered only employees, not their families. Over the next few years, to meet these expenses, Lin had to sell all his company shares and everything else he could part with, including my own hard-earned nurse's savings. That hurt!

It took weeks to put me through all sorts of wearisome tests, for I wasn't well enough to endure them all at once. The final report showed no malignancy, but a condition even more stubborn to cope with. The dysentery amoeba had done such a thorough job of destroying the lining of my intestine and invading the whole of my alimentary track that they warned me it would probably take well nigh the rest of my life to regain the ability to digest and assimilate food. And how right they were. Not until years later, when I settled quietly in Stowe and stopped traveling around, did I begin to regain my health.

From Rochester we proceeded to London, where Lin was asked to stay on in I.C.I.'s London office for six months. We got a nice apartment on the Kensington High Street, and Lin was able to get around some and see his mother's family. A lot of time had passed and I'd had no word of Mother and Father, or Mary or my older sister Dor. Then all of a sudden, the telephone rang in the apartment. I answered and it was the overseas long-distance phone. They said there was a call for me from the Philippine Islands.

This was my very first long-distance call. I thought, "Well, it has to be Neil Starr" — but the call came through and it was Mary. We could hardly hear each other and we both burst into tears. She'd got into Shanghai and now she and Neil were in Manila, and that was fine and she'd had word from Mother and all. After, I picked up the phone to call Lin at the office, and I was so excited that I told him the whole story. Finally the voice at the other end stopped me long enough to say I wasn't talking to Lin at all, it was somebody else. But I finally did get to tell him.

I improved in England, I got a little stronger, and when Lin's tour of duty there ended in May 1938, it was time for us to return to Shanghai. But to escape the enervating Shanghai summer, Lin persuaded me to accept an invitation from my father's family to spend the summer with them on their lovely farm in Ontario, near Lake Huron. It was so beautiful there, and recalled for me many almost forgotten memories of when Mother had taken us children to spend a month there in the summer of 1909, just before going back to China for good.

On October 8, I sailed from Vancouver for Shanghai. The day after I arrived home, I was seized by acute abdominal pain. My doctor whisked me off to the hospital and removed an acute appendix. I was given a course of liver and iron injections to build up my flagging energy; at last my appetite improved, and I began to gain weight and feel more like my normal self. But during the summer of 1939 the international situation was rapidly worsening.

One day I looked out and the place was on fire

I was back home with this refugee camp outside the compound walls. From upstairs you could see all these little mat sheds, and all the people there collecting water morning and evening — and then one day I looked out and the place was on fire. All the mat sheds were in flames and I was terrified, but the fire brigade came and was able to put it out.

Gradually the refugee camp was built up again. I think it burned twice. The fire brigade used bamboo poles as troughs; they would cut them into halves and use them to tunnel water in.

On September 1, 1939, England declared war on Germany. Together with all other British military-age men, Lin was required to report to the British consulate for possible duty. Most of them were then told to go back to their jobs and remain there until·further notice. For the moment, it was most important to England that her trade routes be kept open as long as possible.

At this unlikely moment I found to my surprise and joy that I was pregnant. I was so elated that I forgot about wars and everything else.

Philip Lintilhac with two friends, Tientsin, 1946.
Right: Shanghai, 1949.
Both photos (and captions) by Claire.

PART 4

Wartime and a Changed World

1939 – 1950

That first wartime winter of 1939-40, Father and Mother gave up their house in Chefoo and came to live in Neil's lovely home in Huangqiao, a suburb of Shanghai. My sister Dor and her two boys, David and John, came too. Lin's mother, Dolly, went home to England, but his dad Chussie stayed on in Shanghai. No one knew what the future had in store for any of us.

Ever since 1937, all the China coast had been under Japanese military control. Little "incidents" were forever cropping up, making the atmosphere very tense. Lin had joined the Shanghai police as a volunteer and was frequently called up for riot patrol. With other police he patrolled the back streets of that nervous city in the backs of lorries, covered with vegetables as camouflage.

Spring of 1940 came, and in spite of wars and riots I was serenely happy at the thought of having my baby. It was supposed to be an elective cesarean birth, but in the middle of the night I found myself in labor. I called Lin and I said, "I'm having pains." And he said, "No, you're to have a cesarean, you're not supposed to have labor." And I said, "I know, but I am — quick, let's get cracking!"

On March 12, 1940, Philip was born. When the doctor told me I had a baby boy, I could hardly believe my ears. I could see Lin was having trouble believing it, too. Then the nurse came in with a little bundle and laid it in my arms.

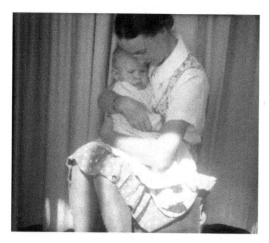

Claire and Philip.

It was hard to believe that this lovely baby, with a golden glow on his almost bald head and blue eyes wide open, was my very own. He had been spared the rough journey of blazing his own trail into the world so was feeling no distress, but instead was gazing around at his new world.

My next joy was being able to breast-feed my baby. I nursed him for three months and stopped then only because I came down with the flu and was very sick. From the beginning Dor came and took care of both Philip and me, as I had cared for her and all three of her babies. What a comfort and a blessing that was.

All that summer, with the war in Europe in full swing, the situation in Shanghai became more and more tense. For me it grew increasingly difficult to find milk powder for my baby. No sooner would I discover a new supply than Shanghai would run out of it. I changed the brand four or five times. Phil thrived on them all.

Crescent Avenue, the I.C.I. company compound, consisted of eleven homes and eleven gardens filled with lovely trees and flowers, all within a high surrounding wall. The avenue was a crescent-shaped, dead-end road. *Gno mei-yueh-lu* (Eyebrow-shape Moon Road) was its Chinese name. Originally this compound was on the outskirts of the settlement, but gradually the city had spread and grown up all around — so now the compound was in the middle of the vast city, and it was a veritable bird sanctuary. In the spring the air was filled with the exquisite songs of birds. Within this peaceful, quiet place it was hard to believe there was a war on. Watchmen were stationed at the gate round the clock.

Yuantasao, Mother's dear old amah, would come from time to time from Huangqiao to visit me. She thoroughly approved of my baby, especially as he was a boy, and presented him with a suit of traditional red satin embroidered in flowers of all colors. The suit had a jacket and long pants, the legs of which were attached only at the waistline in front, leaving each leg conveniently independent of the other. There was a little red satin hat to match.

But Yuantasao didn't approve of Ah-chin and Ah-sah, my amah and cook. Because she couldn't understand a word of their Swatow dialect, she always referred to them as *ya-bahs* (deaf mutes), and it was all I could do to keep her from showing her disapproval by being as nearly abrupt with them as she dared. She did grudgingly concede that they were very clean.

In South China where it was warm and water is plentiful, the people are accustomed to bathing frequently, in contrast to the dry cold north where water is hard to come by, and bathing is not so easily done.

Evacuation

One day in early March, the British Consulate suddenly announced that all British women and children were to be evacuated as soon as possible. This meant Philip and me! Where would I like to go, Lin asked. Where indeed? With no home anywhere in the world outside of China, where *could* I go?

To be faced with such a decision so unexpectedly was bewildering. When Lin suggested England, I suddenly realized I wasn't English and felt I wouldn't be at home there. But with Lin's salary in pounds sterling, where else could I afford to live?

Hurriedly I agreed with some of the other wives that California was less far away from China, and from husbands and homes, than most other places in the world. On the strength of that, it was decided that I would share a cottage with a friend in Laguna Beach. Lin was able to arrange with the company to allow me 200 U.S. dollars a month living allowance.

We cabled Mary and Neil Starr in New York City about this sudden move. When I told Ah-sah that Philip and I had to go away, he asked where we were going.

"America," I replied vaguely. I felt just as vague, for I hadn't the least idea what it was all going to mean.

"Who will cook for you?" asked Ah-sah.

"I will."

"But you don't know how to cook," he pointed out. How true.

He asked me to come right away to the kitchen so he could show me how to prepare a few things for Philip, who was just one year and two weeks old — and for me, too, for I was still far from well and on a very restricted diet. One of the things he showed me that day was how to make his very special bread pudding. To this day, "Ah-sah's Pudding" is still Philip's favorite dessert.

I hastily began to pack. There wasn't much time. Lin advised me not to take anything but absolute necessities. One important thing he did insist on was that I make a note of all our vital statistics. He listed for me his passport number and bank accounts, then gave me his insurance policies, telling me what to do about them. He also gave me all our birth and marriage certificates. At the time, I took this procedure for granted — but later during the war, when all mails were cut off, I heard so many wives say they didn't have any idea even what companies their husbands were insured with.

Claire and Phil on the unusually broad decks of the *Yawata Maru*.

After Pearl Harbor, the Japanese liner *Yawata Maru* was converted into an escort carrier, a smaller type of aircraft carrier.

Lin got leave to accompany me as far as Kobe, Japan. Three days later we boarded our ship, the *Yawata Maru*. We were still in port having lunch when a messenger rushed in and handed Lin a telegram. It was from Mary and Neil, urging me to come to New York and stay with them. I hadn't wanted to be a burden to them, as well as not wanting to be so far from home as the East Coast. When Lin got back to Shanghai a week later, he cabled Neil to that effect.

The *Yawata Maru* was a brand new Japanese luxury liner. She sported no less than three beautiful swimming pools, and the most enormous promenade decks I had ever seen. Shortly after Pearl Harbor I noticed a report in the New York Times that the *Yawata Maru* had been hurriedly converted into an aircraft carrier. So that explained it — she had been built as a carrier, and was only temporarily a passenger ship.

The trip across the Pacific was uneventful except that I was not well enough to leave my cabin very often. Philip's playpen was lashed to the bulkhead on the promenade deck, and each day one of the other I.C.I. wives would take him up there. They told me all sorts of people kindly helped to entertain him.

When we arrived in San Francisco, I didn't have the energy even to go up on deck to look at the famous Golden Gate Bridge. I stayed in my cabin and was giving Phil his bottle when who should appear in my doorway but Mary and Neil!

They had flown over to meet me, and they urged me to go back with them to New York, where I could get good medical care. I said I had made plans and felt I should at least give them a try. But I lasted only 11 days in Laguna Beach — I had no car and couldn't cope with the hills, and there was no telephone in the cottage. I then flew, gratefully, with Mary and Neil to New York.

As if by magic, we were suddenly in their lovely penthouse overlooking Central Park, and were greeted by their Chinese cook, Tzu Ah-ching, a welcome touch of home. To find myself under Mary's tender care lifted an enormous weight off my shoulders, and off my heart.

A Cottage Far from Home

In June 1941, after many weekends of exploring, Mary and Neil decided to buy the lovely home they named "Morefar," near Brewster, New York.

Toward the end of the month they moved there for the summer, taking Philip and me with them. After Labor Day, Mary and Neil moved back into the city. I had to decide whether to stay alone with Phil in Brewster for the winter or move into a small apartment in New York. I decided to stay. That was probably for the best, but oh, how lonely and homesick I was before that year was out.

Mother had remained in Victoria, B.C., hoping to return to Shanghai in the spring. Lin's sister, Marge Pouncey, was also refugeeing with her three children in Victoria, along with many other wives from Shanghai. One day in late September, Mary received a call from Marge saying that Mother was very ill. The doctor suspected widespread cancer.

Marge accompanied Mother to New York City, where the diagnosis was confirmed at the New York Hospital. With expert care and careful nourishment, Mother gained enough strength to leave the hospital and to live for the next six months with Philip and me in our little cottage at Morefar.

During that autumn I received long letters from Lin every week, saying he was counting the days till he could join us six months later. He and all the British civilians in Shanghai had gone to the consulate and offered their services, but they were told, "Go back to your jobs — we've got enough men to carry guns. It's more important at this point that England keep their trade routes open, so go back and carry on until we tell you otherwise."

Then on Sunday, December 7, 1941 — in Shanghai, it was Monday, December 8 — the whole world was staggered with the news that Japanese planes were bombing Pearl Harbor.

"Time Has Come"

Before Pearl Harbor there had been two schools of thought in Shanghai about what turn the war in the Pacific might take. Some reasoned that the Japanese had more sense than to antagonize the Western powers, and they were right as far as the Japanese government was concerned. But the powerful military clique in Japan had taken the reins into their own hands.

On Friday, December 5, Lin received a cable from the I.C.I. office in Hong Kong saying simply: "Time has come." This was the message arranged beforehand between the Shanghai and Hong Kong offices, signaling the moment to put into operation their emergency plans. What was about to happen Lin had no way of knowing, but without delay he went to the banks and withdrew in cash all available company funds, as well as all his own personal cash, and simply took it home.

When Pearl Harbor was bombed, it was early the next Monday morning in Shanghai — before any of the banks were open.

My nephew David Pearson, then just nineteen, was to have sailed from Shanghai for service in Singapore on December 9. Instead, all military-age men were interned, so he and his younger brother, John, were interned in Lungwha camp, where they remained till after VJ Day in late August 1945.

When Japanese officers came to Hong Kong on December 13, 1941, to seek the island's surrender, they brought two British women with them as hostages. One was Mavis Lee, whose husband was the Hong Kong governor's private secretary. She brought her two dachsunds, Otto and Mitzi. *Image courtesy of Historical Photographs of China, University of Bristol.*

Father was now eighty-one. As old people were not put into camp, my sister Dorothy was also left out, to take care of him in Shanghai. This turned out to be a questionable advantage to her, for food and all other necessities were increasingly hard to obtain. Also, she and Father were now at the mercy of groups of unruly Japanese soldiers who came thundering into the house at all hours of the day or night. They were in search of Father's wireless set, which he had, with foresight, already given away. But the soldiers refused to believe this and truculently ransacked the house several times in search of it, roughly pulling everything down and bayoneting the wood paneling.

By now Chiang Kai-shek, leader of the Nationalist government, had moved his capitol from Nanking to remote Chungking far up the Yangtze River. He was still preoccupied with challenges to his personal authority, posed by the many disenchanted factions within his own government. But Japan was on the move.

Suddenly the United States found herself committed not only to war in Europe but also to all-out war in the Pacific. There seemed no alternative but to commit to unconditional support of Chiang and his "reluctant" fight against Japan. To help control the vast quantities of money and war materials now being poured into Chungking, the U.S. government was looking for men with business experience in China who would be willing to go out to Chungking. Neil, with his 20 years of experience in Shanghai, offered his services.

But Mme. Chiang adamantly refused to consider the appointment of any "Old China Hands," insisting instead that she wanted "unbiased" men in this position. What she wanted were novices to China, men who would be less critical of the Nationalist government that was now so riddled with corruption and nepotism. So Neil's offer was turned down.

Chungking and Mme. Chiang

As a Wellesley College graduate and a professing Christian, Mme. Chiang (Soong Mei-ling) had become thoroughly Westernized and had a brilliant command of English. As her husband spoke no English, she became his official interpreter and on many occasions represented him in Washington. I recall in early 1943 hearing her speak in Madison Square Garden. Pleading for more aid to China, she held the whole place spellbound. Later during that same visit she spoke in Washington to the Senate. When she finished, the whole room rose, giving her a standing ovation.

From the beginning she had swayed public opinion about China in the United States. Her popularity gave her an overwhelming influence in both educational and government circles as well as on the press, and she had always maintained close relations with the influential missionary societies in the United States.

Chiang himself had never been to the United States. He had received much of his education and military training in Japan, and his only foreign language was Japanese. During his rise to political power in China, whenever things go too hot politically he would seek asylum in Japan, as did most of his government and family. Though Chiang had formally accepted Christianity, his government was not Christian.

Even so, the United States felt at last able to communicate with China's leaders who now, through Mme. Chiang, spoke a language the West could understand. But while this seemed desirable, it was also misleading, for the Chiangs' claim to Christianity blinded the West to the fact that they were first of all Chinese, the natural product of their own long history and culture.

So by 1942 in Chungking, Mme. Chiang held all the cards. Familiar as she was with Western ways, she refused to accept in Chungking anyone equally familiar with the intricacies of Chinese thinking. The story is long and all too familiar.

In the past, China had boasted that though she had been conquered many times by barbarians from the north, she had ultimately defeated her conquerors from within, systematically exposing them to the luxuries and indulgences of her rich and sophisticated court life. But what China failed to perceive was that this practice was to filter down through the whole fabric of her own society, eventually paralyzing it with decadence. Her proud culture became inextricably linked with a nightmare of corruption and misery.

In many ways this was the state of affairs in Chungking during World War II. "Court life" there was as fascinating to the unsuspecting Westerner as it had been in the past to the barbarian invaders from the north. Envoys from the U.S. who came on official business were immediately caught up in a web of intrigue, where the right hand was never permitted to know what the left hand was doing. These men regularly succumbed to Mme. Chiang's charm — for it was genuine, but also very subtle and sophisticated.

By now the only faction to survive Chiang's campaign of suppression was the hard-core Communist Party, living mostly in caves in Yenan. Toward the end of the war, Chiang's troops were defecting by the thousands to the Communists — not so much because of dedication to Communism as because they had suffered so much from hunger, disease and neglect at the hands of their own government. They had lost all faith in it.

Chiang Kai-shek and Mme. Chiang (Soong Mei-ling)
Image courtesy of C.H. Foo, Y.W. Foo and Historical Photographs of China, University of Bristol.

"He'll Be With You Soon"

I knew the attack on Pearl Harbor meant the end of any further communication with Shanghai. It also explained the very serious tone of Lin's more recent letters. Lin and his father had been interned by the Japanese in a camp for civilians called Pootung, in Shanghai. I didn't know what was going to happen to them now — or to my father, my sister and her two sons, all still in China. All my world.

The next four years the only news I got from Lin was six Red Cross forms, in his handwriting, saying always the same thing: that he and his dad were well and hoped that we were well. Those messages took so long to reach me, from seven to 15 months, that they were almost meaningless.

I often wished I had remained in Shanghai and been interned with Lin. But afterward, Lin told me he seriously doubted that, in my state of health, I would have survived those years of poor and meager prison-camp diet. When the war was over, there were instances of fathers who, after they were released from camp, died later from malnutrition. There were fathers in camp who denied themselves much of their own meager ration to provide a little extra for their families. That, at least, didn't happen to Lin.

That winter went reasonably quickly, for I was busy taking care of Mother and Philip, who was not yet two, in the cottage at Morefar. By the spring of 1942, Mother was getting noticeably weaker. She had a couple of serious blackouts. In April she had a third setback and was taken to hospital. She kept asking for word from Father, who was still in Shanghai with Dor — but there was no word. No word. Toward the end I said to Mary, "We can't let her die without any word from Father, we just can't. We've got to tell her there's a message."

Claire with her mother and father, before the war.

So we braced ourselves and went in. Mother asked if there was any word, and we said, "Yes, we've got good news for you, a message from Father telling you that he's thinking of you and that he's going to come home as soon as he can. He'll be with you soon."

We were waiting for some awkward questions. But she just said, "Oh thank goodness for that."

A couple of days later, on May 21, 1942, little Mother died. She is buried in the small Milltown Cemetery near Morefar.

Pootung: Lin's Internment Camp

Some 13,500 foreigners caught in China by World War II were held by the Japanese in civilian internment camps. About a dozen of those camps were set up in Shanghai — including Pootung camp, where Lin Lintilhac and his father Chussie where interned.

Pootung's British, American and Dutch detainees, all of them male, were housed in a rundown, three-story industrial building, just across the Huangpu River from the International Settlement. The British American Tobacco Company had built the structure in 1901 as a factory, later converted it to a warehouse, and then abandoned it, as too deteriorated for use, in 1931.

Riddled with bedbugs and infested with rats, "the cavernous rooms were dank, filthy and filled with an almost unbearable stench," writes Greg Leck in his 2006 book *Captives of Empire: The Japanese Internment of Allied Civilians in China.*

"Food supplies were notoriously bad," Leck writes, "and it was only International Red Cross parcels, and parcels sent by Chinese or non-interned neutrals, that allowed many to survive the war. The official daily Japanese ration was down to only 300 calories by June 1945."

The detainees built hot-water boilers from old steel drums, and next to the old warehouse they cleared the rubble of a Chinese village, destroyed in the 1937 battle, to create gardens and sports grounds. Climbing to the upper floors of the warehouse, they could look across at the Bund, Garden Bridge and Broadway Mansions, all landmarks of the old International Settlement.

On August 5, 1945, an American C-46 transport plane flew over Pootung, "causing the camp to go wild with excitement," Leck writes. Ten days later, on what became known as V-J Day, the Japanese Empire surrendered to Allied forces aboard the U.S. battleship *Missouri* in Tokyo Bay.

At Pootung camp, a detainee tends the fires beneath four steel drums the prisoners fashioned into hot-water boilers. Photo from *Captives of Empire*, courtesy of author Greg Leck.

Amazed at the Dump

Some of my first impressions of Morefar still linger. The ground, even the dirt, seemed clean to me compared with China, where all fertilizing was done with the ubiquitous night soil, or human waste. One rarely dared to sit on the ground there, or even walk barefoot on the grass. But I suppose the greatest luxury of all was the beautiful clear, pure, cold water that came straight from the tap at Morefar. No boiling was necessary. I could hardly believe it.

Here I am reminded of a visit from a young friend one day here in Stowe. She had been skiing. When I opened the door and invited her in, she announced that there were five other friends in the car and would it be all right if they came in too? Of course.

They were nice young people, finished college and all now working in New York. During the course of conversation, one of the young men was holding forth about his experience in communal living. He related with amusement the novelty of having been bitten by a flea. I couldn't resist interrupting the conversation to describe how, at their age, one of my constant concerns was the omnipresent threat of being bitten by fleas, well-known carriers of the dread bubonic plague and typhus fever (not to be confused with typhoid, an intestinal disease).

There seemed to be enough discarded material here to build a whole village

I pointed out that, thanks to their forebears, whom they had been criticizing, this land had been rid of the devastating diseases that used to take such a heavy toll of lives — and still do, especially in Asia. Today in the United States even doctors have never seen these diseases; they only read about them in their textbooks.

I begged them not to be so ready to blame their elders for what they hadn't done, but instead to recognize the great advances in health and hygiene they had wrought, all without the benefit of miracle drugs and today's wondrous technology.

At Morefar, one of the places that was a continual source of amazement to me was the dump. I would go stare at it with unbelieving eyes, for there seemed to be enough discarded material here to build a whole village. And it was all going to be burned! Bales of unused fence wire; great demijohn bottles, worth a fortune in the world I came from. A whole bathtub, with four old-fashioned legs! I could understand that it was no longer wanted in a newly furnished house, but surely *someone* could use it.

There were also the beautiful cartons and crates that the new furniture had come in. I couldn't help thinking of all the poor refugees in Shanghai whose homes were made of less. This brings to my mind another story that the chairman of the Shanghai Municipal Council used to tell on himself.

He had ordered for the city, at great cost to the community, a huge new incinerator.

It arrived and was installed. Then he discovered that by the time the refuse reached the incinerator, it had been so picked over by Shanghai's poor that there was literally nothing left to incinerate. All that remained were clinkers and bits of iron and stone.

A Dislocated World

The years that followed are a blur of memories. It bothered me that in the lap of luxury I would sometimes become so depressed. What was worse, all this time I never heard from Lin. I knew neither what was happening to him nor what was to become of Phil and me. I would get these Red Cross messages, but the very fastest was seven months old when I got it, and it was just 25 words and I could only reply by writing on the back of that message. That was their way of verifying that whoever was replying was a relative of the prisoner.

When I finally got back to Shanghai, the Red Cross messages still kept coming in, ones that I had never received. I had sent Red Cross packages to Lin in camp — and other prisoners got Red Cross packages, but he never got any. Not one. After we got to Shanghai, they started to come to us. They were all mildewed and falling apart.

Everyone we knew in those days was more or less displaced. The war in Europe and now in the Pacific had dislocated the whole world. Everyone had money problems, and many of our friends came to Mary and Neil for both advice and financial help. They were unstinting and untiring in their efforts to ease the problems of others.

Mary and Neil would come out to Morefar every weekend and bring a retinue of Philippine chauffeurs and Chinese cooks and everything. On Mondays they would all go back to the city, and their chief cook would bring me a tray full of wonderful food

he had cooked that they hadn't finished eating. He knew I didn't know how to cook. But I was trying to learn!

By the winter of 1942-43, I had got to know our neighbors in Brewster. The men were away on war assignments, but their wives and families were there, and at their invitation I would take Philip to play with their children while I visited with the all-too-busy mothers. I recall how curious I was to watch how they lived.

I had never before seen a home

operate without servants, and was fascinated to see how these young women managed to take care of their children and at the same time do all the cooking and housework. It didn't take me long to catch on, but I had the drawback of still not being well, so I often got overtired and depressed. Even now, the effort of trying to recall those days casts a gloom over me.

One day in autumn 1943, the telephone rang. A man's voice said "Mrs. Claire Lintilhac?"

"Yes," I said.

"Do you know anybody by the name of Dr. William Malcolm?"

"Yes, he's my father."

"Do you know anybody by the name of Mrs. Dorothy Pearson?"

"Yes, that's my sister. Why?"

"Well, they're on the SS *Gripsholm*."

They asked me a few questions, and I said, "Who's asking me these questions, who am I talking to?"

"It's the FBI." They were confirming that Father and Dor did have what they claimed they had, somebody in New York who could support them. The *Gripsholm* was scheduled to arrive soon in New York, bringing exchange prisoners of war from Japan and China — and Father and Dor were among those on board.

They had embarked from Shanghai on a Japanese ship, which took them as far as Lourenco Marques [Maputo, Mozambique] on the east coast of Africa, where they were exchanged for Japanese prisoners from the U.S. There they were transferred to the *Gripsholm*.

When the bus arrived we banged on the window

The *Gripsholm* finally arrived in New York, but Dor and Father weren't allowed to come ashore in New York. They were both Canadian so they were bonded through, all the way to Montreal.

We went down when the *Gripsholm* was arriving. Someone had tipped off Mary and me that the bonded-through passengers were being taken off the boat and put on a bus, to go straight up to Canada. We found a narrow place in a ramp where the bus had to stop and move backward and forward, to make an elbow turn. Mary and I posted ourselves there, and when the bus arrived we banged on the window.

Father looked out and he burst into tears. Dor said, "It's Claire, and it's Mary!"

We said, "We'll come get you! We'll come get you in Montreal."

Well, eventually, Neil did that. Neil did so many wonderful things for so many people. Mary and Neil rented an apartment for them in New York City. I moved in from Brewster with Philip and set up housekeeping, to be there when they arrived. It turned out they had been at sea for 68 days. Dor had been seized with appendicitis; in the ship's infirmary, they operated and removed her appendix.

The World-Bridging Life of Neil Starr

Cornelius Vander Starr, better known as C.V. or Neil Starr, married Claire's younger sister Mary in 1937, in the midst of a pioneering international business career. Based for many years in Shanghai, Starr built one of the first truly multinational corporations — and in World War II, he co-founded the U.S. government's ultra-secret Insurance Intelligence Unit, which used insurance industry expertise and behind-the-lines representatives to gather information about the Axis Powers.

"He was born American — the kind of man who wonders how to make elephants bigger and better," wrote John Ahlers, a correspondent for *The Economist*.

The son of a railroad engineer in California who died when he was two, Starr quit college to open an ice-cream parlor, and soon saw great potential in the insurance business. After serving in World War I he sailed for Japan and then Shanghai, where in 1919 he organized American Asiatic Underwriters, Inc. "He broke tradition by making life insurance policies available to the Chinese and giving them responsible positions," wrote *The New York Times*.

Starr also developed the English-language *Shanghai Evening Post and Mercury*, in whose pages he strongly criticized Japan's expansionist efforts of the 1930s. The year he married Mary, the Japanese attacked Shanghai; in 1939, the Post's offices were bombed, its editor was assassinated, and Starr took to traveling in a bulletproof limousine. During the war he moved AAU's offices to Hong Kong, expanded his insurance operations into South America, and joined "Wild Bill" Donovan, founder and head of the U.S. Office of Strategic Services, precursor to the CIA, in creating the Insurance Intelligence Unit.

"They knew which factories to burn, which bridges to blow up, which cargo ships could be sunk in good conscience," wrote the *Los Angeles Times* in 2000, after declassified files revealed the existence of the long-secret unit. As Claire relates, Neil and Mary were also untiring in their efforts to help hundreds of friends, relatives and employees of the Starr companies cope with the dangers and stresses of the war years.

After V-J Day, Starr returned to Shanghai, then left again following the Communist takeover of China. His insurance companies grew throughout the 50s in Asia, South America, Western Europe and the U.S. In 1968, the year he died, most of the many companies he had built were incorporated as the American Insurance Group, or AIG.

Mary and Neil's marriage ended in 1952. Mary then pursued her passion for art, became a painter, and lived the rest of her life in Paris.

Neil Starr, Phil Lintilhac, and Mary Malcolm Starr at Morefar during the war.

Surviving the Camp

In New York toward the end of the war, Neil came to me one day with a proposition. "I think I could get Lin out of camp," he said.

"What?"

"I think I can get him out of camp."

"How?"

"Bribe the Japanese sentries," he said. "It might take a million dollars but I think I can do it. I would have to have a letter to Lin from you, not signed but clearly in your handwriting, that could be taken into camp and given to Lin, saying, 'Follow me. Trust the bearer.' That sort of thing."

It was a terrible decision for me to have to make. There had been lots of escapes from different camps, but there'd never been an escape from Pootung. They called it the "bull-pen," an all-male camp.

I detected a note of uncertainty in Neil's voice. I knew how much he was given to over-enthusiasm when stimulated by a difficult challenge. Also, I knew Lin's dad was in camp with him, and I had no way of knowing whether Lin would be willing to leave him behind.

"I think he will," Neil said. "I think he'll feel strongly enough about his right to escape and to join his family that he will, if we can organize it."

There were many other considerations. I had no way of knowing how well Lin was. Also, Shanghai was the very hub of the Japanese occupation, and far from Chungking and freedom. I finally declined Neil's offer, but my decision cost me many sleepless nights.

After Lin got out, he told me that with two other Britishers in camp he had indeed been making plans to escape. Of the three, Lin was the only one who spoke Chinese. Their plans had gone along well, for all three had good connections in the city; but when zero hour came, their contact on the outside failed to turn up. During all those years there was never an escape from that camp. The Japanese were well-entrenched around Shanghai.

Later when I heard about the atrocities in Manila and Hong Kong after the Japanese took these places, my heart trembled. But as it turned out, Pootung camp was liberated without incident, and Lin and his dad were both safe and well.

The food there had been awful. Lin worked in the kitchen — he said the lowest point was one cup of boiling water at breakfast, half a beet root at lunch and a cup of very thin rice gruel for supper. The rice they got was full of the sweepings from the bottoms of the rice barges; the men who transported it would put in fine-ground white stones to make it weigh more. These would break the prisoners' teeth. Lin had one broken tooth, and lost another after he left camp.

Oh, the stories Lin told about camp. They had rigged up a radio receiving set, and they would get the news from London and then very carefully pass it along. Everyone longed for news. Then one night, the Japanese sentry came in; he went straight to the bed where this radio receiver set was, and confiscated it. It's hard for that many people to keep secrets. After that, the men rigged up another set. But this time they didn't pass the news on, because they didn't want the set confiscated.

Both before and after his internment, Lin was in charge of all arrangements for the welfare of company personnel. The Japanese military took over our compound at Crescent Avenue, and occupied our homes there for the duration of the war. So on V.J. Day, September 2, 1945, without waiting for any formalities, Lin hastened out to Crescent Ave. With the help of four other I.C.I. men from camp, they claimed possession and took up residence in the compound, heading off otherwise inevitable looting.

To Lin's surprise and delight, he found that old Chao, our houseboy, and Yin, our gardener, were still there. They had remained in the employ of the Japanese throughout the war. It was thanks entirely to them that we were able to locate and eventually recover quite a few of our household belongings.

At the time of Japan's sudden capitulation, Shanghai was surrounded by Chinese Communist troops. But the Japanese commanders there were given orders not to surrender to any other than Chinese Nationalist troops. So it wasn't until six long weeks later, when U.S. planes air-lifted Nationalist troops into Shanghai, that the Japanese were able to formally hand over the control of the city.

During that interval the Japanese army of occupation, consisting of mostly very young men, stood point duty throughout that hostile city, maintaining order and preventing looting. Lin was impressed by the discipline among those young Japanese soldiers, for he often saw them being kicked, slapped in the face and spat on, with their fixed bayonets. They never even flinched.

American and British warships moored on the Huangpu River in October 1945, after the Japanese surrender in August. Behind the ships is the warehouse district of Pootung, where Lin and other civilians were held in a wartime internment camp. The vessel at center is the USS *Nashville*; to its right is the USS *Rocky Mount*, and just beyond that is the British ship HMS *Belfast*.
Image courtesy of Dave Evans and Historical Photographs of China, University of Bristol.

"I Wasn't Free to Tell Them"

I forget the exact date, for my heart was trembling a lot in those days, but Neil was just about the first civilian to get into Shanghai after V.J. Day. When he left to return to the United States, he persuaded Lin to leave with him, getting out on U.S. Army planes to Manila and from there to New York.

It was during this trip that Neil first began trying to persuade Lin to join his organization, the Starr Companies. But Lin had a good job with Imperial Chemical Industries; he had got a number of promotions just before and after the war, based on his performance not only in handling office affairs under difficult conditions, but also in coping with the Japanese military and managing the nervous circumstances of company personnel before and after internment.

Lin and Neil arrived in New York in early December. The Washington office called me to say they were expected to arrive there from San Francisco late in the day, but that all planes out of Washington to New York were full. At 10 p.m. the office called again to say they still hadn't arrived. They suggested Mary and I go to bed and rest, for at the very earliest, Lin and Neil would arrive on the 9:30 train the next morning.

Mary went back to her apartment and I went to bed. Philip was in his own room adjoining mine. At three o'clock something wakened me.

Motionless, I listened. Then I heard the door of my room slowly opening and Lin's voice in a whisper calling my name! After five years we met again — but it was so dark we couldn't even see each other.

Soon after arriving, Neil arranged a small dinner party at the St. Regis Hotel in New York for Henry Luce, William Bullitt (former ambassador to the USSR and France), Mary and himself, and Lin and me. The idea was for Luce and Bullitt to get firsthand news of conditions in Shanghai, for Lin was one of the first civilians to get out. It was a pleasant evening and many penetrating questions were put to Lin. But when we got back to the apartment I asked why he hadn't mentioned some of the things he had hinted at to me.

I had never suspected this

"Lin," I said, "why didn't you tell them this and why didn't you tell them that?"

"Well, I wasn't free to tell them," he said. "I haven't told you because I didn't want you to worry, but I've been working with British Intelligence." He'd been with them since before Pearl Harbor.

I had never suspected this. Better still, the Japanese didn't suspect it. Had they known, instead of being a civilian internee, Lin would have been locked up in the infamous Bridge House, Shanghai's political prison, where prisoners were regularly tortured to extract information.

Neil and Mary made plans for the whole family to spend the holidays together in Stowe, Vermont. Right after Christmas, Lin left for London to report to I.C.I. and to

British Intelligence. While he was away, darling Father, now age 85, died following a stroke on February 19, 1946. He is buried beside Mother in the Milltown Cemetery.

Early in March, Lin rejoined us in New York. While in England he had had a return of the severe jaundice that he had contracted in camp. For the next few weeks he was very ill, and was still not well enough to be given the required innoculations before setting out on our return trip to Shanghai.

On April 6, 1946, we drove to Galveston, Texas, where we picked up our boat to return to Shanghai. The SS *Dr. Lykes* was a new cargo ship that carried only 11 passengers. Phil had a cabin to himself adjoining ours, which was just next to the dining saloon where we joined the ship's officers at meals. The trip took five weeks and was peaceful and relaxed, giving Lin a much-needed opportunity to convalesce.

Return to Shanghai, Overwhelmed

We had to lie at anchor for three days in the mouth of the Yangtze and Huangpu rivers to wait our turn for a ship's berth at Shanghai, fourteen miles upriver from the sea.

I'll never forget when we stepped ashore again at Shanghai. I looked around and said to Lin, "What's going on?"

"What do you mean?"

"All these people milling around," I said. "There must be a demonstration or something."

Lin laughed and said, "No, it's always been like this. You've been out of this country for the first time in your life, and you're seeing this with new eyes." Lin had been behind barbed wire all that time, so to him it looked pretty good.

But it was absolute chaos. After all those years of war and deprivation — ten years of war with Japan, and 20 years of civil wars before that — Shanghai was in an appalling state of delapidation and squalor. Everything was filthy, and so was everybody. As we drove through the streets to our compound on the far side of the city, my heart grew heavier and heavier at the awful confusion everywhere.

The city was overflowing with three million refugees from the surrounding countryside. Walking along the streets past one-room open-front shops, one could see, beginning about halfway back in each room, a sort of platform suspended about four feet from the ceiling. These were sleeping areas, little more than crawl spaces, teeming with women and children and crying babies.

People were living in doorways and on the streets, with nowhere to go, nothing to do and nothing to eat. Many were begging or, worse still, were too weak to beg. Later I read in the daily paper that the sanitation department claimed to be picking up as many as 600 bodies from the streets every morning, and carting them off to the incinerator.

I recall one day shopping with Lin at Wing On, Shanghai's largest department store.

As we left by the rear entrance, out from a roll of matting and rags emerged a woman. Beside her in this roll of matting was the body of her husband. With hopeless despair on her face, she was gently shaking him and calling to him, even though she knew he was dead.

That first day when we arrived at our home, I walked into the ground floor where the kitchen and pantries were and the servants' quarters, and found the floor covered with half an inch of smelly black water. Shanghai was so full of refugees that the public utilities couldn't cope with the demand, so the drains had backfired. The sewers all over the city were overflowing into the streets and into the houses, and the houses were full of rats that had been flushed out of the sewers.

I burst into tears. What to do? I got a cat, but the poor thing was petrified of the rats. It climbed onto the highest perch it could find and wouldn't come down even to eat. I went upstairs and looked outside: the refugee camp was still there. They were still making that eternal trek, out to the main roads to get their water at eight o'clock in the morning and five o'clock in the afternoon. But they had organized themselves; they had little industries going on, and they had electric light in there now.

I had no kitchen equipment, and the streets were lined with camp beds covered with U.S. military PX supplies from the war — so I went out there and bought spoons, knives and forks, all marked USN for U.S. Navy. I still have them. You could buy anything on the black market: clothes, equipment, food of any kind, all straight out of the American PX. Shanghai was just flooded with all that.

It was now May. We were in Shanghai for that long hot summer. After going for a swim just once in the French Club's lovely pool, Phil picked up an acute eye infection. He was very sick with a temperature of 105° for days. The hospital put us in touch with a splendid eye specialist, a German Jewish refugee. At first he thought the infection was trachoma. It turned out not to be, but it was almost as serious and the treatment every bit as drastic.

During the rainy season in July the whole city, including our compound, was flooded with unbelievably dirty water from all around. The water was too deep for the cars, so Lin and the other men had to be taken to and from the office in trucks that were high enough to negotiate the flooded streets all the way to the Bund.

Washing clothes at the hydrant outside the I.C.I. compound, 1946.

Embroidered Holes

Rats seemed to be everywhere. They even ate holes in my table linen, presumably around spots where something had been spilled. All foodstuffs had to be put into tins and bottles, and those were hard to come by in threadbare postwar Shanghai.

One night I woke with a shudder, insisting I had felt the whiskers of a rat on my face. Typically male, Lin pooh-poohed this, saying it served me right for putting cream on my face before going to bed. The next night I felt the same thing.

Jumping up, I threw the bedding back; I distinctly heard a thud, then a scuttling on the bare floor. Lin said I had been thinking too much about rats, to just forget about them and go to sleep.

Two night later, his bellow wakened me. "The damn thing has bitten me!" he shouted. When I turned on the light, Lin was sitting up in bed, blood running from one of his ears all over the white sheet. I would say the joke was on him, but it's no joke to be bitten by a rat.

The next evening as I opened the door into the bathroom, a gray streak flashed across my foot into the bedroom. Quickly shutting all doors, I shouted for Lin and Chao and Phil and amah and coolie and everybody to come. Even Sally, the dog, joined in the hue and cry. We began by pulling all the furniture away from the walls. Then with brooms and rolls of paper, we gave chase to the terrified rat. Finally the cook got it with one mighty swat.

I still have one of the tablecloths that the rats ate holes in. Lee Ta-sao, the amah, skillfully embroidered over the small holes and stitched lace medallions over the larger ones. Today one would scarcely suspect the reason for the random embroidery.

Yin, our gardener, had worked at the compound for the Japanese during the war. His wife was sick, and I arranged for her to have a checkup, which led to a hysterectomy. I then brought her home to the little house where they lived, just beside our compound. She and Yin had four or five other children, all different ages.

I said to Yin, "Wasn't your wife expecting a baby when I left to go home before the war? That baby should be about five or six years old now, shouldn't it?" (I have told this story earlier, I know, but I can't help repeating it here.)

He looked defeated. He said, "Well, T'ai-t'ai, after you left and before the Japanese moved in, I didn't have any work. I didn't have a job and there was no money coming in, and my wife had another baby. We didn't have enough food to feed the mouths we already had — and when the new baby came, my wife nursed it as long as she had milk. Then when she had no more milk, we didn't have anything to feed it.

Yin, 1946.

"So, T'ai-t'ai," he said, "I had to sell that little girl. But I found a good home for it."
I said, "I understand, Yin. Those were hard years for you."

Back to Tientsin

In November we were transferred to Tientsin, a three-day boat trip up the coast from Shanghai. North China was home to me; and drab as it was to look at, I had always loved Tientsin. For one thing, the dialect there was the one I grew up with and spoke.

Soon after we arrived, Phil came down with whooping cough, so he couldn't go to school. But just next door were two little Chinese boys the same age, sons of the next-door cook. They were immune, as both had had whooping cough — so for his six weeks of quarantine, Phil played exclusively with those two children. At the end of that time he came to me, puzzled, and asked, "Mommy, who taught me how to speak Chinese?" I said, "Well, Phil, your two little pals did."

I asked the servants to speak only Chinese to Philip, so he would learn. He got really a quite nice vocabulary, and was able to express himself and understand what was going on.

Tientsin at this time was still full of U.S. occupation troops. The foreign residents were nearly all old friends, most of whom had been interned in Weishien camp during the war. As in Shanghai, the main streets of the British Concession were lined with a thriving black market, mostly of U.S. Army PX supplies.

But what preoccupied me most at this time was the delicate business of bringing Lin and Philip closer together. They had accepted each other but didn't really know each other. I discussed it freely with Lin, of course, but felt a subtle responsibility that I kept to myself. I even discussed it with Phil on occasion, and he was as understanding as a seven-year-old could be expected to be. On the whole I felt it was really harder for Lin than it was for Phil.

Lin was all too aware of the wide gap between him and Phil, and gave a lot of serious thought to it. He showed Phil how to handle

Lin and Phil, skating in Tientsin.

his small gun, and took him into the country to shoot duck. They bicycled together, and when winter set in, we took a picnic lunch on most weekdays to the club's splendid skating rink. Though the weather was cold, the skies were cloudless and the sun shone bright and warm. But the political scene was everywhere tense, and the future uncertain.

By the spring of 1948, a barbed-wire fence topped by an electric wire was thrown up around the British Concession, not so much to protect foreigners as to safeguard Chinese government officials, most of whom had homes within the concession. Their fear was of the rumored approach of the *Balu-Jun*, the Communist Eighth Route Army.

Between Tientsin and Peking the railroad bridges were constantly being blown up. On our visits to Peking, the train would crawl slowly across creaking, temporary bridges. I found myself holding my breath till we reached the other side. But it didn't stop us from making these trips.

Our personal lives and activities were circumscribed during these times, but not actually threatened. Yet there was a strong undercurrent of anti-foreign feeling in the air.

Old Man on an Island

A rash of strange pedicab crimes took place about this time, and they always happened to army enlisted men. Maybe this was because the enlisted man carried money on his person. Officers also used pedicabs, as we all did, but officers had the privilege of signing personal "chits" wherever they went.

Pedicabs at this time were makeshift vehicles and were forever being put to too-heavy duty, so it was not uncommon for the gear chain to slip off the wheel at the back. When this happened, the puller would dismount from his bicycle in front, go around to the back of the cab, slip the chain back on, then return to his bicycle.

I never thought anything of it until it was reported that numbers of enlisted men were being found by the side of the road, having been knocked unconscious by a blow on the back of the head.

Eventually one of the victims was able to describe what had happened to him. It turned out that the puller, when he went to the back of the cab, dealt a knockout blow with a heavy instrument to his unsuspecting passenger, then robbed and dumped him by the side of the road. After this, enlisted men were given the privilege of signing chits, too.

We used to have these picnics, out along the moat that surrounded the city, and there was an old man out there. He lived on a tiny mud island, no more than a dozen feet square, in the middle of the moat. I asked him, "Why are you in a little crawl-in mat shed like that?" It was weighted down with a rope that had bricks tied to either end, to keep the mat shed from blowing away. I said, "Haven't you got any sons to take care of you?"

He said, "I have had three sons."

I said, "Where are they?"

"They've all died."

"What did they die of?"

"Just died," said he. "I have nobody to take care of me."

This was why it was so important for Chinese to have sons. Daughters married and went to their husbands' homes, but sons stayed with their parents and brought their wives into their homes, and this was the parents' guarantee for old-age security.

The old man said, "People give me one bowl of noodles a day to live here and watch their fish traps." They were bamboo traps, and he would watch these traps and see that nobody took the fish away. Every day, the owners would come take their catch and give this old man a bowl of noodles. He was just skin and bones. We would give him our leftover sandwiches, or anything else we had. We used to make a thing of taking him all sorts of things.

Philip, right, with Tientsin friend and the old man of the moat.

A Rising Storm

In April 1948, Lin received word that he had been made an I.C.I. company director. This meant being transferred back to the head office in Shanghai. My most vivid recollection of leaving North China that July was our flight out of Peking.

We took off and started to climb. As we climbed, the pilot circled around a couple of times, giving us a dramatic view of the whole city, walls within walls within walls, directly below. There was the mysterious Forbidden City, with its Imperial-yellow tiled roofs. To the south, still within the Tartar City, could be seen the azure blue tiles of the lovely Temple of Heaven, and nearby the pure white marble Altar of Heaven.

The family at a gate to the Forbidden City, Peking, 1948.

As we climbed still higher, there was the feeling of an approaching sandstorm in the air. It was just bone dry, and a great yellow cloud could be seen rolling in from the direction of the Gobi Desert, just northwest of Peking. Suddenly the view of the city below was blotted from sight. We continued climbing into the clear blue sky — and from this height, we could see the whole dramatic outline of the storm.

Thick yellow swirls swept in one after the other, like ostrich plumes, then curled up and up till they reached just below the plane. Here, suspended motionless for a moment, they turned and, like Roman candles, slowly began to descend on the city, shrouding it in the fine yellow powder that is the despair of all homemakers there. No wonder such storms are called dragons; this one looked just like a dragon, whisking its many tails.

At Home, for Now

All during the war the Japanese had used our compound of 11 homes and gardens as residences. The only alteration they made was to convert the master bedroom in each house into a Japanese-style room. The floors were fitted with the lovely four-inch thick *tatami*, felt-lined matting that the floors of all traditional Japanese homes are furnished with. They sit on this soft floor, needing no furniture save a low table at which they both work and eat.

Along one wall in each of these rooms was built in a Japanese closet with sliding doors and shelves, where their bedding is rolled up and put away during the day. At night, for sleep, the bedding is spread out on the floor. So when we moved back into our house, the first thing we had to do was to have the closets and tatami removed. It was great fun redecorating our new home with fresh curtains everywhere, then laying down some beautiful rugs we had bought in Peking. Lin especially appreciated this, for he had spent all those years living with 160 other men in a barren warehouse behind barbed wire.

We weren't planning to leave unless forced to

We had been settled exactly four months when we had to accept that the approach of the Communist forces would sooner or later mean yet another uprooting. How and where to, we couldn't yet foresee; we weren't planning to leave unless forced to. In the meantime, Lin's job was here.

It so happened that our periodic home leave was coming. It was due in April 1950. There was always the possibility that we might have to leave in a hurry before that, perhaps with only what we could carry. We decided to pack a couple of boxes with irreplaceable things, such as photograph albums and other treasures, but mainly with some suitable clothes for hot Hong Kong and cold England. We needed so little these days in Shanghai. The city had been so elegant in days gone by — the Paris of the East, she had been called.

When the boxes were finally packed and ready to go, we shipped them to Hong Kong, where they could be stored till we knew better what the future held for us. It so happened that a year and a half later, we did have to leave in a hurry. At that point, the Communists forbade any photographs or printed matter to leave the country. Not a letter, not a snapshot was allowed to be taken out. We had been lucky.

The Foreign "Y" (YMCA) in Shanghai, just across from the Race Course Bubbling Well Road, was an American institution, managed by a paid American secretary. But it was considered desirable, to give it an international flavor, that its Board of Trustees be composed of men of different nationalities. An I.C.I. man on the board was heading off on home leave, and Lin was asked to take his place as the British member. It was just an honorary position — but when our home leave fell due, Lin was to regret this appointment.

Crossing to Blue Water

The autumns in Shanghai are beautiful, lasting well into December, and 1949 was no exception. We went for lovely walks in the country and picnics along the Soochow Creek, and up the Huangpu to Minghong. This was so full of memories for Lin. His Dad, Chussie, had served as Commodore of the Shanghai Yacht Club, and it was here at Minghong that Chussie moored his beloved Sister Ann, a schooner he himself had had built.

Every Friday evening after office, with family and friends on board, Chussie and his crew of three Chinese sailors would sail the 14 miles down the crowded, muddy Huangpu, past Woosung at the mouth of the river where it joins the even muddier Yangtze River delta. They sailed on out till they reached blue water. That was always their goal.

As a girl, when I'd travel home to Chefoo from Shanghai on different vessels, the high spot was always the excitement of crossing this sharp dividing line, where the muddy river water collided with the blue salt water of the ocean. That dramatic line was always there. Not until we crossed over it into the deep blue of the ocean did I feel I was really on my way home.

Useless Money

With Japan now defeated, Chiang Kai-shek had a golden opportunity to pull his country together and restore the confidence of the people in their government, with the full support of the U.S. and recognition by the other Western powers and the Soviet Union. Instead, by 1948 he had abused this opportunity and forfeited what little confidence there was left. The cost of living was skyrocketing.

Three separate times he betrayed the value of the national currency. The first was when he called in all the U.S. dollars that had flooded the economy, the result of generous funding from UNRRA [the United Nations Relief and Rehabilitation Administration, of 1943-47], the Red Cross and all kinds of American war aid. His government promised to issue value-for-value in Chinese paper money for the greenbacks; but after it did, the value of the paper money went down, down and down.

It's terrifying for people on local salaries to have your pay halved overnight. People who were working for foreign firms were lucky; my husband's salary was put on a cost-of-living allowance, and three years later his cost-of-living allowance was five times his salary.

At the end of that year the Chinese currency was valueless, and Chiang demanded that people surrender all their gold. The Chinese tended to hoard things like gold, because it was their only security. They didn't bank very much, as such, and really there was no point in banking money because it devalued anyway. So Chiang called in the gold — gold bars, gold money, gold anything. This was compulsory. People traded in their gold for Chinese currency, which Chiang again promised to stabilize. Another year and the paper money was absolutely valueless.

The third time, Chiang called in all the silver — silver dollars, silver 50 cent pieces, and everything else. This just demoralized people, for it was taking away their last faint hope of any kind of security. Again he issued soon-to-be-useless paper money. Little did the people know their leader was getting ready to abandon them and flee to the island of Taiwan.

By now the streets were actually littered with this useless money being trampled underfoot. I saw even destitute beggars looking, then not bothering to pick it up. It was no longer possible to carry enough paper money to pay for even one day's groceries. By now Lin's cost-of-living allowance had been increased to six times his salary.

One Sunday when Phil was getting ready for church, he said to me, "Mommy, don't forget to give me my Sunday School collection."

I asked Lin how much I should give him. Lin suggested 10,000 dollars, and handed Phil a note for that amount. The following Sunday when Phil again asked for his collection, I gave him another 10,000 dollar note. Looking at it for a moment, Phil exclaimed, "But this can't be half enough! You gave me 10,000 dollars last Sunday."

I gave him another 10,000 dollar note. He thanked me, murmuring something about not being able to understand Chinese money. I said, "Well, you and all the rest of us, Philip."

In spite of all these conditions, somehow Shanghai was home and it was lovely to be home. But the people were, not so much hostile, as resentful toward foreigners — and by the autumn of 1948, the Chinese Communists were beginning to close in.

Street vendors, Peking.

A Bowl of Flies

One day Philip and I were walking along YuYuen Road when a passerby deliberately spat on Philip. It landed right on the front of his little jacket.

"Don't touch it," I said quickly, holding his hand firmly. "We're nearly home and when we get in, I'll take your jacket off and clean it."

Hacking and spitting was a common and ubiquitous fact of life in China, one the foreigner learned, albeit reluctantly, to accept as part of the Chinese scene. But even the old China hand never quite got used to it. Even had hygiene and sanitation been better understood, there was nothing the man on the street could do about it. When a man had to spit, he had to spit and without the price of a handkerchief, where else but on the ground.

A handkerchief, as we understand it, didn't exist in China. To this day an instinct that stays with me is to avoid touching a lamppost or a telephone pole, or the corner of a wall or even a tree trunk, for it was on these places that the passerby wiped his fingers after having used them to blow his nose onto the ground.

Tibet Road,
Shanghai, 1948.

One day in Shanghai I went to take something to my tailor on Bubbling Well Road. It was 11 a.m., the time when most Chinese working people have their midday meal. When I went into the shop there was no one around, but I could smell food cooking. At the back of the room a table was set with bowls and chopsticks. On the table was what looked for all the world like a bowl full of raisins. As I approached the table, calling to ask if anyone was there, suddenly the "raisins" flew off and, behold, a bowl full of pure white rice.

Today they say there are no flies to be seen in China.

The Settlement on Edge

By the spring of 1949, the Communist Party's Eighth Route Army was advancing on Shanghai. The local authorities set about building cement pillboxes from which to defend the city. They also threw up a solid stockade around the perimeter of the International Settlement. To provide the manpower for such a labor force, each household, foreign and Chinese alike, had to supply a man equipped with either a pick, an axe or a shovel every day. Other work gangs were sent into the countryside to cut down trees, to make the heavy spikes that were embedded in all the main roads leading into the city, to impede the approach of Communist tanks.

The Bund S'hai

The cement for the pillboxes and the logs for the stockade were UNRRA supplies, intended for reconstruction in the city. But when the time came, the Communist troops filtered into the city in sneakers. They didn't have tanks.

With the approach of the Communists, the consulates in the International Settlement determined that some sort of emergency plans should be drawn up. The British Consulate decided to establish a temporary refugee camp down on the riverfront, where Navy ships could have easy access if things got serious. The Settlement was marked off into districts, with each district electing someone to represent them. Lin was chosen to be responsible for our area.

I was on the committee to help organize first aid for the camp. We met several times at the British Consulate to discuss arrangements. To equip the camp, it was decided each family would be asked to send, for each member, a camp bed, a blanket, and a case containing one week's ration of tinned food. Kitchen and toilet arrangements and a first-aid center were hastily built. In the event of an emergency, we would be told when to leave our homes and concentrate in this camp, where we would await developments.

Some sort of emergency plans should be drawn up

I'd had more than one experience during a civil war and knew the street was the worst possible place for anyone, especially women and children, during an emergency. On the other hand, to leave our homes and go to camp before an emergency arose meant abandoning our homes to looters. I put this to the planning committee, but admitted that I had no alternative to suggest other than to stay in our homes and take our chances. Most homes were within company compounds — not that this was any guarantee of safety.

The Last Flight Out

Staying with friends near Shanghai at that time was Claire Chennault, the American general who had led the "Flying Tigers," the American volunteer air group, and then the Chinese air force during the war. One day General Chennault asked me if Philip and I were planning to leave before the arrival of the Communists. If so, he would like to offer us a flight out on one of his planes. I thanked him but said I was planning to stay.

Each day, the Communists were reported to be getting nearer. On the evening of May 22, we were sitting in our living room at 9 p.m. when the front doorbell rang. Standing on the doorstep were three Americans in aviator uniforms. Not a little surprised, Lin invited them to come in.

They said they were pilots with Gen. Chennault's Civil Air Transport [later called Air America], and they had come to offer Philip and me a seat on their last plane out. It was leaving Lunghwa airfield at eleven the next morning. Lin turned to me and

How the Communist Party Won China

The rise of the Chinese Communist Party toward power in its nation began with an epic retreat.

In 1934, an encirclement campaign by Nationalist forces drove nearly 100,000 Communist fighters out of southern China. In what became their legendary Long March, the Communists walked some 6,000 miles, averaging almost 17 per day, to reach Shensi [Shaanxi], a northwestern province with a small Communist base. Nationalists harassed the Communists throughout the journey; only about a tenth of the original marchers reached Shensi.

But what looked like a defeat only proved the resilience of the Communists. One of their leaders, Mao Tse-tung [Mao Zedong], emerged as the head of the Communist Party. He built a new base for his movement in Yenan [Yan'an], a small city surrounded by mountains in north Shensi.

After Japan attacked in 1937, the Nationalist and the Communists formed a United Front, and the Communist forces were reorganized as the Eighth Route Army. They joined in the 1937 battle for Shanghai, and organized most of the resistance to Japan in North China. But tensions again grew with the Nationalists, whose army surrounded and destroyed a 4,000-man Communist force in January 1941.

That ended the United Front — and for the rest of World War II, Mao directed a Communist military whose numbers grew enormously, from about 20,000 fighters in 1934 to some 880,000 by 1945. More and more Chinese were drawn to the Communists by their effectiveness in fighting, and by the Party's support for policies such as land reform and ending government corruption.

In contrast, the Nationalist government under Chiang Kai-shek was weakened throughout the war by its corruption and infighting, and by Chiang's inability to control runaway inflation. Headquartered in the southwestern city of Chungking, Chiang's government was supported by the U.S. and Great Britain. Because the Japanese both controlled the coastline and blocked land supply routes into China, some 650,000 tons of military and other supplies were airlifted by Allied planes over the eastern Himalayan mountains, from India to what was called Free China during World War II.

After the war ended in late 1945, Chiang and Mao met to discuss China's future. The Americans persuaded them to join in a ceasefire and a political conference, where both sides agreed to merge their forces into a national army. But relations remained tense, and in February 1946, large-scale fighting erupted in Manchuria in the north.

The Nationalist army held a three-to-one advantage in numbers when the postwar conflict began. In June '46 they captured Yenan, the Communist capital. But the Communist army continued to expand while the Nationalists grew weaker, and in late 1947 the Communists won major victories. By now the Communists outnumbered the Nationalists, who surrendered Peking and Tientsin in January 1949. Chiang and his government moved southward twice — and in late 1949, they fled to the island of Taiwan.

On October 1, 1949, the Communist Party under Mao Tse-tung declared that the nation was now the People's Republic of China.

From 1908-1950, Oberlin College in Ohio coordinated a program that sent American teachers to rural Shensi [Shaanxi] Province, which became the base of the Chinese Communist Party after the Long March of 1934. Here, a young Mao Tse-tung greets American teacher Herbert Van Meter. *Photo courtesy of Tom Van Meter.*

said, "What about it, do you want to go?"

Before Pearl Harbor, the evacuation of women and children had been compulsory. This time I had a choice — and to leave Lin again was the last thing I wanted to do. It's one thing to run away from your home and save your life, but then what have you got?

"Thank you very much, but I'm not going," I said. "Life's too short."

After a little discussion and a round of beers, the men got up to go. As they left, one of them said, "Right up until five minutes before takeoff at eleven tomorrow morning, if you turn up you'll get a seat on that plane."

They left. The plane left without me. And then came the Communists.

"I Can See the Fire!"

Two days later, on the morning of the 24th of May, 1949, Lin went to the office as usual. At about 2 p.m. I heard shooting in the distance. Small arms fire. Very quickly it came closer, till the bullets were whining past our open windows. I phoned Lin to let him know what was happening, suggesting that if he was planning to come home, he had better come quickly; he might have trouble getting through even now.

After warning me not to leave the house, Lin set out across the seven miles of city streets that separated the office from our compound. Soon one of the company's big trucks arrived, bringing all the men, including Lin, with the news that the British Consulate had just informed him that Communist troops had quietly taken and were now occupying our carefully equipped and provisioned camp, down on the riverfront.

All that was to be seen were piles of discarded Nationalist uniforms

All night the shooting around our compound increased in volume, punctuated by large booms that shook the house. We learned later that the booms were bridges being blown up. Lin phoned around, warning all those in his charge: "Stay in your homes, don't move, don't go out on the streets, just lie low." Dragging our mattresses onto the floor of the inside hallway upstairs, we waited out the night with the shooting and firing all around us.

By morning all was quiet. Venturing out of the compound, Lin half expected to find the streets strewn with dead and dying; but all that was to be seen were piles of discarded Nationalist uniforms. Presumably those soldiers were now mingling anonymously with the crowds on the streets. I don't mean to say they weren't brave soldiers; they just didn't have anything to fight for, and they weren't supported by anything. All those pillboxes, tank traps and stockades — they were never used.

By that afternoon, Nationalist planes were flying low over the city, machine-gunning the streets that were crowded with civilians. Suddenly I heard one coming in low, directly over our house. When I looked out, there standing in the middle of the lawn was Philip, fascinated as he watched bullets plowing a furrow down the middle of the lawn, missing him by only a few yards.

Horrified, I rushed out, shouting, "Philip! Philip!" He was full of excitement: "Mommy, I can see the fire coming out!" I dragged him back in the house.

Lin, now back at the office, phoned to say, "The Nationalists are coming back. They're bombing and it looks as though they're heading for the power plant." If they hit it, he said, we would be without not only lights but also water. "Quickly," he said, "draw water, fill the bathtubs and lock the bathroom doors." I got the tubs filled just in time.

We were a full week after that without running water, and of course no electric light. When Lin got home, he organized a crew to dig three emergency wells inside the compound. Shanghai is basically a mud flat, so low-lying that water lies just below the surface. This water was foul, but useful in the event of fire.

After that, no Nationalist planes came back.

A Quiet Takeover

It took the Communist combat troops five days to complete the occupation of the sprawling city. There were small pockets of resistance and a lot of small-arms fire all around us, but in the end the troops just walked in.

The Communist troops all had metal helmets; they were in ordinary clothes, and they had tennis shoes on. Rubber-soled sneakers. On their backs they had rolls of bedding, and a long stocking in the shape of a horseshoe around their bedding that was full of cooked rice. Each man was a self-sufficient unit: he had an enamel basin, enamel mug and everything he needed for survival, an extra pair of shoes dangling from his pack. You couldn't hear them, there was no marching of soldiers' boots. They just walked past us.

It was a full two weeks before the power station was repaired. In the meantime, Chiang Kai-shek and his government had gone happily off to Taiwan with all of China's gold, silver and U.S. dollars and settled like a plague of locusts on that lovely island, which had been wrested from the Japanese at the cost of many American lives. All with the blessing of the West.

The first, most noticeable thing about the takeover in Shanghai was the orderly behavior of the Communist troops. These were highly disciplined, well-organized soldiers. You'd see them in little clutches on the street; they were everywhere, but kept strictly to themselves. They didn't enter a home or a shop or touch a person, and they never asked for so much as a cup of water, anything to eat, or a cigarette. At meal times throughout the city, they could be seen eating their ration of noodles and tea on the street. This amused the rice-eating Shanghai Chinese, who as a term of ridicule referred to the Northerner as a noodle-eater.

A bamboo fence separated our garden from the Fushoo Gardens next door. Originally Fushoo Gardens was a luxury residential area like Crescent Ave. But for some months before the Communist takeover, it had been occupied by Nationalist troops. Every day at the crack of dawn at that time, there began a discordant blowing of bugles, followed by the noisy drilling of troops on the tennis courts. We could see it all from our upstairs windows.

When the Communist troops took over and occupied Fushoo Road, their disciplined quiet was a welcome relief. It was from here that our servants would watch with some amusement these Northerners eating their noodles.

Immediately upon the Communist occupation, a citywide holiday was declared. Schools, banks and businesses were closed and elaborate street parades were organized. Long serpentine lines of *yangko* dancers, accompanied by noisy bands, wound their way along the crowded streets. I was curious to see them, but Lin discouraged me from going out on the streets. From our top-floor windows, though, we could see and hear enough to imagine what was going on. The servants, who did go onto the streets, filled in the rest of the story.

Communist troops arriving — → may 24, 1949.

Yuyuen Road

The New Regime

Another of the first things the new authorities set about doing was to try to restore confidence in the government by stabilizing the currency. To do this, the value of the currency was staked to basic market commodities or staples: rice, cooking oil, a yard of cloth, and coal balls. Next, the people were encouraged to bank their money, a thing they had long been unable to do because of the runaway inflation.

To illustrate the new banking procedures, let's say a man wanted to bank a hundred dollars (more likely a million by then). On the day of deposit, the bank would first determine how much of that day's staples the hundred dollars represented. The ratio was then recorded, along with the hundred dollars. The one stipulation was that the money remain in the bank for a minimum of one month. After that, when the time came that he wanted to withdraw his hundred dollar deposit, the man would receive the original dollars plus the amount of staples his hundred dollars had represented at the time of deposit.

As a result of this, people gradually began to regain confidence and to feel, at long last, a sense of security. No longer did they have to rush out as soon as they were paid to buy more and more perishable food before the value of their money dropped. The top floor of our house was full of bags of rice and flour that we'd been storing for the servants. Already this rice and flour was full of weevils, and the house full of mice.

Another thing that had been in short supply, in this city so overcrowded with refugees, was water. Up to now, in order to provide water for the many makeshift areas, fire hydrants on the streets were opened twice a day, each morning at eight and again at five in the evening. Then began the long procession of people with pails, out to get a supply of the water for their daily needs: men with buckets on either end of shoulder poles, or two bound-footed women walking tandem with a pail swinging between them from a pole across their shoulders. And endless numbers of children with little pails, all carrying water. Day after endless day, this trek had gone on since before Pearl Harbor.

The new regime installed water faucets on every second street corner. To prevent abuse and waste, a man was stationed at each faucet. People would turn it on and fill their pails; I think they had to give a copper cent for two pails.

Along with this, people were directed, from loudspeakers on street corners, to carry flyswatters for the purpose of killing flies and cockroaches and all kinds of pests. This in the interest of health. They were also told to kill rats and mice and sparrows in the interest of conserving grain, for the houses and warehouses were full of rats and mice.

At the same time, people everywhere were encouraged to organize themselves into unions. The merchants were unionized, the police were unionized, the teachers were unionized; the school children, the rickshaw coolies, even the beggars were unionized. Everybody had to register, and there were more parades with the *yangko, yangko* dance: three steps forward and one step back, all to a rhythm. People were dancing in the streets and rejoicing.

Having got all the people unionized, the Communists now had everybody listed, and they began to put the squeeze on. Cadres went from shop to shop requiring people to buy "Victory" bonds, each according to his financial capacity. Then the administrators came around to look into the accounts of the different firms, all the different little businesses.

The custom in China of keeping two sets of books was traditional, one for the operation of the business and the other to show the tax collector. But the Communist officials would have none of that; they insisted on seeing the real statement of accounts. If there was any argument, they simply looked around, made a quick estimate of their own, and demanded payment accordingly.

Slowly the screws were tightened. The same thing was happening to big business, Chinese and foreign alike — to foreign banks and shipping companies, oil and tobacco companies, and to our company, I.C.I.

Employees were encouraged to present "complaints" against employers. I.C.I. had its full share of employees and ex-employees, men who had been pensioned off before the war with Japan. They all jumped on the bandwagon, demanding more money. Hearings were held.

Pressures were increasing every day, especially for the Chinese

Lin was chosen to represent the company at these hearings. This meant reporting to the "Peoples' Courts" at seven o'clock each morning. All foreigners were deliberately kept cooling their heels in the cold corridors till about eleven. This was to wear down the notoriously impatient foreigner, to the point where he would be more amenable to pressure. But the company picked the right man when they chose Lin to represent them.

Clothed each morning in his warm shooting underwear and fortified with a thermos of hot coffee, Lin would set out for the Peoples' Court. Each day I pinned my faith not only on his patience, but on his understanding and respect for himself and for his fellow man. Lin liked his fellow man.

Day after day the court presented enormous claims on behalf of employees, in an effort to force Lin to commit the company to unwarranted payments. Lin patiently but firmly reasoned and argued. Fortunately I.C.I. enjoyed a good reputation as an employer, although even that couldn't be counted on. In spite of all this, Lin continued to have the respect of the court and never had any personal trouble with them.

Pressures were increasing every day, especially for the Chinese. Employers of every sort — businesses, landlords, money-lenders, even farmers, especially the rich farmers, unable to meet the demands for payments — were committing suicide. And often foreigners who were on the point of leaving would find at the last minute that a "complaint" had been lodged against them, so they would not be permitted to leave.

Although our home leave was not due for another six months, Lin decided it might be wise for him to resign from the board of the Foreign YMCA. With the cost of living soaring, many former residents could no longer afford to live there, so the place was half empty; at the same time, the Y was not permitted to dismiss any of its employees. Thus far there had been no trouble, but they were feeling the pinch. In order not to be involved when the time came for us to leave, Lin resigned.

A Relative Safety

That year of May 1949 through April 1950, the first under Communist rule and our last in China, was staggering for Shanghai. For us personally it was relatively quiet, beyond the general anxiety of not knowing what the next day held in store. We heard stories of street executions and poisonings at banquets, and of suicides and compulsory "confessions."

The public humiliations of landlords, money lenders and those caught breaking or ducking the new laws were daily occurrences. All affluent Chinese went about dressed in their oldest, shabbiest clothes to remain inconspicuous. Once or twice we witnessed street-corner incidents but dared not tarry, hurrying home to the relative safety of our compound.

We had a car, a fifth-hand Hudson. We had taken it over from Lin's predecessor when we arrived from Tientsin because it already had a license, a thing that had been harder to come by, under the Nationalist government, than a car itself. We had also kept on Yang, the driver, for after the Communists took over it was advisable that foreigners avoid driving. In the event of an accident, no matter who was at fault, the foreigner, or any capitalist, was not only obliged to pay all damages but was often whisked off to jail.

Affluent Chinese went about in their oldest, shabbiest clothes

In the "good old days" under the Nationalist government, the reverse had been true: anyone with money or influence could buy his way out of most situations, at a price. The poor had no recourse but to pay and to suffer.

It constantly surprised me how little our personal lives were affected by the change-over to Communist rule. The thing we missed most was our mail, for no papers, no magazines, and no letters were allowed in. All communications had come to a complete halt — all except the telephone.

Surprisingly, we were permitted to put through calls to Mary and Neil in New York, providing we could guarantee that the calls would be paid for at the other end. Although we took for granted that our conversations were being monitored, it was still great fun just to make contact with the outside world. It had a surreal quality about it, though.

It was not just the Foreign YMCA that was forbidden to dismiss any employees.

The same injunction applied to all businesses and private citizens — and was soon to affect us, for just at this time, our house coolie took sick and had to leave. In his place he sent a substitute. Watching this man work, I began to suspect that he had never worked in a foreign home before, or in any kind of home for that matter.

Then one day our houseboy, Chao, confided to me that he was worried about this man. He said all the other servants suspected he was an informer. They had somehow learned that he had previously made his living as a professional blackmailer. I was horrified, and the awful part was that we couldn't dismiss him.

"Foreign Children Never Die"

My indifferent health began to go downhill again. I had long since got rid of the amoebic dysentery, but was plagued with an inability to normally assimilate my food, so I chronically suffered from a degree of malnutrition. As this condition increased, my energy lagged. My blood count was less than half what it should have been.

The only food that appealed to me was the modest amount of milk and butter I was still able to get from Shanghai's only remaining reliable dairy. But the price of butter had increased to ten U.S. dollars a pound! One of the reasons was that fodder for the cows had to be flown into the city.

Chao, the family's Shanghai "houseboy."

My doctor prescribed B-12 for me, but none was available in Shanghai. Lin phoned Neil in New York, who had a supply flown out to Hong Kong, but the Shanghai authorities denied us permission to bring it in. In the end, the doctor decided to give me a series of blood transfusions. Numbers of kind friends and Lin too donated their blood. This seemed to help for awhile, but the benefit wore off all too soon.

In the meantime, the price of dairy products was still going up. It now represented almost half the total wages of our seven servants. This seemed out of all proportion. With so many hungry people around, I was embarrassed at paying such prices. I called in Chao and told him I had decided to discontinue the butter and milk. At such a price, Philip and I would just have to get along without it.

Pausing for a moment, Chao replied saying: "*T'ai-t'ai*, I know the milk and butter is very expensive, but you aren't well and are eating too little. Also, we Chinese people know that the reason foreign children never die is because they are given milk and butter to eat, and orange juice and cod liver oil.

"You have only one child and are too old to have any more children," he went on, "so if you can possibly afford to pay for the milk and butter, you would be very unwise to discontinue it. Look at me — I have had four sons and one daughter. I am nearly 60 and shouldn't be working any more, but I have to go on working until my 14-year-old son is old enough to support me, for his three older brothers and their mother all died when the boys were still very young, 13 years ago. My daughter is married and looking after her husband's old people."

"What did your wife and sons die of?" I asked.

"I don't know, T'ai-t'ai, they just died, all within a year or two of each other."

From his account I gathered that the mother had had tuberculosis, and that the three boys had probably contracted it from her. After the mother's death, the youngest son, still an infant, had grown up without the close care of his TB-infected mother, so he had lived.

I continued to get my milk and butter.

"We Risk Being Accused"

From time to time, Communist police came into our compound. They never asked to see me, but instead went around the back to talk with the servants. When I asked Chao what the police had come for, he parried, saying it was concerning their personal affairs. But on one of these occasions they stayed rather longer than usual. After they left I asked Chao what they had wanted this time.

"Oh, they wanted to know about the dog license," he replied vaguely.

"But we've got the dog license," I reminded him. "What did they really want, Chao?"

"Well, it was the gun license they were asking about."

"It can't be that, Chao. You know they've taken the guns away and are not going to give them back to us. We no longer need a gun license. Can't you tell me what they really came for?"

Anxiously, Chao confided that the police had been asking about us, wanting to know if they were satisfied with the way we, as employers, were treating them. Obviously distressed, Chao now carefully checked to make sure that all the doors were closed so that no one could overhear our conversation.

Then he exclaimed, "Oh, T'ai'-t'ai, why don't you and *Lao-pan* and *Hsiao yeh* leave Shanghai? I have no choice, I have to stay, but you can get out. Why don't you leave? If we tell them that we are satisfied with the way you are treating us, we risk being accused of being running dogs of the foreigner. If we say we're not, then it could make trouble for you. And we don't want to do that."

It turned out that it wasn't going to be as easy for us to leave as Chao thought.

At the Police Station

For the Communist troops to take Shanghai was one thing. It was quite another for their relatively small number of civil administrators to cope with such a large and sophisticated city, with its wheels within wheels of intrigue and outright corruption. As they didn't begin to have enough personnel to do the administering, they had to make use of the existing government officials. These ex-Nationalist officials, now bending over backwards to behave more Communist than the Communists, were tricky people to deal with.

Lin was very busy at the office, as well as having to spend much of his time at the People's Court. So when one day he phoned to ask if I would be willing to go to our local police station to get our car license renewed, I readily agreed.

The police station was only about six blocks away. As the car had gone for Philip, Chao called a rickshaw for me. As I left, Chao told me that if I wasn't back by noon, he would phone my husband at the office. I agreed this was a good precaution.

When I got to the police station, I asked the rickshaw man to wait and went inside. I found myself in a wide corridor. On the right was an open door. Hesitatingly I went in, not knowing if I was in the right place or not, for all the English signs had been removed.

The room was large and divided by a long counter that extended the full length of the room. On the other side of this counter were many desks, all occupied by men busily poring over papers. On my side of the counter I was alone.

Not wanting to appear presumptuous, I just waited. I couldn't help overhearing the quiet exchange of conversation between some of the clerks, and was interested to note that they were all speaking Mandarin, the dialect of North China. These were not Shanghai men; these were true Communists.

Presently one of them came up to the counter and asked in Chinese what I wanted. I explained that I had come to renew our car license. He went to his desk, returned with a sheaf of papers in Chinese, and handed them to me. With a formal smile and bow, I thanked him and started to leave.

These were not Shanghai men; these were true Communists

As I got to the door, the clerk called to me. Pointing to the forms in my hand, he said, "These must be filled out in Chinese, not in English." Smiling politely, I said that I understood and thanked him, starting again for the door.

Once more the clerk called me back. Pointing again to the papers, he said, "They must be written not only in Chinese but with a brush pen, not a foreign [fountain] pen." Once more I said that I understood, and thanked him and left.

When I got outside into the corridor, a policeman was waiting for me.

"Come this way," he said, beckoning me to follow. I was reluctant to go anywhere without knowing why, but I hadn't much choice. I couldn't help being inwardly glad that

Lin and Chao both knew where I was.

I followed the policeman across the wide hall through a door on the other side, into another large room that was also full of desks but with no long counter. The desks were all unoccupied, save for one at the far end of the room. I followed my guide to this desk.

Seated there was a police officer. Without looking up, he spoke to the orderly, who then left the room. When the orderly had gone, the officer stood and courteously motioned me to "*Ch'ing tzo*" (please be seated), indicating the chair on the other side of his desk. When he asked what I had come for, I showed him the papers in my hand, explaining that I had come for a car license.

He took the papers and was shuffling them on the desk when the orderly returned, carrying a parcel wrapped in newspaper. The officer took it and dismissed him with a nod. As the orderly left, the officer rose and reached across the desk with the parcel in his hands, proffering it to me.

Slightly surprised, my own good manners prompted me to rise and put out my hands for the parcel. It felt hot — and wobbly. It was a rubber hot water bottle!

For the first time, the officer looked directly at me and said, with a faint smile, "I apologize for this cold room." (It was January.) "If you just hold that and keep warm, I will fill out your papers."

Mystified, I thanked him, protesting that while this was very kind of him, I thought I should take the papers home to my husband, who could have them filled out at the office.

Shuffling the papers around and again without looking up, he casually remarked, "*Wo jen-te ni.*" (I know you.)

"You know me?" I asked, puzzled.

"Yes, you used to work in the British Municipal Hospital in Tientsin."

"But that was 14 years ago! How did you know that?"

"I was with the British Municipal Police there then," he explained. "Now if you will please answer a few questions, I will fill out your papers."

When he had finished, he rose and handed the papers back to me, telling me to take them to the other room and get my license. Still puzzled, I made one more protest, saying that I thought I had better take the papers home with me and bring them back the next day. We both knew what I meant. I didn't want to implicate him in any way, especially with a foreigner.

"*Pu yao p'a*" (don't be afraid), he said. "Take them now and get your license."

Still completely puzzled, I thanked him and took the papers. He smiled faintly at me, and I smiled back and bowed, not knowing what more to say. Then I left.

Returning to the first room, I handed the papers to the clerk who had given them to me. With a suggestion of a smile, he said, "You're back very quickly. Do you write Chinese?" I replied that I spoke a little Chinese but that I didn't know how to write.

"Well," he asked, "who filled out these papers then?" Hesitating for a moment, I replied that a friend had. Smiling to himself, he went to his desk and made out my license. I got the impression that, without looking up, the other clerks in the room were all covering up faint smiles.

When Lin got home that night, I gave him the license and told him the story. He was as puzzled as I was. But we had our car license, and there were no more police visits to our servants after that.

It wasn't till long after we had left China and come to the United States that I really thought much about this episode. It's perfectly possible that all the other clerks in the police station, all Northerners, were also ex-employees of the Tientsin British Municipal Police. In the maternity home where I worked for four years, there had always been a policeman on duty at our corner.

When those police had questioned our servants, they must have learned all there was to know about us, and that Lin had been in charge of our Tientsin office for the past two years. So I prefer to think that not only do bad reputations follow a person around, but sometimes good ones do too. But we never really found out.

Exit Permits

Just before the Communist takeover, about two million members of the Nationalist civil, military, and business elites and their families fled with Chiang Kai-shek from China to Taiwan. Thousands of China's wealthy also left at this time, going to Europe and the Americas, and to nearby Hong Kong seeking the protection of the British Crown colony.

By now too there was a steady exodus of foreigners from China. The passenger liners out of Hong Kong to Europe were being booked up months in advance. So although our home leave wasn't due till the following year, Lin took the precaution of booking passages on the P&O liner *Carthage*, due to sail from Hong Kong for England on April 30, 1950.

The winter passed, and our departure time drew near. For the trip from Shanghai to Hong Kong, we were booked on the *President Hoover*. We didn't know it at the time, but the *Hoover* was to be the very last passenger ship to leave Shanghai.

Communist regulations stipulated that anyone wanting to leave must first obtain an exit permit. The procedure was to apply in advance for a permit, wait one full month, then look for one's name in the daily paper among the names to be granted permits. Having confirmed that one's name was there, all that remained was to go to the police station and get the permit.

Lin followed these instructions to the letter. When the day came, sure enough there were our names in the paper. He had already arranged with the office for an interpreter, Mr. Wong, to accompany us, for all foreigners were required to communicate through an interpreter, who had to be able to speak not only English and the Shanghai dialect but Mandarin as well, for most all the Communist police were Northerners and spoke only

Mandarin. The next day Phil was kept home from school for he, too, had to appear in person with us at the police station.

We arrived early and joined the queue outside the Exit Permit Office. Our turn came and Lin gave his name. There was the usual amount of delay while they looked for the name. Then, to Lin's surprise, he was told to report to Room 108. When he questioned this, he got no answer, so we had no choice but to move along down the corridor till we came to Room 108.

There in large block letters over the door it read: INVESTIGATION DEPARTMENT. As Lin and I looked at each other, my heart missed a beat.

Lin knocked on the door and we went in. Seated on either side of a very large desk were two police officers. The one facing us was a woman. But neither of them looked up or indicated in any way that they even noticed us, so we just stood and waited.

Presently the man, who had his back to us and the door, still without looking up, spoke to our interpreter, asking what we wanted. Mr. Wong explained that the Exit Permit Office had told us to report here.

A long pause.

"What is the name?" asked the officer, still speaking to the interpreter.

"Lintilhac," Mr. Wong told him. Then followed a lot of shuffling of papers.

"F. E. Lintilhac?"

"Yes," said Mr. Wong. More shuffling of papers and another pause.

Then, looking directly at the interpreter, the officer said, "Tell Mr. Lintilhac that he is not going to be granted an exit permit."

All this in Mandarin that both Lin and I understood. We were stunned into a puzzled silence.

Lin thought carefully for a moment, then said to Mr. Wong, "Would you ask this gentleman if he could tell us why we're not going to be allowed an exit permit?"

Over the door it read: INVESTIGATION DEPARTMENT. My heart missed a beat

Taking his time and shuffling more papers, the officer finally said, "There's been a complaint lodged."

Mr. Wong went through the motions of relaying this message back to us. Lin replied that he thought there must be some mistake, for he had had no trouble with anyone, either at home or at the office.

"You say the name is Lintilhac, *Pu-Nei-Men* (I.C.I.)?"

"Yes," confirmed Mr. Wong.

"Then there is no mistake," replied the officer.

Not wanting to appear impatient, Lin again asked if the officer could give us some idea who had lodged the complaint. There followed another long pause. Then, still through the interpreter, the officer replied, "the Wine Union."

"The Wine Union!" exclaimed Lin. "But I have nothing to do with the Wine Union."

Finally the officer turned to Mr. Wong and said, "Tell Mr. Lintilhac that if he wants to know anything more, he will have to go to the Foreign Affairs Bureau. But that department is now closed for the day."

By now we had been in Room 108, standing all the time, for almost three hours. Phil whispered, "Mommy, are they going to put us in prison?" I shook my head and smiled at him, with an assurance I didn't altogether feel.

When we got outside, Lin took Phil and me to the car, asking Yang to take us home — for, late or not, he was going to the Foreign Affairs Bureau. He was there till after five o'clock. He learned that the complaint had been lodged by the restaurant of the Foreign YMCA. It seemed that because the restaurant served beer, it came under the aegis of the Wine Union.

The next day Lin went to the Y and spoke to the restaurant manager, telling him what had happened. The manager was full of apologies and explained that a few months earlier, when the Board of Trustees informed them the Y was planning to reduce the staff, the manager notified the police, insisting that until the Y agreed to keep them all on, no one on the Board of Trustees should be allowed to leave.

"But that was a long time ago, all of that has been settled," he said. "We no longer have any objection to your going, go ahead and get your exit permit. Tell the police, we no longer have any objection."

"I'm not telling the police," said Lin. "*You* are."

Off they went to the police station. Eventually the misunderstanding was cleared up, and we got our permits without any more trouble — but it took three days. In the meantime, the *President Hoover* had come and gone, leaving our trunks standing on the wharf.

A Silent Goodbye

Normally it was possible to go by train from Shanghai to Canton, which is right next door to Hong Kong. But now no trains were running, because the tracks had been torn up in the fighting. Besides, our permits were for Shanghai and not valid for Canton. What to do?

After collecting our trunks from the wharf, Lin spent the next few days making inquiries and discussing our dilemma with all kinds of authorities and shipping companies. All the time our sailing date from Hong Kong to England was getting uncomfortably close. If we missed that connection, it could be next to impossible to get another booking. As the Canadian trade commissioner and his wife were planning to occupy our house while we were on home leave, I was leaving the house just as it was, fully furnished.

Two mornings later Lin phoned from the office to say he had just confirmed that a

Norwegian freighter, the *Heinrick Jessen*, was due to sail from Tientsin the following week, and there was a vacancy on her. If we could get our Shanghai exit permits exchanged for Tientsin ones, and if train accommodations could be had, would I be game to take a chance on the three-day train trip north to Tientsin, and hope to be able to leave from there?

"Of course," I said.

The servants knew we had been refused exit permits. They also knew the last boat had gone. Chao was genuinely concerned for us. But our concern was now the substitute coolie, for the situation was ready-made for anyone wanting to make mischief.

When Lin got home that night he showed me the new exit permits. He had managed to get them exchanged for Tientsin ones, with the caution that they could not be changed a second time. On enquiring about trains to Tientsin, it seemed that the military had commandeered all rail travel. But there was just the chance that, at the last minute, we might be granted standing room on the train the very next day.

This couldn't be confirmed till the morning; the important thing now was to not let the substitute coolie get wind of our change of plans. So we told no one, not even Philip.

The next morning Lin left for the office, and Philip went off to school. The beds were made and the pajamas tucked under the pillows. Giving the amah some washing and mending to do, I followed my usual daily routine of inspecting the kitchen and ordering the next day's meals, giving the cook money for the market as though nothing was changed. Our suitcases had been packed for days. We were living half in and half out of them, for I was reluctant to unpack.

It seemed so sad to be leaving home like this

At 11 a.m. the phone rang. It was Lin, saying he had confirmed standing room on the train, leaving Shanghai at 6 p.m., and that he would be home at 3. He asked me to send the car to the school for Philip but to tell him nothing, and not to touch the suitcases till he got home, but instead to think up things to keep the coolie busy, so that he would have no opportunity to leave the house.

On the dot of 3, Lin arrived. He called Chao in and told him of our plans, asking him to not let the coolie out of his sight till after we were gone. Chao understood and agreed. Lin gave Chao a generous bonus and asked him to remain with the house till the Patersons arrived, for they planned to keep him on.

Now Lin called in all the other servants, including Chao again. He paid them their full wages plus a bonus of one month's pay each. Wasting no time, the suitcases were packed and locked and put into the car. (The pajamas were still under the pillows.) At 5 p.m. we walked out of our lovely home, leaving everything just as it was. There were tears running down my face as I said goodbye, especially to dear old Chao. It seemed so sad to be leaving our home like this.

After boarding the train, Phil and I sat on our suitcases in the corridor while Lin went in search of someone in authority. Before long he had secured two upper berths, in separate compartments but happily in the same coach. With Phil sharing my bunk, we were thankfully assured at least of our night's sleep.

When we arrived at Tientsin early on the morning of the third day, we found we had to go through three separate police inspections. Two were routine, but the third was a thorough check through the contents of all our trunks and suitcases. Luckily I had always followed a routine of not only numbering the trunks but of attaching complete inventories to the inside of each lid, while carrying duplicates with me.

For the most part the inspector used my inventories and, after spot-checking, found them to be accurate. But there were a few boxes of trinkets that he went through with a fine-tooth comb. This was when I became a little anxious, for a Chinese friend, Shoufen, had asked if I would be willing to take some family heirlooms, including precious pieces of jade, to Hong Kong for her, to be held there in safekeeping at the office. She and her husband, a colleague of Lin's, were hoping to leave Shanghai later, but as Chinese they knew they would be subjected to very close scrutiny, and would stand almost no chance of taking out any valuables.

Except for my own engagement ring, which I was wearing, I owned nothing but some costume "junk" jewelry, bracelets and dangles and bangles that I had planned to abandon. I now felt the best hope of getting Shoufen's valuable things out would be to mix them in among my "junk."

When the inspector came to this box he examined every piece. But clearly he was not an expert in jewelry, for he passed over the jade. Instead his eye was caught by some glittery trinkets of mine. What fascinated him most was a shiny folding Coty vanity case that had been given to me and that I had never used. Inside on the left was a little mirror and on the right a cake of the usual pink scented powder and puff. But its biggest attraction was six tinkling little bells on the outside along one end. The inspector was young and perhaps had visions of delighting a young bride, for he clearly found this trinket irresistible. He put it to one side. After that he lost interest. All Shoufen's lovely things got through safely.

After seven days of very cramped accommodation on the *Heinrick Jessen*, we arrived in Hong Kong. Here we were carefully frisked. They were looking for gold bars. Needless to say we had none.

We had only 36 hours before our boat was due to sail for England. We were met at the wharf and taken straight out to Lookout, Mary and Neil's lovely home overlooking beautiful Repulse Bay.

Voyage to Another Life

The next 36 hours were spent hurriedly getting our boxes out of storage. These were the boxes with all our better clothes that had been shipped out of Shanghai the year before. As I was still not all that well, Lin gave his full time to helping me sort and repack and finally get on board the *Carthage*. This had given him no time to report to the office about the situation in Shanghai — so when we sailed, Lin stayed behind in Hong Kong, catching up with us four days later in Singapore by BOAC flying boat. [British Overseas Airways Corporation, BOAC, was the predecessor of today's British Airways.]

After leaving Hong Kong, our first port of call was one hot, sticky day in Saigon. Next came three lovely days in Singapore, where Lin joined us. I was so relieved; it was not easy to shake the feeling of anxiety that we had had for the past year in Shanghai.

Next we sailed up the west coast of the Malay Peninsula to the idyllic little island of Penang, then west across the Bay of Bengal to Columbo, the capitol of Ceylon [Sri Lanka],

just off the southernmost tip of India. Here Phil saw his first snake-charmer, blowing on his reed pipe while a big cobra reared up out of a basket, waving its hooded head to and fro.

From Ceylon we sailed up the west coast of India to Bombay, the "gateway of India," then due west again across the Arabian Sea to Aden on the southwest corner of the Arabian peninsula, near the entrance to the Red Sea.

In Aden Phil had his first ride on a camel. Lin then hired a taxi with its Arab driver/guide, who drove us out across the dry sands to a green oasis surrounded with towering date-palms. He was eager to show us Aden's reservoir. When we got there we got out of the car and peered down into this yawning place, with great boulders at the bottom all bone-dry and covered with dust and sand. I asked how often it rained in Aden.

"Rain?" he asked, as though he had never heard of such a thing.

The Suez Canal was fascinating, as

Above: The SS *Carthage*.
Below: Lin and Claire in Hong Kong, just out of Shanghai, 1950.

always. Finally we docked at Port Said, the Mediterranean end of the canal. When we got to London, I was seeing doctors at London's Hospital for Tropical Diseases; in the meantime the Korean War had broken out, and Shanghai was now virtually cut off. The London office informed Lin that, after our leave, instead of returning to Shanghai, he would be asked to go to Hong Kong to take charge of the office there.

Snake charmer
and king cobra,
Sri Lanka, 1950

In June we crossed the Atlantic and spent a lovely summer with Mary and Neil in Brewster. Again Neil urged Lin to consider joining his company. Lin would be expected to make extended trips to Asia, but he would be based in New York City. The thing that finally decided Lin was the London doctor's advice that I should not go back to the climate in Hong Kong. Lin felt that life was too short to be separated again from his family. So after some sleepless nights, he decided to accept Neil's very generous offer.

It was a sad day when Lin tendered his resignation from the I.C.I. After 25 years of good and happy service, this was not an easy thing to do.

We rented a nice furnished flat in Putney Heath, London, to be our headquarters for the next six months. After getting Phil settled in boarding school, I followed Lin out to Hong Kong to collect the remainder of our things and try to retrieve some of our household belongings from Shanghai. The next year and a half was spent going and coming between London and Hong Kong, Manila and Singapore, to be with Lin as much as possible, but always getting back to London in time for Phil's holidays.

After 1950, our trips were so numerous to and from Asia, the Middle East, Europe and Bermuda and Cuba, that I can't begin to recall them separately. The winter of 1953-54, we moved from an apartment on the 30th floor of the Carlyle Hotel to our own lovely apartment at 930 Fifth Avenue, overlooking Central Park in New York City.

As time went on, Lin's arthritic hip began to give him more and more pain, with an accompanying loss of mobility. His doctor wanted to operate, but was reluctant to do so until Lin could be reasonably sure of staying here more than six months. In autumn 1957, Lin was admitted to the Presbyterian Medical Center Hospital in New York to have his operation.

One week later, in the middle of the night while still in the hospital, Lin suffered a pulmonary embolism and suddenly died. It was October 16, 1957.

I was devastated by my husband's death. After a time, Phil urged me to consider making our home in Vermont, pointing out that neither of us liked living in a big city. So on June 11, 1958, we moved to Stowe. Time has proven how right he was — for, oh how happy we have been here among so many warm friends in this lovely valley.

AMERICAN INTERNATIONAL ASSURANCE COMPANY, LIMITED

AMERICAN INTERNATIONAL BUILDING

HONG KONG

CABLE ADDRESS:
"AMINTASCO"

POST OFFICE BOX NO. 456
TELEPHONE 26681

THE CHINA MAIL, OCTOBER 17, 1957.

Hongkong Man's Sudden Death In New York

Mr Francis E. Lintilhac

New York, Oct. 16.
Mr Francis Eugene Lintilhac, executive Vice-President and a director of C. V. Starr and Company, New York, senior company in the world-wide American International Insurance organisation, died unexpectedly of a heart attack in New York today.

Mr Lintilhac was also chairman of the board of directors of American International Assurance Company, Hongkong.

He was born to British parents in Shanghai in 1908. He joined the American International Underwriters Organisation in 1950.

He had previously been a director of Imperial Chemical Industries in China, leading British chemical organisation in the Far East.

His grandfather founded P. E. Lintilhac and Company, of London which, for many years, was prominent in the export of raw silk from Shanghai.

Mr Lintilhac is survived by his widow, the former Claire Malcolm, whom he married in Shanghai, and a son.

Page 4   Friday, October 18, 1957.

HONGKONG TIGER STANDARD

F. E. Lintilhac, Starr & Co. Executive, Dies

NEW YORK, Oct. 16 — (Reuter) — Mr. Francis Eugene Lintilhac, Executive Vice-President and a Director of C.V. Starr and Company, New York, senior company in the worldwide American international insurance organisation, died unexpectedly of a heart attack in New York today.

Mr. Lintilhac was also Chairman of the Board of Directors of American International Assurance Company, Hongkong.

He was born to British parents in Shanghai in 1908. He joined the American International Underwriters organisation in 1950.

He had previously been a Director of Imperial Chemical Industries in China, leading British chemical organisation in the Far East, with which he was affiliated for 24 years.

His grandfather founded P. E. Lintilhac and Company, of London, which for many years was prominent in the export of raw silk from Shanghai.

Mr. Lintilhac is survived by his widow, the former Claire Malcolm, whom he married in Shanghai in 1936, and a son, Philip.

SOUTH CHINA MORNING POST,

Friday, October 18, 1957.—15

OBITUARY

Business Executive Dies Suddenly

MR F. E. LINTILHAC

Mr Francis E. Lintilhac, Executive Vice President of C. V. Starr & Co., passed away in New York on Wednesday after a heart attack while successfully recovering from a recent operation.

The late Mr Lintilhac, who was also the Chairman of the Board of the American International Assurance Co., Ltd. (AIA), Hongkong, and a Director of the American International Underwriters Far East Inc., is survived by his wife, Claire Malcolm, and his son, Philip.

Born in Shanghai in 1908, Mr Lintilhac spent many years in the Far East. He was formerly a Director of the Imperial Chemical Industries (China) Ltd. in Shanghai, the firm with which he had been associated for 24 years.

He first joined the American International Group in London in 1950, serving as an executive in foreign companies for which C. V. Starr & Co. is American consultant. He was elected Executive Vice President and Director of C. V. Starr & Co. in 1954. He served as a Director of AIA since 1950 and was elected Chairman of the Board on May 6 this year when he last visited the Colony.

Francis "Lin" Lintilhac's obituaries in Hong Kong English-language newspapers, 1957.

Claire's Later Life, and Her Legacy

After she and Philip moved to Stowe in 1958, Claire lived in the Vermont community for the rest of her life.

Lin had left his widow with a certain amount of stock in the international insurance business that Neil Starr persuaded him to join in 1950. In 1968, a number of companies that Starr had founded were incorporated together as the American International Group, or AIG. Under Starr's successor, Hank Greenberg, AIG grew over the coming decades into the largest insurance company in the world, operating in some 80 countries. Claire's stock exploded in value.

In 1975, Claire created the Lintilhac Foundation. The initial, primary aim of the family foundation was to support Claire's efforts to help bring nurse-midwifery into the American health care system.

Since her professional years in China, maternity nursing had been a passion for Claire. In the late 1960s, she began collaborating with Dr. John Maeck, then the chief of obstetrics and gynecology at the Medical Center Hospital of Vermont in Burlington, to develop one of the first hospital-based nurse-midwifery services in the United States. In 2018, the Certified Nurse-Midwifery Service celebrated its 50th anniversary at what is now the University of Vermont Medical Center.

In 2004, the medical center opened a new maternity unit, centered on the home-style birthing rooms for which Claire had advocated, and named it the Claire M. Lintilhac Birthing Center. "We are commemorating her dedication to perinatal care, and paying tribute to her energy and spirit," said Dr. Melinda Estes, president and CEO of the medical center, as she opened the new facility.

Claire's son Philip graduated in 1963 from the University of Vermont (UVM), and earned a Ph.D. at the University of California. Today he is a research associate professor in plant biology at UVM, with an active teaching schedule.

Claire passed away on August 15, 1984, at her home in Stowe. She was 84 years old. Since then, the Lintilhac Foundation has been led by Crea Sopher Lintilhac, who married Philip in 1983, with Phil serving as a member and officer of the Board of Trustees. Also serving on the Board today are Phil and Crea's three grown children, Louise, William and Paul Lintilhac.

Under Crea and Phil's stewardship, the Lintilhac Foundation has been an influential supporter of progressive environmental action in Vermont. Its top priorities are clean water, renewable energy and land conservation. The foundation also continues to support maternal and child health care, children's well-being, and informed public discourse in Claire's adopted state.

Late in her life, Claire wanted her son to know the whole story of her years in China. She wrote a memoir, which remained unpublished for many years, and she recorded some 15 hours of oral history and storytelling. She also preserved a number of photo albums, compiled by both the Malcolm and Lintilhac families. From those materials, we assembled *China in Another Time*.

Claire and Chinese friends in Stowe. At far right is Aileen Pei, stepmother of the world-renowned architect I.M. Pei.

Afterword

by Louise Lintilhac

Every once in a while during casual conversation with others, I enjoy dropping the fact that my grandmother was born in the 19th century. As a 34-year-old myself, this usually inspires a fun reaction and many more questions, most of which have a similar answer: my grandmother was a woman both ahead of and deeply embedded in her time.

Grandma Claire gave birth to my dad, Phil, at the age of 40, an act that would be considered unconventional even by today's standards. But this choice exemplifies why she has been such a strong female role model for me: she did not let what others might think she *should* be doing get in the way of what she *was* doing.

Claire found fulfillment in helping others, and this work dominated her career for many years. It's hard to say what her life would have looked like if she hadn't lived through two world wars — but she leaned in to her circumstances. When life's path veered and offered her an opportunity to be in love and start a family, she leaned in to that as well. I think you can hear a healthy dose of selflessness in her accounts. She used her life as a lens through which to tell the stories of others, not the other way around.

I never got to meet my grandmother Claire — she died three weeks before I was born — but I do absolutely have a relationship with her. I have read her book and heard the tapes she recorded; but most importantly, I have listened to the stories my dad lovingly tells of their life in China and then in my home state of Vermont. What's at the heart of these stories is compassion for the unique and varied experience of being human, and anyone who has had the pleasure of meeting my dad knows these traits were passed down to him as well.

In this way, people remain with us even if we don't get to know them in person. So it makes me happy to know that through this book, my grandmother Claire will be able to grow her circle of compassion even more.

Acknowledgements

We are particularly grateful to Doug Wilhelm, a writer and editor in Weybridge, Vermont who envisioned this book for what it could become, wove together the text of Claire's book from her writings and recordings, and wrote the historical articles that accompany her narrative. We also thank Rootstock Publishing of Montpelier, Vermont for their consummate care in producing this book; and we thank Nicholas Clifford, late professor of history at Middlebury College, for his introduction and for his expert suggestions, corrections and advice. We were very saddened to learn of Nick's passing in May 2019, just a few months before this book was published.

We acknowledge with gratitude the efforts of Terri Parent, Kim Quinlan, and their colleagues at Stride Creative Group in Burlington, Vermont for the design and page layout, along with Mason Singer of Laughing Bear Associates in Montpelier, for his cover design, and Tim Newcomb of Newcomb Studios, also in Montpelier, for his map. We also thank Nancy Brink, longtime administrative assistant of the Lintilhac Foundation, for all her help.

We thank Jamie Carstairs, manager of the Historical Photographs of China project at the University of Bristol, U.K. for his help in securing permissions to include many of the photos in these pages. We're grateful to Prof. Richard Kent, at Franklin and Marshall College, for helping us find and secure the photo on the front cover. And to all those who gave us their permission to use their photos, we extend a warm thank you.

The Lintilhac Family

CPSIA information can be obtained
at www.ICGtesting.com
Printed in the USA
FSHW010247251119
64387FS